WHAT IS ROMANTICISM?

WHAT IS ROMANTICISM?

Henri Peyre

Translated by
RODA ROBERTS

The University of Alabama Press
University, Alabama

Library of Congress Cataloging in Publication Data

Peyre, Henri, 1901—
　What is romanticism?

　Translation of Qu'est-ce que le romantisme?
　Bibliography: p.
　Includes index.
　1. French literature—18th century—History and criticism. 2.
French literature—19th century—History and criticism. 3. Roman-
ticism. I. Title.
PQ287.P5413　　　　840'.9'14　　　　75-42374
ISBN 0-8173-7003-X

CONTENTS

INTRODUCTION

The title of this book presents us with a question that has often been repeated. There have been many attempts to respond to it but the answers have been inconsistent. It would be fruitless to make yet another effort to invent a unique formula to explain a group of phenomena that frequently vary considerably from country to country and generation to generation. This work is intended specially for those who wish to understand the great importance and intensity of the romantic movement which stirred our emotions, enlarged the horizons of our imagination, gave free rein to individualism, and made modern man eternally dissatisfied with his destiny. We have made no attempt to write a history of the various stages of French literary romanticism; all we have done is replace it in its historical framework. The history of this movement has already been recorded, although only too often it has been purely anecdotal, tracing the progress of the *cénacles,* the literary cliques and second-rate reviews of little importance; in short, scholars have dealt chiefly with the outward, clearly observable aspects of men and works. We preferred to study literary and artistic romanticism in the context of its social and political milieu and to try to understand this ambiguous phenomenon through what was and still is its essence: the sensitivity, anguish, suffering, and joys of the great romantic writers and artists.

Contrary to what is generally believed, it is not only, and perhaps not even principally, in the genre of lyric poetry that French romanticism caused the greatest ferment, but in the novel, in history, in criticism, in social awareness, in painting, and in music. Nor do we feel that romanticism can be restricted to the period between 1820 and 1845 as textbooks have deliberately endeavored to do. So we have tried to trace the main elements that brought about this transformation of man and society from a much earlier date, from the moment when the first wave of romanticism began to swell in about 1760. Throughout the book, we have made an effort to reveal the interdependence that existed between the successive manifestations of romanticism in France and other European countries. In our opinion, the originality, intensity, and vitality of French romanticism, perhaps the most widespread and certainly the most stable in Europe, have not been properly appreciated. Because classical values and traditions had been more firmly established in France than elsewhere, its romanticism had to struggle all the harder to thrive and had to embrace the more meritorious aspects of classicism.

We have made no attempt to conceal the excesses, weaknesses, and at times the absurdities of French romanticism. In any case, since it made its appearance, and even more so a century later, it has had many opponents. These were often people suffering from nostalgia, who, exasperated by the mediocrity of their times, as well as by the pettiness of their compatriots, dreamed of improving conditions by returning to a stricter discipline; they exemplified what the English critic Basil de Selincourt noted in 1923 in an essay on "a French romantic" (who was none other than Charles Maurras) in *The English Secret and other Essays:* it is possible and even customary to detest romanticism in a very romantic way. These adversaries of the new movement, deluded by their dreams, announced repeatedly that the revival of classicism was imminent. However, every attempt they made to turn the clock back was frustrated by a fresh onslaught of romanticism. One of our best contemporary critics, Gaëton Picon, has rightly concluded: "Classicism would not be dead if we could revive it." Never before perhaps has this romanticism of sensibilities and dreams, with its extreme individualism and rebellion against an over-mechanized society and its hierarchies and bureaucracies, been so intense as it has since 1965, as witnessed by the very romantic and utopian revolution of May 1968. Today, even the most inflexible anthropologists are becoming more receptive to Rousseau's ideas and are ingeniously discovering to their delight an order among the varied elements of a primitive culture, an order that is almost logical in its unity. The younger generations are beginning to read the most extravagant, utopian works of previous centuries, perhaps because they foresee the possibility of realizing today the ideals expressed in them. Entire nations are daring to try to save their natural environment from being destroyed by the pollution caused by the presence of man. Young and old alike are rediscovering the so-called total, uninhibited, and natural love and are delighted by works that exalt this unique blend of eroticism and very naive sentimentality. Something of Musset has been reborn in Aragon and a great deal of George Sand is found again in Simone de Beauvoir. If the signs noted in our concluding chapters are correctly interpreted, they indicate that in the last third of the twentieth century there will occur a romantic cataclysm unparalleled at any time except during the preromantic period of 1760, when men were weary of rational understanding and intense analysis. A few words uttered by one of the wisest and most cultured of the novelists and essayists of the period of 1955–70, Michel Butor, seem to express clearly what this book is trying to prove. In answer to an American critic who questioned him on this subject, Butor said:

> Camus is certainly a romantic. Moreover, we are all romantics. There is in some respects a literary school of romanticism which had its heydey in 1830. Obviously, that school is included in literary manuals. But there is also a movement which began at the end of the eighteenth century and has evolved continually up to the present time. . . . There is perfect continuity between the romantic writers and contemporary literature. The constant revival of classicism which took place approximately every ten years in the eighteenth century will certainly never occur again.[1]

1 Romanticism Before the Romantic Period

To be sure, there has always existed a romantic nature and sensitivity, these terms implying a predominance of passion over reason, the lure of the extraordinary, dissatisfaction with the present and delight in suffering. Modern scholars have found indications of such a temperament in the *Odyssey,* in which Ulysses weeps profusely, in Euripides' *Medea* and the *Bacchae,* in the moving grief of Dido, who, as she is about to die for love, casts one last glance at the daylight, only to wail as she sees it. Those critics who particularly enjoy classifying and categorizing have gone a step further and characterized the medieval period—the era of Tristan and Iseult and Lancelot—as an age of romanticism that preceded the period when romanticism reached its full development. The French romantics of the nineteenth century considered as their precursors the "grotesque" writers belonging to the age of Louis XII and portrayed in Moliere's *Don Juan,* writers who have since been called "baroque" or "burlesque" writers and to whom the romantics gave other names. There is nothing wrong with making the past seem more modern in this way and at the same time paying it rather ingenuously the compliment of having been like us and consequently considering it original and still in vogue. It has been eloquently maintained that every new work acquired by a museum transfigures the objects already exhibited, or at least it changes our image of the latter, which are suddenly shaken out of their dusty state of repose. The same principle holds true in literature where the preciosity of Mallarmé and Giraudoux has revived what one might venture to qualify as *précieux* in the works of Thibaut de Champagne

1

and in *Aucassin et Nicolette;* likewise, it is Baudelaire's influence that has caused us to be more deeply affected by Villon's verses on death or some of the rather libertine sonnets of Théophile.

This subtle interplay allows us to transcend and sometimes disregard the dull chronological filiation of works; instead, we can cut vertically into the past and recognize kindred spirits who are separated by hundreds of years. However, this can also lead to confusion of certain concepts that are not very easy to define by themselves. We may take sentences out of their context, cryptic remarks, and fairly insignificant confessions and read into them more than their authors ever intended to convey. Sometimes we may even play on words, like the surrealists who described as "surrealistic" Young's *Night Thoughts* (which they had probably never read) and the disappointing works of Xavier Forneret (1809–84), or like writers of dissertations who think they detect analogies between the symbols of Vigny and those of the symbolists of 1890.

There is no doubt that every mood, every flight of creative imagination, including the most passionate love of nature, the longing for death, and a taste for the morbid could be found in certain men as far back as ten, twenty, or even twenty-five centuries ago. The only difference between those times and the romantic period was that during the former it was not the fashion to express such emotions and the vocabulary needed to do so was lacking. Lyric sentiments could have been best expressed in the novel and perhaps in the epistolary genre; unfortunately, however, they were not developed at that time, even the latter only becoming well-known after its use by Cicero, Abélard, and Petrarch. The concept of originality had not yet been affirmed. Whatever cannot be fully expressed or is not able to break with convention and create a form for itself is quickly repressed or stifled. It has been argued, fairly logically too, that there could not really be any atheists or total disbelievers in the Middle Ages and even in the sixteenth century when in Western Europe men were immersed in Christianity "like fish in an aquarium." However, there were certain "fish" like Pomponazzi and Bonaventure des Périers who were not at all silent or satisfied! There were certainly rebels in the Italy of Benvenuto Cellini or the England of Marlowe. In retrospect they may be considered romantics by temperament. But comparing them to the creative geniuses for whom we are in the habit of reserving the name of romantics, ever since the end of the eighteenth century, might only result in doing away with the clarity that the history of the arts and literatures must have.

The romantic label served as a rallying point in France, although at a later date than in Germany or England. Peculiarly enough, in this country, where everyone prides himself on being an individualist and likes to attack established authority, men of letters, philosophers, and artists tend to group together in schools, movements, and academies, like disciples acclaiming a common master. The literary and artistic milieux of France are so rigidly organized that the only way innovators can seize control of these solidly defended bastions is to work together with others who are at variance with their time or who share, temporarily at least, the same radical convictions. It was only after the famous battles in 1820–30 that the renaissance of history, criticism, the theatre, and painting could take place. At first glance, there seems to be no resemblance between the most "preromantic" of all decades, 1760–70, and the period during which the first works of Augustin Thierry, Sainte-Beuve, Hugo, and Delacroix appeared. But their affinity is revealed if one considers the sentimental effusions, mental disorders, agonies, and reveries of writers such as Rousseau, Diderot, and their many admirers and followers (those of *La Nouvelle Héloïse* particularly) like Mirabeau, Laclos, Rétif, Léonard, Loaisel de Tréogate, and Julie de Lespinasse. However, these writers who loved sentiment, passion, and even sentimentalism were not followed immediately by Chateaubriand, Balzac, and Michelet. It is unrealistic and simplistic to expect a symmetrical progression of tendencies, although at one time Brunetière had been in favor of this concept and had tried to present classicism as something that gradually asserted itself, then triumphed and personified the essence of France for a while before passing on to a stage of decadence. For various reasons—social, political, and aesthetic—or perhaps due to a series of accidents that results in great geniuses not always appearing on the scene when necessary, this first thrust of romanticism was not prolonged. In the last fifty odd years, we have gotten into the habit of calling this stage "preromantic," for lack of a better term.

THE CONCEPT OF PREROMANTICISM AND THE TERM "PREROMANTICISM" ARE MISLEADING

"Preromanticism" is not a very appropriate term, although it is better than the designation "preclassicism," which has been used to characterize everything that seemed to announce the very brief period of classicism (1660–85) from the Pléiade onwards and certainly for the sixty years extending from Malherbe to Boileau. These appellations would tend to make someone who is not too familiar with the subject or very observant believe that a period of several decades holds no interest except for the fact that it helped to develop what followed it and was better known. In the same way, the pagan world (symbolized by Virgil and Statius in the eyes of some, by Dante and Ovid in the opinion of others) was formerly considered important only as a period that prepared the way for Christianity and even today Simone Weil

tends to view antiquity in this light, in spite of her eagerness to gain
new vigor by drawing on the "Greek source." In the final pages of *The
Purgatory,* Virgil gave way to Beatrice and Saint Bernard. At one point
in his work *La Pensée et le Mouvant,* Henri Bergson has very rightly
warned historians of literature and ideas against what he calls "the
logic of retrospection," which induces us, for instance, to link together
the romanticism of the nineteenth century with what was already
romantic in the works of the classical writers. However, he notes:

> . . . the romantic aspect of classicism only emerged as the retroactive
> effect of romanticism, once the latter had appeared. If there had not
> been a Rousseau, a Chateaubriand, a Vigny, a Victor Hugo, not only
> should we never have perceived, but also *there would never really have
> existed,* any romanticism in the earlier classical writers, for this romanti-
> cism of theirs only materializes by lifting out of their work a certain
> aspect, and that slice thus cut out, with its particular form, no more
> existed in classical literature before romanticism appeared on the scene
> than there exists, in the cloud floating by, the amusing design that an
> artist perceives in shaping to his fancy the amorphous mass. Romanti-
> cism worked retroactively on classicism on the artist's design worked on
> the cloud. Retroactively it created its own prefiguration in the past and
> an explanation of itself by what had come before.

It is indeed far too easy to qualify a certain period of the past that
was too complex or too inconsistent to have established its own
identity as a "period of transition," and consequently take away from it
any semblance of coherence, and consider its talented writers who
might have been too diversified or too modest to pass for chiefs of
literary schools as either "late-comers and exceptions" or as "forerunners." It is far better, despite the greater effort involved, to try to
understand the so-called transitory period for and in itself and to
discover the reasons—if indeed any exist—that might explain its lack
of strong unity and the absence during this time of avid creative
geniuses, like Voltaire, Hugo, and Goethe, capable of leaving their
mark on their entire "age." However, this kind of understanding can
only be arrived at after the particular period is over, and it is the
authors of textbooks who have the responsibility of accomplishing
this. It is anything but certain that the years 1920–30 in France,
England, and Germany will be called "the age of Proust," "the age of
T. S. Eliot and Joyce," and "the age of Thomas Mann." It is even less
certain that André Breton and J.-P. Sartre, both leaders of intellectual
groups and doctrinarians, will be looked upon in the histories of the
year 2000 as men who had the greatest influence and who accomplished the most during the years 1930–60. If a cultured man of 1760
or 1780 had been asked which of the great writers of his time would

probably give his name to an entire period, he would certainly not
have replied "Diderot" or "Sade" or even "Rousseau"; instead, after
Voltaire, whose influence over literature was diminishing, he would
have mentioned L'abbé Delille and, at a later date, Beaumarchais or
Bernardin de Saint-Pierre rather than Rétif or Laclos.

In every period of history, contemporaries, particularly the critics,
who are generally more irascible than others, have complained about
the poor quality of the works of their age and deplored the apathy of
writers who, incapable of producing anything original, only seemed to
be marking time on the path beaten by their more enterprising predecessors. The more criticism becomes accepted as an established institution and shapes public opinion, the more sullen it becomes. This
is the case today, at the beginning of the last third of the twentieth
century. A similar situation prevailed during the Second Empire,
when critics found fault with the authoritarianism of another regime;
however, it was at that very time that poetry, the so-called realistic
novel, painting, and even the theater experienced one of their most
illustrious stages of development (although Sainte-Beuve refused to
accept this fact at first, in his articles on poetry in 1852 and those on
the novelists of the period). Artists indulged in their melancholy and
flaunted their pessimism, as they love to do in times of general
prosperity and in so-called consumer societies.

Of course, even men like Voltaire and Diderot suffered quite often
from pessimism. But accusations of sterility or apathy can certainly
not be made against the man who continued to write militant articles,
polemic letters and tracts, until he was over eighty, or the man who,
along with his collaborators, slaved tirelessly over the Encyclopedia.
And new and invaluable ideas were unexpectedly introduced at this
time by moralists, political and economic reformers, travelers to the
New World and explorers of Iran, India, and the Pacific Isles. The
most original works written between 1760 and 1775 are not solely
those of Rousseau or Diderot and his friends. If literary history were
better linked with the history of ideas and what we now call the human
sciences, attention would be focused on works such as Chastellux'
Voyage dans l'Amérique (1764), l'abbé Raynal's unmethodical but very
influential *Historie . . . des éstablissements des Européens dans les Deux
Indes,* the remarkable *Essai de tactique générale* (1773) by Guibert,
whose ideas Bonaparte was to put into practice, and the admirable
translation of the *Avesta* (1771) done by that non-conformist
Anquetil-Duperron, who had such a "romantic" career. Lamarck,
Carnot, Champollion, and many, many others who became famous at
the time of the Revolution and Napoleon owed a great deal to the
richness of the ideas disseminated by these predecessors.

It should be pointed out that, from the political point of view, the period between 1760 and 1788 was affected by what we describe today by the stock phase "disintegration of structures." In other epochs, literature seems to have taken delight in depicting that kind of imminent breakdown of the system. The greatest Viennese writers of the pre-1914 period had no richer source of inspiration. Novelists, particularly since Balzac, have been fond of such gloomy subjects as the decline of a family and the squandering of a patrimony or savings accumulated honestly and with some difficulty by one's ancestors. Acts of folly seem to follow after and take the place of too much judicious prudence. Political writers and reformers let fresh air into these moldy institutions and reveal clearly the hypocrisy that the conventional respect for vested interests barely concealed. Poets, curbed by rules of meter and traditional genres, and dramatists, bound by the habits of a public that is hostile to innovations, give less evidence of originality than their colleagues who experiment with less venerated genres. The established genres, which Napoleon spoke highly of to the author of *Faust* at Erfurt and which Brunetière loved so dearly, are not sacrosanct for us. Nevertheless, they correspond to some reality or legitimate exigencies of our mind. In certain genres, progress, or even just development, is slower, either because they depend greatly on material means and techniques as in the case of music and architecture or because those who devote themselves to them are more timorous and feel they should, above all, give to the public what it expects from them. This explains why many of the novels of the eighteenth century are anachronistic; they are closer in spirit to the moralists of the preceding century and the writers of memoirs than to the preoccupations of their time, which were principally political and philosophical and oriented towards the future. They do not reflect what was important and new in their age any better than the works of Giraudoux and Cocteau did in the years 1920–35. Their tendency towards escapism, even when escapism leads them to a facile libertinism and erotism, has less originality than that revealed in *L'Astrée* and *Clélie*. The occasional and very happy success of certain of these novels, *Cleveland, Manon Lescant, Monsieur Nicolas,* and especially *Les Liaisons dangereuses,* stands out all the better against the rest of the superabundant work of Prévost and Rétif. As far as Laclos is concerned, there is a complete contrast between the man and his work—and the same can be said of Bernardin, a hypochondriac who had quite an unhappy life but who managed to produce *Paul et Virginie,* a novel of mawkish sentimentalism. From the prison of Picpus, Laclos, an artillery officer who became a Jacobin but was suspect to the revolutionaries of 1793–94, wrote letters to his wife that can only be described as those of an excellent father, a bourgeois and banal moralist, and a boring preacher of domestic virtues.

COMPLEXITY OF THIS PERIOD

It thus becomes obvious that the period which we may call "preromantic," like any epoch, and perhaps more than any other, was confused and complex. Everything coexisted during it, the most conventional and timid side by side with real originality, at least in the manner of feeling, if not always in the way of expressing imaginatively the sentiments experienced. A great deal of the past continued to thrive at this time. Homer and Racine have never been praised as much as they were by Diderot. Voltaire became, in literature, the high priest of values and sometimes of conventions that will later be called classical. The poetry of Léonard, Bertin, and Parny, the three Creoles who were famous at that time, frequently brings to mind that of Chaulieu, the amatory elegies of La Fontaine, or even of Théophile and Tristan. The apologists of the Christian faith turn to Fénelon and Massillon for inspiration. The moralists revive occasionally the style of La Rochefoucauld or La Bruyère. However, there exists at the same time an intensely harrowing tension, with the mind and heart of man often in conflict. Many of the elements that will be found again in romanticism are present at this time. It is doubtful whether any one of the "romantic muses" has ever been as passionate as Julie de Lespinasse, whether the *mal du siècle* or disenchantment with life has affected any man or woman as much as it did the unhappy Mme. du Deffand. It is by situating them in this preromantic period that one can undoubtedly best understand Sénancour and Benjamin Constant, who were late-comers rather than precursors, and very often Chateaubriand and Lamartine, who were much more Voltairian than one would imagine at first. In France, at least, where the victory of classicism had been particularly decisive and literary traditions were most revered, it took a disorderly succession of "romantic" waves to finally bring about the literary revolution of the years 1830 and after. The most original is that of 1760–75. But it was followed, because of various events, by an equally strong reflux.

The term "preromanticism," like the word "preclassicism," is not a very felicitous one for yet another reason—it suggests that there existed during that period a movement with some common ideas and goals, whereas, in reality, there were only a few writers who worked in isolation and were at times opposed to each other, and even fewer musicians, painters, and sculptors. The most original art form, besides literature, would perhaps be town planning or architecture, and to characterize it as preromantic would be as futile as it would be misleading. A series of very diligent university studies, done principally after Lanson's courses in the first ten or twelve years of this century, and following the rise of comparative literature, has thrown light upon various aspects of this period. It is not our intention to enumerate these works here, nor to present them briefly, but only to indicate their general bearing on any understanding of romanticism.

THE GROWING INTEREST IN FOREIGN COUNTRIES
AND
THE REINTERPRETATION OF ANTIQUITY

One of the first new elements noticeable during the preromantic period was a greater interest on the part of Frenchmen in other countries: Germany, Switzerland, Russia to some extent, but chiefly Great Britain and, soon after, the America of Franklin, Washington, and of course Indians and Blacks. More people traveled to these countries, and they succeeded in understanding civilizations very different from their own. The Swiss assumed then the role of intermediary between Germany and France, and even more England, a role that they have continued to play ever since. But the French, following the example of Montesquieu and Prévost, learned to break away from Paris. With great perceptiveness, they often came to understand civilizations other than their own, and they frequently suggested very sensible plans to modernize countries that they thought could be more easily reformed than France. We are still amazed today by the wisdom of the constitution that Rousseau drafted for Poland. The less well-known program that Diderot worked out to set up a modernized system of education in Russia, after a visit of only a few months to the country, is even more remarkable. However, the men of this period, at least until the appearance of Bernardin de Saint-Pierre, did not have a true sense of local color or picturesque exoticism; in any case, scholars have ridiculously overrated the role of this exoticism in the works of the romantics of 1820–30, who had, however, at their disposal a descriptive vocabulary that was more ample. But several of the preromantics had the knack of going beyond the highly colored and chatoyant outward appearance of apparent diversities and interpreting in depth other cultures: Anquetil-Duperron did this in the case of Iran; various Frenchmen interpreted Indian culture, even though it was the English rather than the compatriots of Dupleix who succeeded in deciphering Sanskrit; still others studied Greece, which was finally visited by travelers instead of simply being idealized through ancient authors; last but not least, in many instances, it was Frenchmen who encouraged various European nationalities to get rid of their fascination for everything that originated in Paris and Versailles, so that they might discover their own true personality.

Scholars have studied closely the development of Anglomania in France during the period of preromanticism: the adaptation of the works of Shakespeare, whom Voltaire had abandoned in his old age, by Letourneur and Ducis, the admiration of the French for *Paradise Lost,* Thomson's *Seasons,* and especially Young's *Night Thoughts.* These English influences were unduly exaggerated by the first comparative scholars in France, like Joseph Texte (who related everything in Rousseau to foreign sources), Robert L. Cru (who saw above all in Diderot a disciple of the British), and even Fernand Baldensperger, who followed the fortunes of Young in France. Carried away by their enthusiasm as pioneers broadening the scope of national literary history, they did not specify in sufficient detail how a foreign cultural importation makes its influence felt. The generosity of certain scholars in thus affirming what a country seems to have received from another is carried at times to the point of undue intellectual honesty. We would be more inclined today to emphasize in this eighteenth century that was the golden age of cosmopolitanism, when philosophical thought tried to be international rather than nationalistic, the autonomy of each of the great nations of Western Europe. The English of that period, from Addison and Pope to Johnson and Blake, are very different from the French. To compare Pope too closely to Boileau, as has been done, can only lead to misunderstanding. The Germans, from Lessing and Herder to their romantics, whom Goethe regarded with alarm (Novalis, Hoelderlin, or Kleist), had nothing French or classical about them. The *Aufklärung* had some common direction and purpose in several countries. But it was as different in different countries as romanticism was to be later on. The tendency of several ideological or cultural historians nowadays is to dwell more upon the influence of antiquity, especially Latin antiquity, on the preromantics and those who were fascinated by the architectural style of Herculaneum and Pompeii than upon the so-called foreign influences. Two American historians of eighteenth-century France have written works full of erudition and enlightening observations on the obsession that the Philosophes had about antiquity: Frank E. Manuel, *The Eighteenth Century Confronts the Gods* (Harvard University Press, 1959) and Peter Gay, *The Enlightenment, an Interpretation: The Rise of Modern Paganism* (New York, Alfred Knopf, 1966). The Stoics, Lucretius, even Horace and Homer, were in fact much more passionately loved by the men of this period than by those of the century of Louis XIII and even of Louis XIV. It looked as if the moderns had won in the famous quarrel. But the blows dealt to the superstition of the ancients to which Boileau and even La Bruyère and Fénelon were able to cling, had been beneficial. They led to the ancients being read with a fresh outlook. Diderot could get excited about Homer and even about Tacitus and Seneca in a way that Racine himself had certainly not done. There is no doubt that these thinkers and writers of pagan antiquity, some of whom had been materialists, Epicurean atomists or, like the Stoics, pantheists, several of whom had already prepared all the arguments of the Sceptics were of great help in the fight against "Intolerance."

A FEELING FOR NATURE

Another aspect of this period that has been greatly documented is the rediscovery of a feeling for nature by the preromantics: their exploration of mountains, attempted very timidly at first, and their even more tentative search for the poetry of the sea. It is certainly easy to make mistakes in these matters by deducing rather hastily from literature to life that what it had not been the fashion to express had not been felt at all. Gide and Valéry liked to say that a culture, just like a person, reveals itself much more by what it conceals than by what it reveals conspicuously. But elaborate research into the memoirs and letters of the seventeenth century has disclosed neither a keen perception nor an intense enjoyment of nature, not even a pantheistic need for man to lose himself in things and to become one with them. Racan and Théophile could dream of solitude and the peace offered by a rustic retreat, with many recollections, besides, of *Hoc erat in votis,* of Tibullus, Propertius and Horace. La Fontaine's evocations of nature are most charming, but this feeling for trees or a clear stream, very similar to that of the Ancients, is, on the other hand, very different from that of Shelley or Lenau. Undoubtedly, one had to begin by descriptive poetry and try at first to draw up a quasi-taxonomic list (one wonders if it will be rehabilitated one day by being called phenomenological) containing the details of seasons, agricultural labor, and days. It must be added that the extension of geographic horizons is not so important as the broadening of inner horizons by Rousseau, Bernardin, and, soon after, Chateaubriand and Sénancour. Like many others among us they only receive from and perceive in nature what they ask of it, or perhaps what they give to it. Coleridge, who was well aware of this, has expressed beautifully what he felt in the most melancholy and moving of his odes, entitled *Dejection:*

O Lady! We receive but what we give,
And in our life alone does Nature live.

These ancestors of the romantic poets of 1820–40 do not, however, go as far as anthropomorphism, and in what Ruskin condemns as

"pathetic fallacy" or delusion of passion, as their successors of the
nineteenth century would do. They had been influenced by the habit
of descriptive poetry and the scientific spirit of their epoch, which had
taught them patient and minute observation. The precision and accu-
racy of several of Buffon's comments on plants, if not on animals (for
he tends to stylize the latter, in the manner of an academician who is
used to extolling his associates or his inferior colleagues), have been
ranked higher than the descriptions of Linné by more than one naturalist. The touching images of Rousseau, fleeing the company of his
fellowmen and taking a keen interest in the plants that he collected for
his herbarium, portray more than a sick man or an eccentric; they
depict an analyst preoccupied with the details of plant life. Rousseau
lacks many qualities of an artist: a colorful descriptive vocabulary, a
picturesque style of expression, the elliptical and suggestive image
that brings together two elements that are very different in appearance, the technique of associating words that Chateaubriand used in
phrases (such as "la cime indéterminée des forêts"—"The indeterminate line of treetops in the forests") that irritated Stendhal. Although
Goethe was greatly indebted to Rousseau, he surpassed him from the
very start of his career in *Werther* and in the love poems of his youth.
The splendid poem that he wrote at the age of thirty-two, when he was
madly in love with the daughter of the Alsatian pastor Brion, entitled
"Welcome and Farewell" ("Wilkommen and Abschied") and the short
work that seems insolent in its happiness, called *Night Thoughts
(Nachtgedanken),* which was inspired by his passion for Mme de Stein
ten years later in 1781, combine the vision of nature and human
passions much more successfully than anything achieved in *La
Nouvelle Héloïse.* Unfortunately, feeling, almost as much as thinking,
needs words to give it form, and feeling becomes refined only by
means of the verbal framework in which one is able to place the
original impressions and emotions that have been experienced or are
semiconscious.

THE INADEQUACIES OF POETRY

There is no doubt that one of the greatest misfortunes of the French
preromantics was not to have produced or come upon extremely
talented poets who could have expressed in verse what they seem to
have felt intensely. A possible reason for this lack might have been
that at this time there were comparatively few tormented souls and
sick minds like Gilbert and Malfilâtre (whom Vigny compared with
Chatterton). This was not the case in England, where, even more than
in Germany during this period (1770–1800), were many neuras-

thenics (Johnson, Boswell, Thomas Gray, William Cowper), individuals who were queer even in their sexual behavior like the extremely rich William Beckford, alcoholics like Robert Burns, men who were mad as Swift had been in his fashion, and as John Clare, William Collins, and Christopher Smart would be later on. On the other hand, however, never has as much poetry been written in France as in the eighteenth century, but nothing makes duller reading than a history (even in the form of a brief survey) of French poetry written at the time of Voltaire and Rousseau. Six out of twelve volumes of Emile Faguet's *Histoire de la poésie française* devoted to the period that extends from the successors of Boileau to Chénier and the First Empire. And although this critic might have been seriously mistaken about Baudelaire and bewailed "the absence of ideas" in the works of Hugo and other visionaries, he did, however, have a flair for a certain kind of poetry. But his diligent review of these many poets has revealed nothing, or almost nothing, worthy of great honour. Parny is certainly not an insignificant poet; his poems, although styled "erotic," are not very sordid. They evoke with sensual charm the conquest of Ellénore, the poet's victory over her modesty, followed by the infidelity of the woman, "the dressing-room scene", and other scenes that delight us in the paintings of Boucher and Fragonard. Strangely enough, however, the poetry of this period has not been able to communicate vivacity, color, nostalgia, or even rhythm to themes that are presented in a moving fashion in the rococo style or in the art works of Pigalle and Fragonard.

Preromanticism in its prose, which is more vigorous, then Romanticism that transforms our ideas on poetics, and finally the cult of imagination for which Baudelaire[1] is given credit have probably made us insensitive to the rather delicate and superficial charm that does exist in preromantic poetry that never raves or takes risks.[2] Dorat, however, wrote some very appealing poems. The same is true of Bertin, who was originally from Ile Bourbon like Parny and who was more unhappy than he. If one compiled an anthology of eulogies of inconstancy, which would certainly be interesting, the Chevalier de Boufflers (Knight of Malta after he had given up ecclesiastical status) would occupy an enviable place, along with another clergyman, John Donne, who, for his part, had started off with a life of passion ("A une jeune fille qui menaçait de me rendre heureux"). The famous hemistich of the poem Le Lac ("Oh time! Suspend your flight!") is found in the work of a poet of the eighteenth century, Thomas; Léonard, whom Musset might well have read, had asked, at the end of his "Stances sur le bois de Romainville", the pathetic question:

Is the last asset left to me
The comfort of crying?

THE UNIQUE CHARM OF THE EPISTLE IN VERSE

Finally, a genre of poetry that we have been led to neglect by the cult of passion, lamentation, and anguish, professed by the romantics and by all or almost all who followed them (Paul Valéry, and Jean Giraudoux in prose are exceptions, being in modern times the most genuine survivors of the eighteenth century), has been excellently handled by some of the poets who were modest and amused, quickly got over their sorrows, and were resigned to old age and infidelity, during the years 1715–60. This genre is the charming epistle in verse, which was more successfully executed during this period than it had been by Horace himself and much more refined than the efforts of Martial or those Latin writers who reviled woman. Voltaire was the great master of this epistle. "L'épître du tu et du vous", with its well-known cry:

> If you want me to love again,
> Give me back the age of love,

the epistle "Tandis qu'au-dessus de la terre" . . . . addressed in 1749 by Voltaire, the quasi-legitimate lover of Mme du Châtelet, to the man who had ousted him from that position, Saint-Lambert (by whom the marchioness had a child and died of it) should have an assured place in all anthologies of the two hundred best French poems. The genre continued to survive with Musset, at times with Hugo (but with less delicacy of execution), and with Mallarmé, and it has as much merit as the cosmic poetry or metaphysical poems of those whom our epoch, enamored of the tragic, loves exclusively.

The reform of poetry undoubtedly demanded much more joint effort and a more persistent determination to improve things than the extremely sensual or excessively timorous temperaments of those whom we call preromantics were capable of. André Chénier himself only dared to renovate here and there; he could have been a poet of subtle and tantalizing sensuality such as Goethe became in his period of maturity in his *Roman Elegies* and *The Divan,* or as Vigny, more clumsily, tried to be. But his few innovations in versification amount to very little. His best poems, "L'Aveugle" (which the poet Paul Claudel, who was usually less indulgent towards unbelievers and atheists, declared one of the two best long poems of French literature, the other being the no less pagan "Satyre" of *La Légende des siècles),* "La Jeune Malade," 'La Jeune Tarentine" have lost none of their appeal for the young, if our experience can be trusted. But it is the hazard and misfortune of any classicism, more particularly in poetry, the theater, music, and even in painting with the pupils of David and Ingres, to allow itself to be too easily reduced to rules and systematized in the form of regulations and prohibitions. The disciples of Banville and Leconte de Lisle, and even those who later would have been tempted to imitate Paul Valéry, have experienced this.

Preromanticism has shown more daring in the less established genres, in which one could innovate freely: the epistolary novel, which only had a few antecedents in the authentic letters of Abélard and Héloïse or the letters exchanged by two lovers of the sixteenth century (*Les Angoisses douloureuses qui procèdent d'amour,* by Helisenne de Crenne, 1560); the personal novel, which will reach the height of its development only in the following century, when ruthless (but at the same time complacent) frankness about oneself will have become the object of those who write in order to find their true identity, confess their faults, and reveal the innermost recesses of their heart (Constant, Mme de Duras, George Sand, Emile de Girardin, Flaubert, Maxime du Camp, and Fromentin at the start of their careers); the *drame bourgeois* and the *comédie larmoyante.* Two literary genres that are almost impossible to reduce to a definable form and that give full rein to the need for disorder and incoherency, of which the men of 1760–75 discover the full value, are going to be particularly original at this time—the philosophical dialogue and the letter.

THE PHILOSOPHICAL DIALOGUE AND THE LETTER

The first of these two had illustrious predecessors, starting with Plato, and closer in time to us Malebranche and Berkeley, or less famous ones like the dialogues of Bouhours and La Mothe Le Vayer, or even the mocking and caustic banter of the "Provincial" with his Molinist interlocutors. It is of course Diderot who is the great master of this genre, and there has been no one equal to him since. In his *Neveu de Rameau,* his "Conversation with the field marshal's wife," and the impressive extravagant talk between d'Alembert and Bordeu, he has done more than merely multiply prophetic views. He has, besides, offered examples of an aesthetics that repudiated order, clarity, deliberate planning, logic, and coherence of ideas. "A man of genius knows that he is taking a risk, and he is aware of this without having calculated the pros and cons: this reckoning is done in advance in his mind." This is what Diderot wrote in his short treatise on *Le Génie.* In a spirited page of *Réflexions sur le livre De l'Esprit,* he finds fault with and jeers (in a very methodical way) at method, which thwarts creative freedom and makes anything paradoxical (that is often the truth of tomorrow) that should be insinuative, concealed, spontaneous, and natural seem clumsy. Georges May, by going deeply into the aesthetics and turn of mind of the philosopher, has been able to present Diderot in a very credible manner as the "artist and philosopher of the incoherent" (*Festschrift für Herbert Dieckmann, Europäische Aufklärung,* Munich: Wilhelm Frick, 1966). Victor Hugo, who composed more flawlessly than any classical writer when he so desired, and he often did, undertook a similar campaign, but in a more ponderous fashion, in his *William Shakespeare,* where he attacks moderation, order, and artistic restraints advocated by those who have never had any spirit to curb or any immoderation to control.

The letter is no less prominent in the second half of the eighteenth century. La Bruyére had conceded that women were better at this type of writing than men; that had been true in the seventeenth century, when the correspondence of men of letters was very often dull and lifeless. But it is men, Voltaire, Diderot, Rousseau, perhaps the greatest of all French letterwriters (along with Flaubert later on), who remain the masters of this form of writing that is all the more expressive as it involves less restraint and cannot be reduced to a particular style or genre. Much more than in the letters, revealing as they were, of Descartes to Princess Elisabeth, or in the letters of spiritual direction or polemical letters of Fénelon or Bossuet, the whole man is revealed with his many interests, his passions, his dreams, and perhaps his multiple and successive sincerities, in the incoherent, spontaneous, and fervent letters quivering with emotion, written by Diderot, Rousseau, and one of the most ardent Frenchmen of that time, the fickle and haughty Mirabeau, to Mme Denis, to Sophie Volland, that old maid watched over by her mother, to Mme d'Epinay or M. de Malesherbes. To invoke the progress realized in literature by the concept of sincerity, in order to explain the abundance of these letters, is much too simplistic.[3] After all, what Diderot was able to affirm about the advantages of composed self-control in an actor, in his *Paradoxe sur le comédien,* is also valid for those who write a great number of sentimental or amatory letters. The Don Juans like Mirabeau, and even Tartuffe in his declaration to Elmire, are, for a moment, inspired by a sincerity that is perhaps genuine, as others (Diderot and Rousseau among the most important) could be inspired by self-pity. Mirabeau, who was very capable of playing false in love, and later in politics, had no doubts when he predicted a memorable future for Robespierre: "That man will go far, for he believes everything he says." The flexibility of the letter will allow the development of the novel of confession, by the German, French, and Russian writers of the following century. What fills these letters with confession, self-analysis, anecdotes, and spontaneous narratives, far from weakening the novel of the nineteenth century, on the contrary enriched it. The use that Balzac makes in his novels of long, almost moralizing letters by women would deserve a detailed study. Long before the pictorial and literary art of the romantic period, the letters of the eighteenth century bear witness to a growing liking for the fragment (so evident in the *Zibaldone* of Leopardi, the *Fragmente* of Novalis, and the essays of Hazlitt and Lamb) and a preference for the unfinished, the sketch, the incomplete, that are more suggestive and stimulating than the artificial and laboriously constructed complete work.

TRANSFORMATION OF LITERARY CONCEPTS

The originality of these years, which saw the birth and often the death of several of the elements that, revived and transfigured, would later combine to make up romanticism, lies ultimately, and perhaps mainly, in the transformation of the aesthetic ideas of the West and in a new philosophical sensitivity.

Literary historians, who are sometimes too fond of studying theories and doctrines, have laid great stress on the first of these two phenomena. There is a danger of their misrepresenting the very complex disorder of reality by isolating from their age and the circumstances that surround them a few theoretical works that poets or novelists have not in actual fact read very much. They imagine that the transmission of theoretical ideas takes place more easily and frequently than it really does. Some expressions that have never been properly defined (like the "je ne sais quoi"—"an indefinable something"—used by Corneille, Méré, Pascal, and other so-called classical writers, or "l' enthousiasme" celebrated in various very cold and conventional odes) are thus given an importance that they never had by these historians who study literary concepts that are detached from literary works. In my opinion, scholars have overrated the role of innovators and precursors of a new poetics, played by Abbé du Bos by his *Réflexions critiques* of 1719, or Rémond de Saint-Mard, or the English aristocrat Shaftesbury (dead since 1713), who was a champion of altruistic morals and the intuition of the conscience, capable of distinguishing good and evil, or even the ugly and the beautiful. His successor, the Scotsman Hutcheson (who died in 1746), resumed this comparison of beauty and virtue. But both men still did not approach the passionate ardor of the preromantics. Their rare intuitions or their impatience with the narrow rationalism that was in vogue at that time do not make them prophets of the future. More particularly, the budding ideas later called romantic, which modern scholars, diligent about reading everything, are able to discover in different countries, could lead us to believe that what has been expressed in Germany by some "magician of the North" unknown then in France, or by a lover of esoterism, or by an illuminist, or in Italy by some daring theorizing aesthetician has necessarily filtered through to creative writers.[4] The latter had many other things to do without reading everything that had been written in several languages. We lose sight of the fact that in those days, when public libraries were only accessible to very few people, when no research grants were awarded to allow men to go and consult some work a thousand miles from home, the young writer or thinker in his formative years was limited to what his father's or grandfather's library contained. And this had been collected thirty or fifty years before and often did not include any recent work. This was Rousseau's case at the home of Mme de Warens or that of that voracious reader, young Leopardi, at Recanati: his work *Zibaldone* shows that he was inspired by the Ancients and especially by the French writers of the eighteenth century, however romantic a sensibility he may have had. His pessimism resembles that of the eighteenth century (it calls back to mind the historic pessimism of Montesquieu and the bitterness of Chamfort), which is very different from that of Schopenhauer or his exact contemporary, Alfred de Vigny. A similar error in outlook makes us look for remote antecedents for anything new, and so the *Discours sur l'origine de l'inégalité,* the *Méditations of Lamartine, and the Préface de Cromwell* seem today only to be centos of citations or reminiscences. If indeed everything has been said, the majority of creative writers, who, at the age of twenty five or thirty, are far from being bookworms, have had the good fortune of being completely unaware of this. Moreover, as Delacroix has rightly noted in his *Journal* on May 15, 1824: "What creates men of genius, or rather what they create, is not new ideas, but this one dominant idea that what has been said has not yet been adequately expressed." Jean Fabre has used very pertinently the word "énergie" ("vigor"), along with the sometimes antithetical but complementary term "nostalgie" ("nostalgia") to characterize the eighteenth-century romanticism, which is really closely related to the Enlightenment and which has wrongly been isolated too much from the great movement of the *Aufklärung.* This first pre-Revolutionary romanticism, like the second one that will follow it, is one of the manifestations of modern man, as this same critic has very clearly shown. Henceforth, it is around man in this world, and no longer around the divine, that the new world, definitely oriented towards the future from the time of Locke and Voltaire, is organized.

NEW PHILOSOPHICAL VITALITY

The vigor of these personalities has been derived from the emotional intensity with which they have recognized the validity—as far as they were concerned—of ideas or moods that might have been felt and expressed previously. Scholars have discovered many of the ideas of Descartes in the works of the scholastic philosophers of the Middle Ages and have found that the wager of Pascal was more or less formulated before him by the Jesuit apologists. They have rightly challenged Montesquieu's claim to have conceived *prolem sine matre creatam* and have pointed out in Rousseau's political ideas reminiscences or distortions of the theories of Hobbes or Locke. That is really not very important. Many forms of this wave of passionate feelings that broke over Western Europe after 1760 (and flowed back into France after one or two generations, twenty or thirty years) had appeared separately since 1670. The public had wept on hearing the plays of Racine and the sermons of Bourdaloue and reading *Lettres d'une religieuse portugaise;* Mme de Sévigné, every time she parted from her daughter, shed as many tears as the devoted Aeneas. But these elements of romantic sensibility were still isolated, timid, slightly ashamed to attract attention. The distinction between sensibility and sentimentalism is very subtle and perhaps artifical. Some modest discretion, a social fear of ridicule, the distrust of exuberant effusions that the mind stops understanding or analyzing had, before the day of Abbé Prévost and Rousseau, obstructed the removal of the dikes and the opening of the sluice-gates that controlled the river within. "Is there such great delight in feeling?" Bossuet, surprised or indignant, had wondered. Religion (quietists, German and Moravian pietists, Quakers, dissidents of several sects, then Wesleyans in England) had moreover channeled many intemperate effusions and filled hearts that might have been considered empty and desolate.

THE ENNUI OF THE PREROMANTICS

On the contrary, in the second half of the eighteenth century, there was an explosion of inexplicable, perhaps morbid moods, which people had been afraid of revealing publicly for a long while. The century that spoke the most about happiness and claimed that everyone has the right to seek this happiness dreamed about it above all, because it clearly felt that it had not found it. Voltaire was not able to avoid ennui, despite his incessant craving for activity, just like the author of *Werther,* who cared very little for a future life in which there would no longer be obstacles to surmount and new worlds to conquer. Both men knew very well that it is man's fate to advance from desire to satisfaction and to say to himself, like Goethe had done, that he is yearning for something new *(und im Genuss Verschmacht' ich nach Begierde).* Georges May has brought out one of the *Four Faces of Diderot* (Boivin, 1951), that of Diderot the pessimist; although his vitality, which was turbulent but productive, surpassed even Voltaire's, discouragement over disputes, lassitude, the ennui of living, the intense fear of the ennui that undermines an existence of which action or passion has been the motivating force almost got the better of him more than once. He thought that solitude was "antisocial," the sign of a villain, and Rousseau did not forgive him for this statement, which was certainly a tactless one. But throughout his life, he tried to run away from himself, just like the frivolous man whom his beloved Seneca often portrayed; he dreamed of passion and power, even cruel and brutal in nature, to escape the dismal monotony of an aimless life that is perhaps made dreary by its extreme virtuousness.[5] Like Erasmus, Rabelais, and Montaigne, Diderot even cultivated an appearance of irrationality, or an irrationality that is partly sham, as the surest way to avoid the ennui that would result from a rational literature. "One often has to give wisdom the appearance of folly in order to have it accepted," he says in a letter written in September 1769 to Sophie's Volland. Baudelaire, in a curious note that precedes his translation of Poe's work, *Mesmeric Revelation,* in *La Liberté de penser,* in 1848 (II, 176), insinuates that Diderot, whom he greatly admired, "Makes deliberate use of his enthusiastic, sanguine and vociferous nature." Indeed, few authors have had to this extent the ability to experience by autosuggestion the enthusiasm that they had just feigned in the first place. The famous and perplexing "Paradox" of Diderot is just as real for the author as for the actor.

A study of the status granted by French romantics to Diderot, of his prestige and his influence among them, remains to be written. But it is more in the second half of the last century (with Baudelaire, the Goncourts, Zola, and the Théâtre libre) and in ours that Diderot has been best understood. Rather, it was Rousseau, in his *Nouvelle Héloïse,* and in some very moving letters written shortly before or after the composition of this novel, published in 1761, and a few authors considered of minor importance today, but more representative of the mood of the epoch, who have expressed almost all the sentiments regarded as romantic since that time. Never again, even in the works of George Sand or Michelet, would these sentiments be as exalted as they were at the very first with "preromanticism."

The ennui of life had certainly been felt quite intensely in former ages. The Epicureans, in Rome, had justified suicide because they felt that the sum total of the bad outweighed that of the good in their analysis of pleasures. Hegesias, in Alexandria, had earned the name of "Peisithanatos" ("one who recommends death"), and he had followers in Rome as well. Rarely has the *taedium vitae* been expressed in a more pessimistic but also stimulating manner and the futility of loving embraces exposed with more relentless rage than in Lucretius' poem. The monks of the Middle Ages had also known *acedia;* and we know how often the sovereign majesty of death was evoked in sixteenth-century English tragedy. Death was tenderly cherished by Cleopatra and even more impulsively solicited by Anthony, Othello, and even the lovers of Verona. But it seems that it was around 1760–75 that this *noia* brought about by an existence that was regarded as extremely futile assailed hearts as weary of pleasure as of the insensitivity of analytical and disillusioned minds. Mme du Deffand bewailed monotonously this depression that underminded every joy. Mlle de Lespinasse was consumed even more violently by a love so voracious that it could only weary the men who were the object or victim of it, as in the plays of Racine, *quaerens quem devoret.* She hated rational people. "Passion alone is reasonable," she exclaimed in one of her letters. Even being betrayed was better than not being loved. She knew and said this long before Musset rediscovered this sentiment. She analyzed herself but did not even want to make use of the weapons of coquetry. She wrote to a lover: "You know very well that when I hate you, it means that I love you with a passion so great that it confuses my reasoning power." Hermione would not have expressed herself differently. Sainte-Beuve, who quoted this sentence in the second volume of his *Causeries du lundi,* did not fail to recall Maxim 340 in which La Rochefoucauld asserted that "the mind of most women is used more to support their folly than their wisdom."

ROUSSEAU, ANALYST OF THE PREROMANTIC SPLEEN

Mlle de Lespinasse was not the only woman in the second half of the eighteenth century who, with more exclusive egocentrism, experienced the anxieties and aspirations of the heroine of *La Nouvelle Héloïse.* Rousseau, in several of his epistolary confessions, has harked back to this obsession with the emptiness that he felt within him. In a letter dated January 26, 1962, he explained to M. de Malesherbes his need to live by romance and imagination: "I felt within me an inexplicable emptiness that nothing could have filled, a certain aspiration of the heart for another sort of pleasure, which I could not imagine, but of which I felt the need." Seven years later, in one of those very fine letters, worded with great fact, in which he played the role of a lay director of conscience, he wrote to Mme de Berthier, who complained to him about being bored in society, that he recognized in this sentiment of impatience and ennui the sign of privileged beings. "This inner emptiness about which you complain is only felt by minds made to be filled; narrow minds never experience emptiness, because they are always full of trifles." There is indeed pride in this feeling of being different from others, and probably superior to them. Sénancour, Byron, Vigny, and Tolstoi will be Rousseau's successors in this respect. There is also a peculiar pleasure in mental suffering, and the masochistic aspect of Rousseau's nature was fully aware of this. This ancestor of romanticism who has been accused of so many failings has examined the depths of his being with more courageous lucidity than many of the moralists of the classical period, preachers, and perhaps Montaigne, of whom he was jealous, had done. A few letters written to Sophie are admirable from the point of view of the author's refusal to delude himself. Jean-Jacques knew how to examine and expose his need for the romantic without inhibiting it. "I was always searching for what did not exist . . . Is it my fault that what I love does not exist?" Marcel Proust would not have disclaimed a declaration like the following from *L'Emile* on the self-deception involved in love: "What is true love but a fabrication of the mind, a delusion, an illusion? We much prefer the image that we form than the object to which we apply it. Julie has a propensity for moralizing didacticism that easily aggravates a man when he finds it in a woman; more than one heroine of Balzac, in *Le Lys dans la vallée* or in *Béatrix,* is in this respect the successor of Julie. Men would like to reserve for themselves the prerogative of educating the women they woo. They like to think that the flighty Manon is more feminine, or more true to life, than the New Héloïse, and perhaps even the foolish Clélia Conti than the Duchess of Sanseverina, whose amused smile furthers the sentimental education of Fabrice. There is nevertheless a very subtle complexity in Rousseau's heroine, who is one of the most credible lovers of the French novel. She can be coquettish and pert when she likes, and she resembles the young female characters of Marivaux more than those of Corneille. Only, she wants to be sure that the passion to which she might succumb is not a trivial fancy. She has the courage to make the confession that could be made by a good half of the eighteenth century: "I am too happy; happiness bores me."

THE MYTH OF HAPPINESS

A considerable number of recent works by historians of sensibility has rectified and broadened our conception of this period that was depicted a short time ago as being entirely oriented towards the diffusion of enlightened ideas and the rate of progress. Pierre Trahard, using good taste and confining himself to men of talent best known to the general public, has clearly shown how libertinage and sensibility, eroticism and pity that was at times declamatory, were blended together at that time (*Les Maîtres de la sensibilité française de 1715 à 1789,* Boivin, 1931–33). Still, he has not emphasized sufficiently the close relationship between this sensibility and the sensualism of the Enlightenment. In 1930, André Monglond traced, with much psychological and stylistic finesse, what he considered an "internal" history of at least some of the aspects of French preromanticism (Grenoble: Arthaud, 1930). One of their successors among the most learned professors of the French university system, Robert Mauzi, after a much more careful study of the so-called secondary works and all the lesser known aspects of the century, has written a remarkable dissertation on *L'idée du bombeur au XVIIIe siècle* (Armand Colin, 1960); this idée-force, or this myth, was neither as new in Europe as Saint-Just was to declare, nor as generally accepted as it might have been believed and asserted. Eulogies of happiness, or fictional works and even works of art (with the exception of music) that have dealt with the subject of happiness, have not really succeeded in presenting their century as a golden age, or in portraying the golden age of the future as something very desirable.[6] But until the regeneration of the Revolution and certain declamations of the artisans of a world refashioned in blood and fire, the preromantic period had the good taste to preserve its clearsightedness and its love of limpid and vivid prose. A modern writer whose profound sympathy would seem, at first sight, to have been directed towards this century of unbelievers or people incapable of believing in the traditional ways, Julien Green, wrote in 1943 in the review *Fontaine:* "The eighteenth century was one of the most alert of all times. French society before the Revolution fell into the abyss with its eyes wide open. . . . What is important for this century is to live and to feel itself living, it could be said that it is well aware that it will fall asleep presently, and for a long time, to the sound of the drums of Sancerre."[7]

THE MAL DU SIECLE BEFORE THE REVOLUTION

It would hardly be paradoxical to maintain that the famous *mal du siècle,* of which Musset thought he had discovered one of the sources in the battles of the Empire and in the chagrin caused by an exaltation that had no purpose or use after Waterloo, had more particularly afflicted the grandparents of these youngsters of the century, in about 1760–80. It would, however, be more sensible to conclude simply that there were in France (and in three or four other countries of Europe) several waves of this epidemic of the sickness of the soul. The first, that of the preromantics, and the third (that of Baudelaire, Leconte de Lisle, Flaubert, Fromentin, and Taine, of Matthew Arnold, Swinburne, James Thomson, and Thomas Hardy, and of Wagner, Büchner, and Kierkegaard, all born around 1813–20) have probably felt their affliction more intensely than the generation of French romantics who complained more loudly about it. For Hugo, Lamartine, Michelet, Delacroix, Berlioz, and even Vigny received more consolation from creative activity and action.

On all sides, towards the end of the reign of Louis XV and during that of Louis XVI, it was not the joy of living, which has been much too celebrated by those who later idealized it in their reminiscences, that was portrayed in letters, memoirs, and novels. On the contrary, what was depicted in these works was ennui, the source of many rebellions of the young who found no use for the talents they thought they had or nobody to lend a ear to their reform projects. At all times, certainly, young people have thought that the conservatism of their elders got in the way of solutions being found. But the more they feel they are educated and competent, the less privileges seem justified by merit, and the more impatient they become. Men in authority call it arrogance.[8] "How it (ennui) undermines and destroys us! What a distaste for life it engenders! It is the most terrible and the most common of maladies," wrote Fletcher—whom Robert Mauzi cites— in 1786 in his *Réflexions d'un jeune homme.* "It is like a tapeworm that devours everything with the result that nothing does us any good," Mme. du Deffand wrote, not very elegantly, about ennui to Walpole in 1773. Men envy trees because they do not think or feel. They envy animals, as Walt Whitman would do, ashamed as they are of their fellow-creatures, human beings, who "lie awake in the dark and weep over their sins" or "discuss their duty to God." They consult doctors about the vapors. They search for gloomy places, abysses and grottos; as in the Baudelairian "Spleen," they feel the dull dark sky "an inflexible providence," bearing down on man and preventing him from breathing freely. Loaisel de Tréogate was not a great writer; he had undoubtedly read the already very romantic *Cleveland,* and he bore it in mind. He cherished his anxieties and his mental anguish. On him as on so many others, the grandiloquent *Night Thoughts* of the Englishman Young have exercised a fascination that is even more difficult for posterity to understand than that of Ossian, but for fifty years in Europe, minds and hearts took pleasure in these moods. Napoleon had a sentimental and melancholy side to his nature, just like Goethe, who was influenced by *Hamlet* when he wrote *Wilhelm Meister,* by Ossian, and also, when he was well past the so-called age "of reason," by Béranger. The Don Juans of this period at the end of the century, the creator of Valmont, who certainly did not experience what he observed and analyzed, and even those who lived the life of a Casanova with less vaingloriousness than the Venetian adventurer, Mirabeau, or the Prince de Ligne, were also sentimental men or sentimentalists, indulging in the mental sicknesses of the epoch and in the pleasure of melancholy while smirking about their acting talents. For what woman did not dearly love at that time the nobility of heart that sadness seems to harbor? Mirabeau wrote to Sophie from his prison cell that he could only be comforted by reading Rousseau; he shed tears as he read him. The Prince de Ligne stifled his stray melancholic impulses in his life as a warrior and traveler, but when the occasion demanded it he knew how to produce tears that effectively touched women's hearts. To Sara, his English friend, he explained in one of his accounts, he wrote the most heart-rending letters. "Young was a clown compared to me. I had even eradicted the stars from the night so that it might be more somber. . . . I would lift up my tombstone to have another word with it." It was true that Sara was English, and "what a stroke of luck for an English woman to have a source of lugubrious ideas!" But he exposed to mothers (by definition termed "virtuous") the maleficence of *La Nouvelle Héloïse,* a book that was more dangerous than *Les Liaisons dangereuses,* "for the poison is clearly visible in it."

Two articles by Armand Hoog have shown with conviction and psychological finesse how greatly this first *mal du siècle,* which preceded the other by some fifty years, had affected minds and how it would be unwise to refuse the adjective "romantic" to writers whose style, clichés, and figures of speech were not the same as those of the generation of 1830. Medical sciences during the years 1750–80 had not failed to take an interest in these psychosomatic ailments, which were manifested by vapors, listlessness, fainting fits, a weak will, and nervous tension. The famous Dr. Tronchin already spoke about "the medical science of the psyche." Voltaire and Grimm praised the perspicaciousness of another doctor who specialized in nervous and emotional disorders, Dr. Pierre Pomme, whose technique has been described by Armand Hoog. He analyzed dreams in order to detect in them symptoms of the anxiety that was felt and to make an attempt at therapy. The great Antoine Pinel, author of the magnificent treatise *Nosographie philosophique* (1801), had had excellent precursors. It is almost boring to read in literary histories how the fashion of meditating over tombs and musing around graveyards spread in Western Europe. If joy quickly palls in poetry, this type of lugubrious melancholy, which remained unchanged in form for a long time, is even more monotonous. But the anxiety of death, the *Todestrieb,* had invaded the novel since Abbé Prévost. Long before Schopenhauer, Byron, and Leopardi, it had been commonplace to declare what Byron would say to himself, certainly with more artificiality, in a famous stanza of the poem "Euthanasia": "Count o'er thy days from anguish free,/And know, whatever thou hast been,/'Tis something better: not to be."

These desires to be reduced to nothingness were less emphatically expressed than in the poetry of Leconte de Lisle. The sorrow of the world was not represented, in verse or prose, with the gravity that is found in Matthew Arnold's "Dover Beach" or the mocking bitterness of Jules Laforgue. But if the expression of sentiments is awkward, the authenticity of the obsessive anguish of these preromantics is not called into question. Even the love of corpses and the incessant preoccupation with the decomposition of bodies are found in several of these writers' works, as they had been in a certain monacal Christianity or as they would be in the writings of E. A. Poe and the Frenchmen of 1835–40: Théophile Gautier, Pétrus Borel, Charles Lassailly, and others of whom the young Baudelaire was aware.

In my opinion today, the poetic expression of such sentiments lacks the vivid imagery and youthful wonder that the romantic writers of other countries were going to recapture by becoming childlike again or by capering in a world of fantasy for which the Latins apparently feel more of a repugnance than the Celts or the Germans. It also lacks music, which could have enhanced these feelings with a dreamy quality. But the most important elements of the French romantic sensibility were present even before the end of the reign of Louis XVI and the outbreak of the Revolution. It was particularly at that time that, under cover sometimes of borrowings from Roman writers and hidden by classical eloquence, this preromanticism was finally experienced. As has been the case more than once in history, these men consumed by ennui, with overflowing hearts, excited by utopian ideas, hankering after a past they idealized in their imagination, and dreaming about the future showed themselves to be men of action and conquerors. It is only in literature and the arts that the expression of this romantic sensibility was interrupted. A reaction of twenty or thirty years followed this first romantic wave and increased the combativeness of the successors of this first romanticism in their struggles during the years 1830–40.

2 French Romanticism and Romanticism in Other Countries

ORIGINALITY OF THE DIFFERENT ROMANTIC MOVEMENTS IN EUROPE

It is not as a result of a foolish sense of nationalism that we are emphasizing the psychological originality and the influence of "pre-romantic" moods and of various books that expressed them, rather clumsily at times, in the France of 1760–1775. Anteriority in arts and letters is certainly a virtue in the eyes of the historian. Raphaël and Racine, Shakespeare and Newton rose to fame by climbing on the shoulders of their predecessors, to use the old cliché. But that does not mean that they were insignificant men; and their reputation is not tarnished by this any more than that of Rousseau, who protested violently against inequality and derived ideas from the travel accounts of missionaries, or of Pascal, who unceremoniously borrowed the most famous of his arguments from the Jesuits Silhon and Sirmond. On various occasions in the course of this work we will put forward the thesis that French romanticism, because it was kept in check or deferred for a long time, finally burst forth with an even greater exasperation in France and has affected more profoundly there than anywhere else the intellectual and even political life of the country. Quite simply, one of the ways in which the study of comparative literature has been useful is that it has made us recognize not only the similarities and at times the curious parallels between closely related cultures, but also the fundamental heterogeneity of the various movements (the Renaissance, classicism, the "Enlightenment", romanticism, symbolism) which have animated West European literatures. The terms, in spite of appearances and even when they have been borrowed by one country from another, cover very different realities and connotations. Political and social events, the aspirations of the people, the influence of their governments on the subjects or citizens varied tremendously from the England of George III and Pitt, from the divided and for a time Napoleonized Germany and Italy, to the France of Robespierre and the Empire. Even today, there is not much synchronism between the socialist thrust of one country of Western Europe, the dictatorial tendency of another, the imperialistic nationalism of the one, the lassitude or the exclusive interest in commercial profits of the other. A classification by generations of the writers and artists of these various countries has been proposed; but these generations do not coincide exactly in their dates, and not always in their aspirations—and of course one must not forget that it is impossible to predict when great men will appear on the scene.

THE FIRST ROMANTIC WAVE IN FRANCE
PRECEDED ROMANTICISM IN OTHER COUNTRIES

In France at the time when Voltaire was exercising his literary royalty, when publication of the *Encyclopédie* was beginning, when the greatest thinkers believed that man could be transformed by reason, education, and more knowledge, other currents led men and women to seek passion, reveal their most intimate feelings, feel melancholic about ruins, and experience nostalgia and a desire for death. This first current did not become a great river which could sweep everything away with it; and looking back from our comfortable position as omniscient posterity, we can come up today with twenty good reasons to explain that what happened had to happen—even if several of these reasons invoke a national character that is very hypothetical. To be sure, historical events exerted more influence, and what can be called romanticism, with its exaltation, its love of adventure and even its imagination, passed from literature and art, into the actions of the enemies and builders of the Revolution, the administrators and warriors of the Empire. Between about 1760 and 1775 or 1780, the works that were "romantic" before romanticism reached its full development were no less original in France than they were at that time in Germany or England. With the exception, once again, of poetry, there had been more ardent passion in *Manon Lescant and Cleveland,* a greater cult of passion in the works of Diderot and Rousseau, more fervour in the lucubration of illuminism by Pernety, Saint-Martin, Fabre d'Olivet, than there was then in so-called "more foggy" countries. Love letters in France were more impassioned or perhaps more declamatory. Even after *Werther (1774),* the *Lettres de deux amants habitants de Lyon* by the poet Léonard, the *Soirées de mélancolie* and *Doilbreuse* written between 1777 and 1783 by that peculiar Breton

Loaisel de Tréogate, works produced by talents that cannot be compared with that of young Goethe, pursue more stubbornly the pleasure that is contained in grief than the writings of the English and the
Germans. Mirabeau may have been a political mountebank and an
eloquent Southerner, but this man who, in about 1777, was engulfed
"in a torrent of sensual pleasure" because he had received a letter from
Sophie, who envied those who had committed suicide for reasons of
love, who cried out: "My heart contracts and swells in turn, so much
that it seems to want to burst or run away from me," was also a
precursor of the sentimentalists and sensualists of romanticism.

It was France which, even before Germany, became the first country on the continent to develop a passion for Shakespeare, the Swiss
Gessner and the Scot Ossian (or the skilful forger who used his name),
the last two of whom were introduced to the country as early as 1760
by Turgot. Letourneur, who adapted fairly freely into French the
Night Thoughts of Young in 1769, and Ossian in 1777, and of course
Shakespeare, is one of the creators of the romantic spirit in France. A
little later, at the very time when the Louis XVI style had made the
study of preromantic passion seem uninteresting and had brought into
vogue the mawkish and the rustic which were considered simple and
good, François Volney dealt most skilfully and even most forcefully
with the theme of ruins. Byron, Shelley and others who travelled to
the Orient read his *Voyage en Syrie et en Egypte* of 1783–1785 and his
Ruines (1791). Letourneur, Turgot and Volney deserve to have their
role reevaluated today, as it has certainly been superabundantly done
for that other preromantic, Sade, whose *Justine,* in 1791, anticipates
the pessimistic and erotic novels of neighboring countries.

If France has become, especially since 1850 or 1860, the country
with the most flourishing poetry in Europe, a poetry which has given
impetus to other schools of poetry, this was not the case up to 1820, at
least not in the ways that we consider the only productive ones today.
Foreign critics are in the habit of finding fault with a certain poverty of
French imagination and the absence of nebulous but exciting theories
on the imagination. Their thesis, which has been complacently repeated, is questionable. It is doubtful if the poems, most of them
second-rate, composed in England during the eighteenth century on
"the pleasures of imagination," and even the aesthetic theories, so
chary of precise definitions, of this enigmatic term or catchcall, have
really helped British writers to discover themselves. But hidden behind these awkward formulae lies an instinctive respect for the forces
of dream, a refusal to become slaves to what is real and positive, and
finally a claiming of the preeminent role of the poet—a claim that had
not been articulated in France since the youthful affirmations of
Ronsard and his friends.

THE FIRST WAVE OF GERMAN ROMANTICISM BETWEEN
ABOUT 1780 AND 1800

The fact remains that in Germany the first manifestation of romanticism, by no means more original than that of Rousseau or Diderot, less fascinated by mystical or illuminist theories, but more oriented towards poetry, took place between 1775 and 1800, when French romanticism had lost its flavor and force. Some Swiss intellectuals had been instrumental, in the preceding years, in creating respect for rustic life, the grandeur of mountains and Christian themes: Lavater by his *Schweizerlieder* of 1767 and soon after by his physiognomic theories, the physiologist and poet Albrecht von Haller who extolled the Alps as early as 1732, the sentimental bookseller Gessner between 1756 and 1772. Klopstock's poem on *The Messiah (1748)* enjoyed a tremendous reputation throughout Europe during those very years that are thought of as being entirely monopolized by the war against the Beast. The work of the Englishman Lowth on *The Religious Poetry of the Hebrews,* written in 1753, was quickly translated into German and French. Herder, born in 1774, published a book on *The Spirit of Hebrew Poetry* (1782–1783) which was admired in France until the middle of the following ceremony.

A few dates pointed the way to the earliest romantic activity in German literature. In 1759, Lessing heralded Shakespeare's renown; he died in 1781. In 1771, the young Goethe, who had had a memorable encounter with Herder the previous year at Strasbourg, delivered a youthful and impassioned speech at Frankfurt to extol Shakespeare, whose suit of armor "the little Frenchman" could not appropriate, just as he could not don the Greek armor that was too big and awkward for him. In 1774, *Werther* troubled European sensibility. At the same time, Goethe was writing the *Urfaust* which became part of the great drama which followed in 1808. *Goetz von Berlichingen,* the most tumultuous of Goethe's dramas, was written as early as 1773. From 1780 on, when he was working on *Iphigenia* and was getting ready to visit the classical land of Italy, his romanticism was tempered. It became less declamatory and more sensual in the *Roman Elegies* (1788–1790) which glorified concupiscence and the delights of love in the town of ruins which had also been the home of those lovers of Roman times, Catullus and Ovid. In 1794–1796, *Wilhelm Meister,* still full of ardor and famous for its unrestrained nostalgia for the land of orange-trees, also presented, as Flaubert and Fromentin later tried to do, means of getting rid of romanticism by making use of illusions of passion to teach moderation of sentiments.

Hamann, solitary and singular, died at the age of fifty-eight in 1788.

Bürger died in 1794, twenty years after his work *Lenora* had delighted an entire generation of young people enamored of fantastic journeys. The great period of the *Sturm and Drang* began around 1781 (date of Schiller's *Robbers*) and 1785. But the revolutionary ferment of these young fanatics did not last long. As far as it is admissible to generalize, the most outstanding of the German romantics quickly became (in the last decade of the eighteenth century) conservatives and traditionalists in religion and reactionaries in politics. No European intellectual had welcomed the beginnings of the French Revolution with such transports of admiration as Fichte, Schelling, Hegel, and Hoelderlin. But, with the exception perhaps of Hegel, who hailed with a famous and slightly ridiculous declaration Bonaparte's ride to Jena in 1806, two days before the defeat of Prussia, they rapidly changed their opinions. Fichte, Wilhelm Schlegel, and the jurist Savigny soon went back to praising original Germanism or the Prussian State, which, they hoped, would remain obstinately opposed to the French emperor.

Be that as it may, it was during the years that immediately preceded or followed the year 1800, when French literature was dormant and romanticism eclipsed, that typically romantic works were written in Germany; the poems of Novalis (who died in 1801 at the age of twenty-nine), those of Hoelderlin, born two years before him, in 1770, and threatened by madness after 1800, the poetry of Tieck, who was born in 1773, and who in 1803 revived the poetry of the Middle Ages in his *Minnelieder*. Schiller, who repudiated at a fairly young age the ardor that characterized his earlier works, died in 1805. Kleist committed suicide in 1811, leaving behind the most unrestrained of Hellenic-romantic dramas, namely, his *Penthesilea* and also his more moving *Prinz von Homburg* (1810). Jean Paul Richter, who was older than them (born in 1763), published his *Hesperus* in 1795, and this was followed in 1798 by the no less strange and formless *Sternbald* of Tieck. Several of these romantic writers, including Schiller and the philosopher Schelling, had published significant texts in their review *Die Horen* from 1795. The same year, Schelling dealt with the topic of *The Self as a philosophical principle*. The very year when the French Revolution ended with the Consular regime (1799), Friedrich Schlegel published his novel of erotic education, *Lucinde*. France knew nothing whatsoever, or practically nothing, at that time, about this first German romanticism. Mme de Staël was not much better informed. The influence of this romanticism, if there was any influence, was exercised much later, when the French dramatists of 1820–1835 read Schiller, and even later than that and much less than we are led to believe by superficial analogies, during the period of symbolism.

It is an oversimplification to trace, in order to satisfy a desire for symmetry, an alternation of a romantic period extending from the *Sturm and Drang* to the beginning of the nineteenth century and a classical period represented by Schiller in his old age and Goethe who, in his tranquil bourgeois situation, was irritated by the eccentricities, often bordering on the morbid, of the young. Goethe, after all, did not cease embodying in his works, and particularly in the second part of *Faust,* many of the chaotic elements of romanticism and experiencing successive passions in his love life, just like his young rivals. But it is true that there was a sort of falling off from the great musing and mystical impulses of the romantics between about 1810 and 1825, at the time when France was plunging into disputes between two rival aesthetics and was preparing for its poetic renaissance. It was to be the role of the generation born around 1800 (Grillparzer of Austria, born in 1791; Platen and Heine, born in 1796 and 1797; Lenau, born in 1802, and Hebbel a little later) to create poetic and dramatic works imbued once more with romantic passion and social rebellion. But these writers were all solitary figures, living in Austria, Swabia, or even France. With the exception of Heine, they did not become well known outside German-speaking countries.

THE POETRY OF NATURE, NIGHT, AND DEATH IN ENGLAND DURING THE EIGHTEENTH CENTURY

A feeling for nature, expressed in labored descriptions that were not inspired as yet by a Rousseau-like pantheism, the contemplation of the night and of tombs, a thinking back to the age of chivalry or to that of the so-called original bards had given rise to a whole current of poetry in England as early as the second quarter of the eighteenth century. The *Seasons* of Thomson was written in 1726–1730, Young's *Night Thoughts* in 1742–1745, the gloomy meditations of Hervey in about 1745. Gray's famous elegy on a country cemetery appeared in 1760 and the *Reliques of Ancient English Poetry* compiled by Percy were published in 1765. Chatterton poisoned himself five years later, in 1770. Ossian had stirred imaginations after 1760–1763. A few reflective works and works dealing with aesthetic renovation were also produced from about 1760 and were contemporaneous with the discontinuous and daring theories of Diderot: the *Letters* of Richard Hurd on chivalry and on the untranslatable word and the very British concept of "romance" (1762), three years after the *Conjectures on Original Composition* in which Young showed himself to be a more daring innovator than in his extremely famous *Night Thoughts* in verse. *The Castle of Otranto* by Horace Walpole (1764) was the first novel to make strangeness a feature of literature that was weary of the picaresque, realistic, and edifying novels. Two great poets, also innovators, appeared soon after: Blake (born in 1757) and Burns (in 1759). If neither they nor Crabbe nor Cowper formed a "school," a very un-British institution, as people on the Continent later fancied that the "Lakists" had done, they did nevertheless constitute a first generation of romantic poets, more oriented towards a modern diction and a popular euphony than the "latecomers" in France.

The appellation "first romantic generation" is usually reserved by historians of literature for Wordsworth, Coleridge, Southey and, possibly, Scott, born in 1770, 1772, 1774, and 1771 respectively. It was when they reached the age of about thirty that they published their aesthetic manifestos and their impressive works, without, however, exercizing a great influence over the public that was at odds with them and even less influence on the quarterly reviews which jeered at them. It was on these poets (Wordsworth and Coleridge particularly, Blake as well) that the upheaval of the French Revolution had had a great effect, much more than on French writers who had lived through or fled from the great collective tragedy.

But the distinction of two very great men among these poets is certainly not enough to warrant calling the whole period "romantic." The public, even the small group interested in poetry, was not in perfect agreement with them. There were few periodicals, if any, which upheld their views or understood them. The representative writers of the period of the Napoleonic wars were in fact economists or philosophers who did not have the characteristics of passion, idealism, and personal effusions that typified the romantics: Sydney Smith (1771–1845), Bentham who was born in 1748 and died ten years after Shelley, in 1832, Malthus (1766–1834), Ricardo (1772–1823), and James Mill (1773–1836). Landor and Lamb, both born in 1775, did not want to be nor thought they were romantics. Peacock, born in 1785, always laughed at the whims of poets who claimed to defy common sense. Jane Austen, who was twenty-five years old when the new century began and who died two years after Waterloo, knew nothing about the poets, so different from herself, who are considered by textbooks today as the spokesmen of their epoch. Alone among the fairly famous prose-writers, Hazlitt, born in 1778, De Quincey, seven years younger than him, and their senior Walter Scott who became a novelist after 1814, can be regarded as romantic in some aspects. English romanticism had made a strong impression upon English personality and history long before the great outburst of Byronism.

The second—or from our point of view, the third—romantic generation, which was also restricted to the domain of poetry, was limited to three or four names: Byron (1788–1824), Shelley (1792–1822), Keats (1795–1821), and the curious and tragic recluse Beddoes (1803–1849). Other writers who were of the same age had little in common with them; writers such as Carlyle (born in 1795), Newman (born in 1801), Macaulay (born in 1800), John Stuart Mill (born in 1806), Darwin (born in 1809), Mrs. Gaskell (1810), Thackeray (1811). How many non-romantics there still were among them! The term "the unromantics" has been invented in English to characterize them. It was perhaps around 1840, when the great romantic poets who were misunderstood or vilified, like Byron, during their lifetime, had been dead for a long time and their posthumous glory had been proclaimed by the younger generation, that romanticism was experienced most intensely by their successors. These were Tennyson (born in 1809, like Fitzgerald), Browning (born in 1812), Clough and Arnold (born in 1819 and 1822), Charlotte and Emily Brontë (1816 and 1818), and later still Rossetti, James Thomson, and Swinburne. But these authors, apart from Swinburne, who extolled Hugo and Baudelaire, had no relations with their Parisian contemporaries, although they belonged to the period during which the latter finally gained victory in France after 1820–1830.

There would be little use in referring to countries beyond the Alps or Pyrenees to corroborate the patent facts which we have been recalling in this chapter. The Spanish romantic movement only dated from about 1830. Before this, the few stray romantic impulses that may be perceived were especially characteristic of Spaniards who had emigrated. Romantic reviews, never very numerous, only appeared after 1835 and owed a great deal to Parisian disputes. Larra, the most romantic of Spanish writers from the point of view of his life, his love affairs, and his suicide in 1837 at the age of twenty-eight, had not only been brought up in France but also spoke French as his mother tongue. Espronceda (1808–1842) fought in Paris during the 1830 Revolution and used his romantic virtuoso's flamboyance to further political causes. Zorilla prolonged Spanish romanticism which was extremely Byronian, colorful, enraptured by fantasy and words, till the end of the century; he lived from 1817 to 1893 and became familiar with the French romantic writers in Paris when he was about thirty years old. He was obsessed by the theme of *Don Juan,* just as Byron, Lenau, and Kierkegaard were at that time, and much more than the compatriots of Molière had been. But the differences of sensibility, imagination, power of understanding and, of course, technique and language are so great between the romantic writers of these different countries (and of the Italy of Foscolo, Leopardi, and Manzoni) that one is induced to return to the study of individuals rather than of groups and to the heterogeneity of romanticisms or to their very diverse multiplicity, according to the thesis maintained emphatically not long ago by a great historian of ideas, Lovejoy. If romanticism is restricted to poetry, it is very certain that the German and English poetic works have preceded those of France. If, as we believe, romanticism should be studied in other literary genres as well (theater, novel, history), in other arts, and in its diffusion among an agitated public, prone to revolutionary riots, impatient to make progress, then, in this perspective, French romanticism has been the most authentic, from the time of its precursors of the years 1760–1775 and especially after 1815. Only Polish romanticism (according to those who are fortunate enough to be able to read this Polish romantic literature in the original language) can be compared and preferred to it. And as Jean Fabre has shown in *Lumières et romantisme,* Polish poetry, with Mickiewicz and Slowacki, has this superiority over others in that it "bears within it the grief of a nation, like a mother bears a child." In the face of oppression, emigration, and exile, it has endured nostalgia and maintained energy as the two poles between which European romanticism oscillates.

RELATIVE ARREST OF LITERARY PRODUCTION
IN FRANCE DURING THE TIME OF THE REVOLUTION
AND THE EMPIRE

The question has often been raised as to why French preromanticism, which seemed daring and full of ardent fervor with Rousseau, Diderot, and a few novelists and travelers who followed them, came to a halt for such a long time. In fact, from about 1780 until appearance of Lamartine in poetry, Mérimée, Vigny, Dumas, and Hugo in drama, Augustin Thierry in history and the few novels between 1820 and 1830 that precede those of Stendhal and Balzac, it is traditional to declare French literature sterile and romanticism suppressed. Napoleon himself has been blamed for this; and yet he was the most romantic Frenchman who ever lived, if to live and act by the imagination can be considered romantic, and the most passionate and chimerical of French sovereigns since the Middle Ages, if one thinks of his love-letters to Joséphine and even of his relations with Marie Walewska or Marie-Louise. The extremely convenient clearcut categories which literary history likes to dwell on undoubtedly distort our vision. It is so satisfying for lucid minds to declare that a neo-classical (or psuedo-classical) reaction put an end at that time to the slightly indiscreet outbursts of the precursors of romanticism, and that the Revolution and later the censorship of the emperor took care of what was left. The conqueror's famous sally, pronounced in Berlin, on November 21, 1806, is taken seriously: "People complain that we no longer have a literature. That is the fault of the Home Secretary." Napoleon knew how to make fun of others and of himself. Certainly, Chateaubriand, Mme de Staël, Benjamin Constant, Sénancour,

Charles de Villers were either foreigners or exiles who were reduced to silence. But English poets from 1812 and after, including Landor and Browning, also lived outside their country, as did many Americans between 1900 and 1938; they are not cut out of the literature of their nation because of that. A literature that comprises such eminent names, and others besides (the two de Maistres for instance, who were much more French at heart than they themselves believed), plus Joubert, Maine de Biran, Courier, Nodier, cannot be despised. There are other periods of fifteen or twenty years in French literature, of which the period 1950–1970 is perhaps one, which are no more illustrious. The truth is that we have not studied in any depth the literature of the First Empire and even that of the Revolution. Sainte-Beuve's work on *Chateaubriand et son groupe littéraire* is perhaps, after his *Port-Royal*, the best of his writings, even if at times he fires off malevolent epigrams at the Enchanter. In this work, one sees how the critic (and this is true of Lamartine, Vigny, Balzac, and Hugo, whose imagination will remain filled with memories of these years of the Empire) becomes immersed in the generation which came just before his own. Any young man who finds in the library of his parents books that were read thirty or forty years ago runs the risk of being more influenced by them than by those which has just been published and have not yet reached his province or his district.

Moreover, it would be naive to wonder at the absence of a prolific literary flowering at the time of the Consulate and the Empire. On the one hand, the army lured and destroyed talented men, who, if they had not been engaged in action, might have left their mark on literature. The tentacular administration of the French departments and of the countries which formed part of France for a time, as well as of conquered territories, also required first-rate men, and they were not lacking; for it is in the task of administration that the Empire has proved to be most lastingly effective. Certainly more than half a million Frenchmen (without counting the Allies) died in the wars of these twenty-odd years, and who knows what budding Pascals and Rousseaus there were among them? Finally, and the parallels between this period and ours are striking, science, more than literature, attracted gifted young men, and Laplace, Champollion, Cuvier, Monge, Bichat, Saint-Hilaire, Lamarck (even if he was unappreciated by the sovereign) have added plenty of luster to the Empire. It is towards science that the most promising subjects were oriented in the state-supported secondary schools of the Empire.

Furthermore, as early as the reign of Louis XVI, except in the case of some isolated writers like Laclos, Rétif, and Sade, or of fiery personalities like Beaumarchais, some insipidity and a liking for what is "nice" and falsely ingenuous had undermined literature. Today we like to associate romanticism with violence and revolt. We think that Sade is more realistic, at least when he is interpreted symbolically, than Bernardin de Saint-Pierre. However, in *Paul et Virginie,* and even in the heroine of *La Nouvelle Héloïse* there is a modest reserve, a lucid refusal to pour out one's heart, which have their value and are closer to the real, or to the average, than are *Justine* and *Juliette* (1791 and 1798 respectively) and even *Les Nuits de Paris,* that fine work that Rétif published in 1788. We like this gracefully poetic and always genuine modesty in Julien Sorel, in Fabrice in his tower, and in Lucien Leuwen who dreams of Mme de Chasteller as he hears the hunting-horns. It has a great deal to do with the fascination that Joubert has for us. This friend of Chateaubriand, who was very different from him and whom his contemporaries were only able to know partially (it was only in 1938 that a complete edition of his *Carnets* really did him justice), outlined views on imagination and poetry which might have made him, as a theoretician, the French Coleridge. Today he is even exalted as a spiritual brother of Mallarmé, but not quite an ancestor, for he scarcely exercised any influence in France.[1] But there is not very often synchronism between the originality of theories on the nature of poetry and poems, hymns, or songs actually composed. Often, one is even prejudicial to the other especially if the theories precede the works and claim beforehand to legislate, or to limit the imagination of temperamental talented people. It is critics of foreign origin, impressed by the slightly naive veneration that their English-speaking colleagues have shown for the distinction between "imagination" and "fancy," who have recently extolled Joubert, as the Englishman Matthew Arnold and the American Irving Babbitt had tried to do in the past. Indeed, Joubert had, with some scholastic awkwardness, deliberated upon the substantives "imagination" and "phantaisie" and suspected at times the value that passivity has for the poet: "wise passiveness," Wordsworth used to say during the same period, and later Keats promoted the curious expression "negative capability." He has also been conscious of what could be revealed by the search for the invisible behind the visible, a guest which also tempted the French Swedenborgians. In the history of romantic writings, Joubert remains a solitary figure without immediate descendants, but one of the most profound of the extremely large number of writers of mediations or discontinuous notations in France.

Thus the style that prevailed during the First Empire is better than it has repeatedly been made out to be, and the great influence that the emperor exercised on literature and art was after his death: from 1821 onwards and until the triumphant moment when his ashes were brought back to France. Even before Bonaparte had affirmed his interest in the arts and sciences by taking along with him a group of scholars and artists to Egypt on his ship in which he read Ossian every night, the Revolution had reduced to silence the survivors of the preceding epoch (Beaumarchais, Laclos, Bernardin) or had put to death André Chénier and Barnave. It has fairly often been said that the Revolutionaries' cult of ancient Rome, following the mode of antiquity that the excavations at Herculaneum and Pompeii had initiated, had interrupted the impetus which would otherwise have led the French to appreciate romanticism. This is to delude oneself considerably with words that one likes to place in contrast one with the other. Very often, men like Michelet, Berlioz, Hugo, and—in other countries—Hoelderlin and Swinburne dearly loved the authors of antiquity with a so-called "romantic" passion that was violent, irrational, almost physical. These artists sought in the works of antiquity a profound admiration for nature, escape from the present, sensual reactions, rather than infallible models to imitate. That was perhaps how it was for Racine at Port-Royal or Fénelon, or Molière when he discovered Lucretius. But that was not the period when confessions were fashionable. During the last twenty years of the Monarchy that collapsed in 1791, there was a remarkable rebirth of scholarship in the arts and letters of antiquity. However, poetry and prose were not at all affected by it. The ancients provided ammunition to attack religious fanaticism. Lucretius, the Stoics, Julian the Apostate provided weapons. Or else, the fragile and the graceful, the erotic elements and the embellished pastoral elements were chosen from the legacy of the ancients, rather than the virile and serious aspects. The contemporaries of Louis XVI, including Chénier, seemed to have a preference for the Ionian and even the Alexandrian. Chénier was so totally in accord with his century that it is difficult to understand how he could have seemed romantic later on because of some innovations of form.

But the salons and the court at Versailles, the entourage of Marie-Antoinette, and the admirers of Delille and Parny only represent one of the phases of France during the reign of Louis XVI. Those who lived in the provinces were champing at the bit at this time, from boredom and impatience, seeing no outlet for the talent they felt they possessed or no possibility of accomplishing the reforms they considered indispensable. Their names were Danton or Robespierre, Saint-Just, Marat or David, Marceau and Hoche. The aesthetic theories and prose of those of them who were writers obviously did not anticipate the *Préface de Cromwell* or the cosmopolitan views of Mme de Staël. But their sensibility and their style were romantic, even when they celebrated the festival of the goddess Reason or exclaimed: "The world has been a void since the days of the Romans." The revolutionary turmoil made executioners or martyrs, or perhaps energetic warriors of some of them, who, like Bonaparte, passed from the stage of literary reveries to that of controlling men and things. Others were dreamers, dissatisfied with rationalism, and even with Rousseau's arguments which aimed to limit reasoning. They were already suffering from an emotional void that nothing could fill, except perhaps a mystical impulsion towards the divine, at times even recourse to some theosophy or magic to arrive more quickly at what they considered divine. "How many men there are between God and me!," Rousseau complained. In his *Oeuvres posthumes* Saint-Martin wrote: "There is no man who can suffice for me. I want God"; and Rivarol, who was at times a very curious psychologist, said: "In men's hearts there is a religious chord that nothing can root out and which can always be moved by hope and fear."

THE INFLUENCE OF EMIGRATION
ON THE EARLY STAGES OF ROMANTICISM

Among those works of our century which have renewed our understanding of the origins of French romanticism, one of the most original and daring from the point of view of the vast scholarship it required, is that of Fernand Baldensperger, published in 1925: *Le Mouvement des idées dans l'emigration francaise (1789–1815)*. Approximately one hundred and seventy-five thousand people, most of them from the cultured classes of society, had more or less voluntarily left France after 1789. Many returned at the beginning of the Napoleonic era. Others settled in Russia, Germany, and the United States. Had it not been for the historical vicissitudes, these aristocrats or bourgeois would probably have formed a public capable of acclaiming and perhaps even of writing the new literature by the end of the eighteenth century. It was people like them who had shown enthusiasm for *La Nouvelle Héloïse* and even for the *Encylopédie,* for American independence, and for *Le Mariage de Figaro.* They had wept over the plays of Nivelle de la Chaussée and been moved by the moral scenes painted by Greuze. Led by Louis XVI, they had subscribed to Letourneur's translation of Shakespeare and dreamed of Fingal and Malvina. Even their liking for the most alluring pictures of Boucher and Fragonard or for the narratives of Crébillon Junior would easily have harmonized with the cult of emotion, as occurred later with Mérimée, Hugo, and Musset. The romantics of 1830, the brothers of Didier of *Marion Delorme* and Rolla, were not the only ones to dream of rescuing prostitutes from their fate and of restoring their virginity by means of true love.

But *dis aliter visum.* This was not to be their destiny. And it is futile to speculate on what could have happened if French romanticism had found its public thirty years earlier. Baldensperger's very diligent research is important because it shows how, in seven or eight European countries and in the new American Republic, the French emigrants had undergone an emotional upheaval, a moral and physical uprootedness, a revision of values, and this helped to form more quickly a public able to sympathize with Chateaubriand, Balzac, and Lamartine. Neither the banishment of Protestants after the Revocation of the Edict of Nantes, nor even the exile of "White Russians" after 1917 or of German Jews after 1933, has been of as much consequence in this respect, although the last group in particular have contributed far more significantly to science and learning outside the frontiers of Germany. It was only the group of French emigrants at the time of the Revolution that included a great number of people who returned to their country after years of ordeal and did their utmost to renew ties with the past somehow or other. The Russians after Lenin, the Spanish republicans, or the Cubans after Castro would not have dreamed of doing such a thing.

These French émigrés had to break completely with society life as they knew it and were forced unexpectedly into contact with common people, working men, sometimes overseas with aborigines such as Chateaubriand imagined or thought he had seen, with humble families of patriarchal customs, with Quakers, Methodists, Moravian or German Pietists leading a very Christian life that the readers of Voltaire and Holbach believed dead. They also had constant, daily contact with new landscapes, a closer contact than the conquerors of the Great Army had with the Russian or Polish Steppes, the Bavarian or Lombardian valleys, as they marched rapidly through them. Haller and Gessner, Thomson who wrote *The Seasons,* and Rousseau were no longer pretexts for bookish idylls for these travellers. A feeling for nature, and awareness of the isolation of man amidst overpowering landscapes or bleak plains, of his estrangement from men whose language he did not always understand, a desperate nostalgia for a more serene past, anguish at the thought of the future, consciousness of the insignificance of man tossed around by events, escaping the guillotine and a nation full of hatred by mere chance: these emotions and many others were experienced by these exiles before they were expressed by a new literature.

Of course those exiles who had some spare time or talent wrote their memoirs, languidly and complacently, with an egocentricity that is understandable in those who had abandoned everything and were complacently alone with their ego, like Rousseau when he wrote his *Rêveries.* Some of them wrote novels, the most successful models of which were those of Chateaubriand, Mme de Staël, Constant, and Sénancour. In *L'Emigré* (1797), the economist and polygraph Sénac de

Meilhan, being less exclusively preoccupied with ego, had somewhat clumsily discovered the dramatic possibilities of an epistolary novel on this subject. Unfortunately, none of these émigrés—men or women—were poets, and this holds true also for the inexhaustible Mme de Genlis, Charles de Villers, Rivarol, and even Chateaubriand, who attempted a ballad in verse. All the lyrical themes were there before them, experienced by them. Their imagination should have been set on fire. The cheap finery of outmoded classicism, the platitudes in the manner of Delille would perhaps have been rejected by those who had had to learn a language that was new to them. But a writer like Wordsworth or Novalis was not destined to appear among these exiles.

At least, they were forced to question their political views. Two foreigners, who were, however, French by inclination, Mme de Staël and Joseph de Maistre, were to write their reflections on the cataclysmic French Revolution and the lessons it taught to those who could manage to understand them. Belief in divine Providence or in the law of irreversible progress had been shaken by the spectacle of the Terror and by the hatreds stirred up within the very frontiers of France. The philosophy of the Enlightenment had been attacked or repudiated by this event. The instability of the oldest and most solidly established monarchy in Europe had seemed illusory. Could it be that these revolutions were willed by God as a punishment and perhaps as a lesson? Was a regeneration inevitably preceded by a blood bath? Greek tragic writers used often in their works the image of a parent devouring his children. Was the same old image to express also the fatal progress of the Revolution as it destroyed first the Royalists, then the Girondins, then the followers of Danton and remained ever bloodthirsty and looking for fresh victims? Many men at that time, including Chateaubriand in London, de Bonald, and several others, reflected on a philosophy of history that had to be reconstructed completely. Conjectures on this subject later enriched the poetry of Lamartine, Vigny, and Hugo. That was not enough to renew poetic language before 1820, and it could certainly have been dangerous to approach this kind of topic in France during the period of imperial censorship. But, between 1789 and 1815, a secret transformation of sensibility had taken place within France and even more so outside France, while poets of other nations were already making efforts to renew the outmoded poetic diction. Chateaubriand's words in his work *Mémoires d'outre-tombe* (Book XIII, Ch. 2)—words that Baldensperger has emphasized in his epilogue—are, to a large degree, true: "The literary changes of which the 19th century is so proud are a result of emigration and exile." But, as so often happens in history—and this will be clearly seen during the imperial epic and the First and

Second World Wars, the influence of which will be felt by the younger writers—it is not those living during the great events who write about them most forcefully or feel their effects most deeply. It is their descendants, impatient and pensive adolescents whose feelings are hurt by the smallest trifles and whose parents were personally engulfed by history in the making. The great events of romanticism will occur mainly after 1802 and 1815.

3 The Word "Romantic" and the Chronology of Controversies over Romanticism in France

Many criticisms have been leveled against the use of words such as "classical," "realist," "symbolist," and, above all, "romantic," which is the most general of the terms in meaning and the most likely to be misunderstood. Paul Valéry, who enjoyed harrassing those who were not precise in their thinking, said that one had to be out of one's mind to play around with such terms; however, even he has not been able to refrain from using them. T. S. Eliot considered that their usage gave a perverse gratification to those who sought futile disputes, and he preferred to leave such games, and the use of these terms, to "professors and literary historians . . . ; for no author in his right mind stops to ask himself as he is writing if his work is going to be romantic or the opposite of romantic" (*After Strange Gods,* 1933). Indeed, the assertion is less valid for certain romantic writers of France and Germany than for writers of other countries. But is equally futile to fight against the use of this convenient term. To ask everyone who uses it to define it exactly is proposing a superhuman task to ordinary mortals. And the few who claim to stand out from the common herd are literary historians and theoretical critics, each of whom puts together his own thesis to give a slightly different interpretation of romanticism as he sees it. The truth is that no brief definition is valid for topics where the subjective point of view and inclination count so heavily. All one can do is to describe, enumerate, eliminate, emphasize certain characteristics, and to do this every time one would need a volume. Others during this period make use of the term which, if not used as an adjective applicable to thousands of natures since those of Eve or

42

Cain, but as a noun ("romanticism"), at least has the advantage of characterizing a period which began in the middle of the eighteenth century or shortly after. It was then that the word made its appearance, first as an adjective, then as a noun, and it rapidly became popular as if, from that moment on, it was subconsciously desired, and then became indispensable.

The history of the adjective "romantic" has been written, at least in part, and we are only going to summarize its main points. As early as 1924, Logan Pearsall Smith, an American living in England, who had a very fine sense of language, wrote a few suggestive pages on the word "romantic" in his *Four Words*. A Swiss professor, Alexis François, had already done some lexicographical research, first on the use of the adjective "romantique," then on the noun "romantisme"; and he published his views in the *Annales J.-J. Rousseau* in 1909, and in 1918 in the *Bibliothèque universelle et Revue Suisse*. He returned to this subject in a short article published in *Mélanges Baldensperger,* "Où en est romantique?" The best clarification was finally given by Baldensperger himself in "Romantique: ses analogues et ses équivalents. Tableau synoptique de 1650 à 1810," a work of about a hundred pages published in *Harvard Studies in Philosophy* in 1937. More precise information on these different essays, all scholarly and interesting, will be found in the bibliography at the end of this work. Finally, the credit for the most recent clarification of the history of this word must be given another Swiss scholar and comparatist who has settled in the United States, François Jost, who wrote "Romantique: la lecon d'un mot," published in *Essais de littérature comparée,* at Fribourg in 1968.

EQUIVALENT TERMS IN
ITALIAN, ENGLISH, AND GERMAN

It took a while for the adjective "romantique" in French to break away from another term, "romanesque," derived from the word "romanzesco" and already found in Cotgrave in 1611. But the adjective "romanesque" was only accepted in English much later and merely to characterize Romanesque art and architecture: it is the word "romantick" that prevails in English and is later accepted in France with the exotic connotation that it will retain for a long time. Of course, the meaning attached to the word was: that which calls to mind the old romances (of chivalry) and the era of the troubadours (in English, "romance" as opposed to "novel," the latter being more realistic and containing less unbelievable adventures). Then the term "romantic" came to be applied to landscapes and ruins which recalled the peculiarities and ingenuousness of the old romances. In John Evelyn's *Diary,* mention is made in 1654 of "a very romantic place" near Bath. Likewise, in 1666, Samuel Pepys speaks of "the most romantic castle in the world," thus evoking the fascinating castles described in stories of the past.

In 1674, while translating Father Rapin's *Réflexions sur la Poétique d'Aristote,* Rymer applies the adjective "romantic" (then spelt "roman-tick") to the poetry of the Italian writers Pulci, Boiardo, and Ariosto. That is already an indication that connotations of liberty and unre-strained æsthetic imagination vis-à-vis rules are given to the word, which will pass from the terminology of nature into that of critical appreciation. In 1690, Furetière only sanctions the word "romanes-que," which he defines as "which is like a romance" and therefore improbable and almost unbelievable. At the beginning of the eighteenth century, Pope and Addison, in their descriptions of the Castle of Windsor and the picturesque site of Chevy Chase respec-tively, find these places "romantic" because of their relative wildness and that indefinable whimsical something that constitutes their charm. In 1766, at the start of his *Vicar of Wakefield,* Goldsmith calls certain first names, such as Olivia, that were then just becoming popular, romantic: and Wieland, in Germany, chooses the name Olivia for its romantic quality, in *Amadis* (1771). Henceforth, English poets will be able to make free use of this term. James Thomson, Thomas Warton Jr., and many others whom François Jost has expertly listed, as well as novelists who were not at all inclined towards reverie and vague yearnings, such as Fielding, use it lavishly. But it is first in Germany, then in France, that the word will become part of the vocabulary of literary polemics.

The term "romantisch" was derived from English and appeared relatively late in the German language. But the Germans' love of the Middle Ages and chivalry, their desire to be free of the aesthetic restraints that originated in France, and their inclination for the whim-sical and strange made them accept this term very quickly. In 1800, Tieck entitles his poems *Romantische Dichtungen;* in 1802, Schiller gives his play *Maid of Orleans* the subtitle *Eine romantische Tragödie.* From then on, the success of the word is assured. The Schlegel brothers make use of it and Goethe will say later, with some unjust rancor, that they seized upon this classical-romantic opposition which he himself had started, partly for the fun of the thing. It is from them that Mme de Staël, in her turn, will borrow this opposition, which she will popularize in her work *De l' Allemagne* (1810, but read in France only after that date). In this book she will peremptorily make the famous declaration: "Here I consider classical poetry as that of an-cients and romantic poetry as that which is related in some way to chivalrous traditions."

ROUSSEAU, LETOURNER, MME DE STAEL

In about 1776–1777, we find the word "romantique" used to some extent in French, but in an uncertain and hesitant manner. The most famous example of the use of the term is found in the Marquis de Girardin's *De la Composition des paysages ou des moyens d'embellir la nature autour des habitations, en joignant l'agréable à l'utile*—long explanatory titles were not avoided at this time—and its celebrity is due to the fact that Rousseau borrowed the adjective "romantique" from this work and inserted it in his *Rêveries* composed in about 1777. Girardin's book was published in 1777 in Geneva, if the date given on the title page is right. It could have been written as early as 1775. The other important text in which the word "romantique" appears is the 1776 Address-Preface of Letourneur's translation of Shakespeare. The publication of the translation itself, which was supposed to be in twenty volumes, was to follow. In this Address, Letourneur announced:

> It is not only in town that Shakespeare should be read and meditated upon. The one who really wants to know him should wander around the countryside . . . , climb to the summit of rocks and mountains; from there, he should gaze at the vast sea, and look at the aerial and *romantic* view of the clouds; then he would understand the great genius of Shakespeare, this genius that paints and animates everything.

Today one may not think highly of Letourneur as a translator, but in this text he already expressed feelings that the romantics would echo fifty or a hundred years later. An annotation to these lines specified furthermore that the adjective used thus in the sense of "exotic" joined together "the physical and moral effects of the perspective." If a valley is merely picturesque, it might well deserve to be painted. "But if it is 'romantique', it evokes a desire to relax in it, it is pleasing to the eye to gaze on it, and soon the imagination is affected by it and fills it with interesting scenes; it forgets the valley and delights in the ideas and images the valley has inspired in it." François Jost has picked out and commented perspicaciously on several other usages of the word "romantique" in about 1780 (de Saussure), 1783 (L.-P. Bérenger travelling to Marseilles), 1786 (satirical reference of the Prince de Ligne). It continued to be applied to sites, and the word was obviously lacking while this particular quality of landscape was keenly felt. In fact, A.-L. Millin, in his *Dictionnaire des Beaux-Arts* in 1806 suggests that this word be borrowed from German and English and used in painting as well as in literature, as no equivalent of it was yet to be found in French.

Soon after, in 1801, in *Néologie ou vocabulaire des mots nouveaux,* Sébastien Mercier, making fun of academic critics who theorize endlessly but are incapable of "romaniser" (writing a novel), contemptuously considers the adjective "romanesque" "artificial and bizarre" compared with "romantique," whose meaning "can be perceived but not defined." In 1802–1803, Sénancour assures the definitive acceptance of the term in the well-known extract that follows Letter 38 in *Obermann:* "De l'expression romantique et du ranz des vaches." No longer is only a site considered romantic but also music and the feeling of melancholy and nostalgia that it arouses. "Romantic" comes to signify a mood and it is associated with "mystery" and "ideals" and venerated as the privilege of "people capable of deep feelings." François Jost points out that Sénancour is undoubtedly the first person to use the noun "romantisme" to designate, not a literary movement which had not yet come into being, but the romantic quality in nature. And in *De l'Allemagne* (1810; but it was actually discovered by the French in 1813, in London) a compatriot of the Swiss Sénancour declares peremptorily in Chapter XI of the second part:

> The noun "romanticism" has recently been introduced in Germany to designate the poetry which originated with the songs of the troubadours, the poetry inspired by chivalry and Christianity. . . . In our opinion, the issue is not between classical poetry and romantic poetry, but between the imitation of the one and the inspiration of the other.

In 1816, when the literary controversy begins to rage in France, Saint-Chamans writes in *L'Antiromantique:* "All I see is that the classical writers are material and the romanticists spiritual."

Undoubtedly the word "romantique" spread from France to Italy where it was less easily accepted in spite of the efforts of Monti and Foscolo. In Italian, the noun changes to "romanticisme" and Stendhal will use that form for a while. Counter to the extremely famous title of a rather mediocre work, romanticism certainly does exist in Italy: it had remote ancestors there in Dante and Petrarch. Foscolo, who italianizes the story of Werther in a very declamatory epistolary novel of a man who committed suicide, Manzoni in his "Lettre en français à M. Chauvet and in his ode on *"The Fifth of May"* (1821) and Napoleon, and even more so at a later date Carducci in his *"Hymn to Satan,"* are definitely romantic. The contrast between Northern and Southern literatures, brought out again by Charles-Victor de Bonstetten, is puerile; for romanticism is after all least prevalent in England in the period 1800–1830, where it is restricted to a few poets estranged from their fellow countrymen. But if one does not count Stendhal, Italy did not play an active role in the aesthetic controversies which France enjoyed before allowing the romantic writers to triumph.

THE BATTLE OF ROMANTICISM IN FRANCE

The chronology of romanticism in the nineteenth century has been extremely well established by several historians, and we need only to mention its main stages here. This history of events, literary coteries, and romantic manifestos is "superficial," often anecdotic, and confused because it presents what happened from one day to the next; nevertheless, it is valuable, for it restores for us the point of view of that period and the particular atmosphere of aesthetic conflicts and literary polemics (often with a political basis or implication) which Parisians thrive on. Also, of course, it distorts reality, for it tends to make us think that the romantic writers knew clearly at that time what they were looking for, what they wanted to become or even what they already were in 1822 or 1825; it also leads us to believe that there was a clearcut line of demarcation between them and their adversaries, when, in actuality, nobody was very sure of the camp he belonged to or the friends he should associate with. Chateaubriand kept aloof from and stayed above all these controversies, scornful of those who claimed kinship with him; he was far more preoccupied with playing a political role during the Restoration than with leading a literary revolt that seemed to flout Homer, Virgil, and Racine. Lamartine shunned the theories and animosities of polemicists. Nodier was considered a romantic, but he really was not one by nature. At one time, Stendhal had seemed to be the spokesman for a bold and modernistic aesthetics, but his *Racine et Shakespeare* (1823–1825) is certainly his most confused and disappointing work; he took pleasure in making fun of Chateaubriand, whom he called M. de Castelfulgens, and of his description of the "indeterminate line of tree-tops in the forests" or of the rising of the moon, written in a style very different from that of the Civil Code; moreover, although his style seems so poetic in several chapters of his two great novels, he did not really have a feeling for poetry (in verse form). If mere numbers have any significance in such matters, one is forced to admit that there were more opponents of romanticism among the writers (Auger, Viennet, Baour-Lormian, and—soon after—the university professors, Villemain, Nisard, and Nettement) than champions of romanticism, who called the former "vieilles perruques" ("old fogies"). It is easy to declare today that the tide of history and of the future was against them. But at that time nobody had the slightest inkling of this. Moreover, many other movements in painting, music, and literature, both before and after romanticism, have vehemently maintained that they are the voice of the future and that, in the wake of this or that great war or revolution, the new society needs a new form of art; nevertheless, four out of five of these movements have amounted to nothing. Perhaps romanticism was indeed "the Revolution in literature," as Hugo declared, but it is difficult to understand why it triumphed so late in a country which had just changed all its structures in 1789–1791 and again in 1800. Or perhaps, as Vitet stated in *Le Globe* on April 2, 1825, romanticism was "Protestantism in letters and the arts"; but if that were true, the romantics were strange Protestants who, at the outset, extolled the monarchy, were thrilled by the coronation of Charles , and claimed rather as pagans their right to their pleasures and whims (Stendhal, Mérimée, Musset). The most persistent claim of the romantics, repeated constantly in the newspapers and reviews which supported the new school, is that of freedom in art and freedom of art. As early as 1824, in Rouen, there took place interesting debates (in which Guttinguer was the most famous participant) during which the complete freedom of genius was proclaimed and the poet refused vehemently to allow any "limits to be placed on the exaltation of thought." Duvergier de Hauranne, the most discerning critic of *Le Globe,* maintained emphatically that the only enemy of the new school was routine: "Subjection to the rules of language; freedom in every other respect: this should at the very least be the motto of the romantics." They claim to copy nature directly rather than imitate the reproductions of nature already prepared before their time, and to discover the real nature of Greek and Roman customs, beliefs, and civilization in order to appreciate the works of antiquity. It must be added that this critic did not support romanticism and that *Le Globe* did not remain favorably disposed towards the new literature for a very long period; it soon began to favor "a happy medium," then it became partial to the Saint-Simonian doctrine, and in 1831 it came to an untimely end. But at any rate it deserves credit for having introduced some relativism into the literary disputes and for having clearly discerned and affirmed that romanticism was not a theory but a "mood," characterised by "spirit, yearning, and dreams".[1]

The very first years of the century were marked by a series of publications which appeared in quick succession: Mme de Staël's *De la Litterature* in 1800, *Atala* in 1801, followed in 1802 by *Le Génie du Christianisme, René,* and also *Delphine,* Charles Nodier's *Le Peintre de Salzbourg* 1803, *Obermann* in 1804. Benjamin Constant's *Adolphe* was completed in 1806 but it was not published until 1814. His preface to his adaptation of Schiller's *Wallenstein,* written in 1809 (the year of *Les Martyrs,* is an important piece of criticism; he was the most knowledgeable of his contemporaries on German literature and aesthetics. *De l'Allemagne* was censured and all copies of it were destroyed in

1810, but it was republished outside France in 1813. In 1811, Chateaubriand published his *Itinéraire de Paris à Jérusalem.* The same year Sismondi, another Swiss belonging to this golden age of Swiss-French literature, published *De la Littérature du midi de l'Europe.* That year witnessed the start of the real dispute over romanticism; and imperial censorship, which had grown less rigid, did not oppose it. Villers, the singular French émigré who became an ardent Germanophile (one of the first of the many Frenchmen who praised the German woman), had led up to it by his *Erotique comparée* (1806); and Bouterwek, whose mind was also open to what was foreign and strange, had published in 1812 his *Histoire de la littérature espagnole,* in which he showed a preference for the "romantic" traits of the Spanish theatre and *romancero* over the stylization of French tragedy. Of course, in his *Cours de littérature dramatique* which appeared in translation in 1814, Schlegel had already extolled the romantic genre as the most capable of uncovering the hidden depths of the universe and being aware of mystery, at the same time as it blended form and subject matter in art, for form is something organic and comes into being like a plant or mineral crystallization. It is not superadded or put on later like a garment. There was some protest against these arguments, in the name of so-called classical criteria (order, unities, reason, cult of antiquity), by A. Jay, in a *Discours sur le romantisme* presented on November 25, 1815 at the Athénée, and by Saint-Chamans, a month later in *L'Antiromantique;* but these protestations were, in our opinion, very feeble and in vain.

The task of reviving some medieval works and translating foreign books—a sounder undertaking than many of these oratorical debates taking place—was being attempted in France during the last years of the Empire and at the beginning of the Restoration period. From 1816 on, Raynouard brought the troubadours into honor. Soon afterwards Fauriel propagated his views on that subject, which made a great impression on all those who were already versed in old Provençal poetry; this was followed in 1824 by his *Chants populaires de la Gréce moderne.* In this way, A. Lovejoy's thesis, that Romanticism is often equivalent to primitivism, is confirmed, at least to some degree. The return to the medieval past was more significant in the case of France than it was as far as Germany, England, or Italy and Spain were concerned. The latter had never made a complete break with their Middle Ages as France had thought it had done or had wanted to do during the period of the Pléiade and the seventeenth century. "Beware of Marchangy" and poetic prose, Victor Hugo exclaimed in *Quatre Vents de l'esprit.* His work *La Gaule poétique,* published between 1813 and 1817, enjoyed a great triumph at that time and contributed to one of the romantic tendencies that most impressed his contemporaries: a renewed interest in the Middle Ages. In 1808 and in succeeding years, Michaud's *Historie des Croisades,* while not aiming at literary effects, narrated, with sympathy for the eras characterised by faith and with psychological insight, the medieval expeditions to the Holy Land. Above all, since 1795, a very young man, Alexandre Lenoir, had succeeded in keeping alive the "Musée des Monuments français," in which were collected works of art confiscated by the revolutionary government, especially from churches and convents. The museum survived somehow or other under Napoleon and it was not till 1816 that it was discontinued by the government of Louis XVIII. Lenoir's taste, his knowledge, and even his respect for these remains of ancient monuments have been called into question. But the many works preserved in this way aroused the imagination of the youth of the Empire, and more particularly that of Michelet, who was still a child at the time; in the thirteenth book of his *Histoire de la Révolution française,* he has recalled this museum with impassioned gratitude.

From 1816 onwards, Byron and the first historical novels of Walter Scott were read more and more in France: seven or eight of Scott's novel's appeared within a period of three years. *La Minerve francaise* did not side with the new school, but it did at least take an interest in it. Charles Nodier, hesitant at first, ventured to praise Mme de Staël's book on Germany; then he emulated the English fantastic tales in *Lord Ruthwen* (1820), a story of vampires, and in *Smarra ou les Démons de la nuit, songs romantiques* (1821). In 1819, Henri de Latouche published the poetic works of André Chénier, whose manuscripts had been entrusted to him by Daunou. *Le Conservateur littéraire,* which was not daring or innovative, acclaimed this poet who was a victim of the Terror, but deplored his audacities of language and particularly of versification; and Victor Hugo, who had not found his own style as yet, criticized the liberties Chénier had taken with grammar and verse structure. Those who were considered romantic writers at that time were Casimir Delavigne, Alexandre Soumet (born in 1786), his friend Alexandre Guiraud (born in 1788), their senior Henri de Latouche (born in 1785), and finally a young friend Emile Deschamps (born in 1791), who joined a small group which sought novelty in art. It was through Deschamps that Vigny and Hugo came to be associated with the first real group of romantic poets. Lamartine's *Méditations poétiques* had caused quite a stir in March 1820 and moved the general public; at that time, the author was staying aloof from all groups; those who most praised this poet destined for success were the royalists and also the upholders of religion. From a political point of view, this romanticism leaned towards the liberal right and monarchical opinions, and this was the position later taken by Vigny, Balzac, and Hugo for at least twenty-five years, and Musset within the bounds of his interest in politics. On the contrary, those who were more skeptical and Voltairian in temperament and did not tend to reveal their feelings with as much complacency (men like Courier and Stendhal) were inclined to adopt a censorious attitude towards the government. And influenced by Charles X's reactionary policies and the growing power of the Congregation, Lamartine, Hugo, and of course Michelet, the champion of tolerance and of the people and the opponent of the Jesuits, soon began also to do homage themselves to Voltaire.

Between 1822 and 1830, promising and poetic works appeared in rapid succession: Hugo's *Odes* in 1822, *Han d'Islande* in 1823, *Nouvelles Odes* the following year, *Odes et Ballades* in 1826, *Cromwell* and its famous preface in 1827, *Les Orientales* in 1829. *Marion Delorme* and *Hernani* were completed in 1829 and 1830 respectively, and in the same year Hugo wrote *Notre-Dame de Paris,* which was published in March 1831, eight months before *Les Feuilles d'automne.* Vigny began his career in 1822 with the publication of his *Poèmes,* which appeared again in 1825 under the title of *Poèmes antiques et modernes.* 1823 was the date of *Les Nouvelles Méditations* as well as *La Mort de Socrate:* 1830 was the year of *Harmonies poétiques et religieuses;* in 1831 and 1834, Lamartine added to his list of published works two very noteworthy essays, *Destinées de la poèsie* (1834) and *Politique rationnelle* (1831). Musset and Nerval began to publish their works in 1830.

In the genre of the novel, Vigny, who was five years older than Victor Hugo, anticipated him in the historical novel with the publication of *Cinq-Mars* in 1826; Mérimée produced his *Chroniques du règne de Charles IX* in 1829; Balzac did not as yet acknowledge his earlier works as his own; Stendhal and George Sand made a wonderful début in the novel in 1831, with *Le Rouge et Le Noir* and *Indiana; Armance,* published in 1827, had not attracted much attention. At this stage, Sainte-Beuve was openly serving the romantic cause with his *Tableau de la littérature française du XVIe siècle* (1828) and *Poésies de Joseph Delorne* (1829). Interest in foreign literatures, heightened by the profound admiration lavished by some on Byron and the hatred that others felt for this writer who was looked upon as "angel or demon," had extended to the Spanish *Romances* translated by Abel Hugo in 1822 and translations of Spanish, German, and English plays published by Ladocat. Viennet, Lacretelle Junior, Auger, and other champions of declining classicism had not managed to put an end to the excesses of the young romantics by ridiculing or insulting them. The new school was extolled for a while by *Le Globe* and between 1823 and 1824 by *La Muse française.* In 1825, the king bestowed the Legion of Honor on Lamartine and Hugo, invited the latter to his coronation and appointed Baron Taylor Royal Commissioner of the "Théâtre

français." After much internal conflict and confusion, the most enterprising of the gifted young writers joined forces to form the "Céna-
cle". Hugo became its spokesman and leader and received the adula-
tion of his friends, Victor Pavie, Paul Foucher, and even Sainte-
Beuve. British actors, playing Shakespeare in Paris, were acclaimed,
often by people who understood no English. The painters of the
period made common cause with the poets and prophets of the new
aesthetics. In 1828, Emile Deschamps also wrote a kind of romantic
manifesto which was the preface to his work *Etudes françaises et
étrangères.* Hugo's esteem for the grotesque, Deschamps' pronounce-
ments on modernism and the obligation to write for one's times,
Hugo's disenthrallment from the reactionary tendencies of the Restoration, revealed in the early years of 1827 in his *Ode à la colonne*—all
these factors helped to make the new school, which felt that victory
was at hand, more daring and confident. The dynamic Alexandre
Dumas joined the romantic group in 1828. 1829, the year when
Vigny's adaptation of *Othello* was performed, and 1830 (February 25),
when the first performance of *Hernani* took place, are usually considered the dates by which romanticism triumphed in France. However,
already Charles Nodier showed signs of dissociating from the leader
of the new school and Sainte-Beuve's attitude towards the play that
caused such a stir was less than lukewarm. As is always the case,
differences in temperament between people brought together for a
short period by a common cause were accentuated once victory had
been attained. But if romanticism did not give rise to further literary
controversy, it did, however, deeply move many more people in the
following years. Romantic emotions were experienced not only in
Paris and the Toulouse of the Jeux Floraux, but also by the younger
generation in the provinces. However, for many years, romanticism
did not seem very different from classicism in its final stages and from
tragedies like Pierre Lebrun's *Léonidas* and Casimir Delavigne's
Marino Faliero, and poems such as those of Chenedollé, Millevoye,
and at a slightly later date Henri de Latouche, whose early works
revealed in fact traces of an almost premature romantic elegiac sensibility and desire for aesthetic liberty. Only gradually, and partly
following the impact of the July Revolution of 1830, did French
romanticism come to realize that it had to become involved in politics
and reap the aesthetic and social consequences of the French Revolution many years after the event. From this point of view, the origins of
romanticism can be traced not only to emigration, but also to the
Revolution and the Napoleonic era, rather than to foreign influences
or the Industrial Revolution, in spite of what might appear to have
been the case or what Lamartine, Hugo, even Vigny, and Constant and
George Sand had believed in their formative years.[2] This explains the

political involvement of French romantic literature, long after 1830, when England, Germany, and even Russia were forced to accept an apolitical or conservative literature. This also accounts for the fervor and passion with which the younger generations of Frenchmen, born around 1810 or 1820 or even later, adopted romanticism and experienced feelings of melancholy and despair. Their extravagant dreams clashed with a reality which they considered materialistic and prosaic; they suffered from the impression of being failures or in advance of their times. No other European literature contains so many works which reveal this bitter disenchantment: these include poems by Baudelaire and the Parnassians, Mallarmé's complaints about his contemporaries' aversion to poetry, Fromentin's *Dominique,* whose disheartened hero gives up his dreams, the novels of Maxime du Camp *(Les Forces perdues),* Le Poittevin and Flaubert *(Mémoires d'un fou,* and *Novembre)* which depict failure and a longing to die or become insane. What had maintained the vitality of the romantic writers of 1825–1830 had been the aesthetic disputes, their opposition to opponents or their attacks against the traditionally classical strongholds like the Académie and the Théâtre Français, and their ambition to emulate Napoleon's military achievements in the field of literature. Once the literary war was over and the victory was won, more lofty ambitions filled the hearts of those who followed the first romantics—ambitions which were not realized because they were impracticable; as Rimbaud said at a later date, they had dreams of changing life or at least the European way of living. The disillusioned Bovary-like attitude of the new generation took the place of the aggressive optimism of its predecessors.

4 Romanticism
and Revolution

Many men have found it entertaining to speculate on the interconnection between the terms "romanticism" and "Revolution," both of which are impressive and even inspire awe in some people. In the first quarter of the twentieth century, there were a great many men in France who were not in favor of the legacy of the Revolution, and their argumentative dogmatism certainly succeeded in making an impression on great intellectuals (such as E. R. Curtius, T. E. Hulme, T. S. Eliot, and Irving Babbitt) in Germany, England, and the United States. They thought that they had discredited romanticism forever by denouncing it for having introduced the worst characteristics of the Revolution into philosophy and art. A hundred years earlier, romantic writers, accused of betraying their cultural heritage, had retorted in their manifestos, which were often contradictory as they were inspired by a particular occasion and by youthful polemic, that their movement merely symbolized the introduction of liberalism, or even the revolutionary spirit, into the literary domain. Thus, Stendhal acknowledged that his "romanticisme" consisted of an acceptance of modern ideas born out of the great upheavals of the period 1789–1815. There was no desire to return to the old pre-Revolutionary order of things even on the part of those who had Royalist inclinations and had been completely won over to the Bourbon cause (at least for a brief while), men whose monarchical convictions were a result either of their own nature or a bitter nostalgia as in Chateaubriand's case, or of maternal influence as in the case of Hugo, Vigny, and Lamartine. Mme de Staël, whose political philosophy was superior to her novels,

54

had declared in *Considérations sur la Révolution française* (published in 1818, a year after her death) that the new literature that was just making its appearance was the logical result of the great Revolution. In 1824, a young poet by the name of Hugo, who at that time professed legitimist opinions and refused to choose between classicism and romanticism, stated wisely in the preface to his *Nouvelles Odes* that it would have been surprising, if not deplorable, had the Revolution that had upset an entire society not made its influence felt on literature. And he added with great astuteness: "Contemporary literature may partially be a *result* of the Revolution without being an *expression* of it. The new literature is authentic. Why should we care if it is a result of the Revolution? Surely a crop grown on top of a volcano is no less edible than that which has been planted elsewhere?" Already at the age of twenty-two, he was fond of making generalizations about history. He declared that the great writers of the past had nearly always appeared unexpectedly in the wake of tragedies and that great political epochs and great literary periods were often connected in some way. In his opinion, something remarkable seemed to be dawning on the horizon, something which would not necessarily be revolutionary, in fact, quite the reverse.

The political views professed by any particular romantic during the Restoration period were really not very significant. What was of far greater consequence was the fervent sensibility, the emotional and almost physical intensity with which ideas of every kind were conceived and experienced. Even the Neoclassical admirers of the period 1900–1910—Maurras, Seillière, Lasserre, and Daudet—with their nostalgia for a past that was definitely over, their raving and ranting, their belligerence and their phobias, were far from possessing the serenity, awareness, discipline, and rationality usually recommended by Classical writers. Maurras could have discovered in himself the weaknesses and absurdities of a peculiar "effeminate romanticism". Likewise, or rather inversely, what the young Vigny and Hugo thought they ought to believe in, out of loyalty to their upbringing and their mother, quickly gave way to the changes brought about by history (after the July Revolution which stirred the emotions of the French and exalted them as the second coming of liberty). Even Lamartine, the poet who was the least favorably inclined towards Napoleon, and one of the very few members of the Chamber of Deputies who realized the danger of the return of the Ashes which excited bourgeois France of 1840, slowly revised his orthodox ideas and affirmed his deep faith in the regeneration brought about by revolution. It is a well-known fact that Marx and Engels, the founders of scientific communism, held in high esteem that monarchical reactionary, Balzac, who was also, in his fashion, a Catholic reactionary or a partisan of Catholicism. Engels maintained that he had learned more from him than from all the works ever written by historians, economists, and statisticians. Balzac's temperament, whatever he might have thought about it, was that of a non-conformist who was both in revolt against his age and fascinated by it. What was peculiar was that it was thirty years or more before the extraordinary events of the Reign of Terror, the war of the Vendée, the atrocities committed by the Emperor's soldiers in Spain or the episodes of Jena and Beresina, which had been noted in authentic or apocryphal memoirs, figured in the literature of imagination and were greatly magnified by writers and artists (with the exception of David and Gros).

THE IMPACT OF THE REVOLUTION ON PHILOSOPHY AND LITERATURE

The immediate impact of the events of 1789–1791 was felt more keenly by German and English poets than by French writers, in spite of the fact that the latter witnessed the development of this astounding series of incidents and some even took part in them. "The Revolution is the child of philosophy," and Fichte hailed it as such. At almost the same time, Hegel expressed the view that the revolt of the Parisians against an ineffective monarchy marked "an important date in the history of the entire world"; and this judgment was repeated in his work *Philosophy of History*. Theory and reality seemed for once to be in harmony with each other. "It is heaven on earth," he declared; and on the anniversary of the capture of the Bastille, he planted, along with Schelling, a tree of liberty in Tübingen, to commemorate the event. Fichte, who was of plebeian stock, was more deeply moved by these occurrences than any other philosopher, and even after the Reign of Terror, in April 1795, he acknowledged that his *Doctrine of Science* "belonged to a certain extent to the French nation," for it was thanks to it that he "had been so greatly exalted and had been able to find within himself the ability needed to comprehend the ideas" he expressed in his work. Kant, although much older, was equally enthusiastic about the Revolution, an enthusiasm which was not dimmed even by the Reign of Terror. Again in 1798, in his final work, *The Contest of Faculties,* he rendered homage to the Revolution, which he considered moral in its essence. "Such a great event in world history will never be forgotten, for it has revealed that there exists deep down in human nature the possibility of moral progress, a possibility which had not occurred to any politician before this time." Even Klopstock, who was, however, much less attached to France by education and feeling, had expressed delight about the Revolution, and he was rewarded for this by being granted the title of "honorary citizen" of

France by the Legislative Assembly. Schiller, who had also been made an honorary citizen with the gallicized name of "Sieur Gille," anxious about morals and forgetting that he had begun his career more daringly with *Kabale und Liebe,* was afraid that the French upheaval would lead to a disregard for moral laws. But a distinguished German, Anacharsis Clootz, adopted insurgent France as his new motherland; he was later guillotined there. Several other Germans also came to France and became fervent French nationals.[1] Goethe however, in spite of his famous prediction on the night of Valmy, when he participated in the campaign against France (which soon proved abortive), did not really like the Sansculottism of the revolutionaries and was only keen on Napoleon, who had been good-natured enough to award him the Legion of Honor in 1808 and to say pompously to him, "You are a man, Mr. Goethe." But the French Revolution inspired other Germans: Kleist, at a certain period, wanted to enlist in the French army camped at Boulogne; Hoelderlin composed his *Hymn to Liberty* in 1793 and later extolled Rousseau for being a man who knew "how to interpret the signs by which the Gods communicate with us mortals"; at a later date, the Revolution moved Heine and Büchner, the latter of whom died at the age of twenty-three in 1837, after having written *The Death of Danton,* one of the finest dramas inspired by the Revolution.

England was one of the first of the European nations to salute the dawn of a new era in world history, through the words of its best poets, Wordsworth, Coleridge, and Southey. In July 1790 and again in 1791, Wordsworth spent more than twelve months at Blois, where he made the acquaintance of a French officer sold on the new ideas, and even fathered an illegitimate daughter whose existence he kept concealed from the great majority of his compatriots and from posterity. But in *The Prelude,* his autobiography in verse, published after his death, he evoked with retrospective admiration those days when human nature seemed to have been suddenly regenerated in France:

> France standing on the top of golden hours,
> And human nature seeming born again.
> (VI, 340-341)

His revolutionary zeal, frustrated by Bonaparte's conquest of Italy in 1796 and the Directory's invasion of Switzerland, turned into almost bitter hatred. Like other disillusioned ex-revolutionaries, he became the "lost leader," an embittered reactionary. But had it not been for Rousseau and the Revolution, he would very likely never have discovered his real talent for poetry. Coleridge had shared his friend's enthusiasm, although he was more inclined towards German metaphysics than French philosophy; his attitude changed, however, with the fear of the Directory's army landing along the English coast and with the French army's violation of Swiss neutrality; his poem, *Fears in Solitude* was composed in morbid dread of an invasion—an apprehension that continued to obsess the English until Waterloo. At all events, a few years later, the day after the presentation of *The Prelude* (1807), Coleridge recalled in a poem, *To William Wordsworth,* the wave of joy and hope that had swept over the world when "from the general heart of human kind, Hope sprang forth like a full-born deity." William Blake also wrote a poem—which he did not publish—on *The French Revolution;* it was to consist of seven cantos and only the first one was composed; it must be added that it is a strange and frenzied poem in which appear the Archbishop of Paris, the commanding officer of the Bastille, and Abbé Siéyès. Shelley, who was born during the period of the Legislative Assembly (1792), never stopped dreaming about what the Revolution could have meant, had it really managed to establish the reign of liberty on earth. Shelley, Blake, Byron, and Manzoni (who belonged to another country and whose ode on Napoleon, who had died on May 5, 1821, was later translated into English by Gladstone) continued, with a peculiar respect born from their sense of fair play and with some feeling of shame about their attitude towards the fallen giant at St. Helena, to meditate upon the death of Napoleon in 1821 and the rise and fall of the greatest revolution in world history.

REASONS FOR THIS PHENOMENON

The attitude of Frenchmen towards the Revolution in their own country was more complex to explain. In 1820 and even a little later, the memory of emigration, the Reign of Terror, compulsory military service under Napoleon, and the invasion of their country in 1814 and 1815 was still too fresh in their minds. It took time and the blunders of Charles X to alienate many of them from the dynasty to which they had rallied in good faith at the beginning of the Restoration period. They also needed some historical works or books on the philosophy of history in order to have a more accurate view of events that their parents had told them about, more often than not with terror. After Mme de Staël's posthumous work, those of Ballanche and Lamennais endeavored to explain the Revolution in terms of the plans of the Creator, while, in about 1823–1824, Thier's and Mignet's histories of the Revolution were published. What was already apparent was that strange feeling which many Frenchmen would continue to have towards their Revolution (and also towards the victories and consequent defeats of Napoleon): dismay at what their country had thus been able to perpetrate in cold blood, dismay about the numerous massacres, but at the same time, pride in such a momentous upheaval which had been more constructive than destructive. Later, even Renan, one of the wisest Frenchmen, who at times condemned democracy, was to reconsider his fairly recent and extremely peremptory judgment on the destruction of the monarchical and religious past of France. He did not hesitate to do so, and he recalled in his *Souvenirs d'enfance* the all-pervading love of the Revolution that his mother had instilled in him: "Since I have noticed how foreign writers are desperately trying to prove that the French Revolution stood for nothing but shame and folly, and that it has no importance in world history, I am beginning to think that it may be the best thing we have ever done, as they are so envious of it."

It would be quite out of the question to draw too precise a parallel between revolution and romanticism in France. A strong wave of emotion and of aesthetic revival, such as that which characterized romanticism, is brought about by many different forces and therefore cannot be explained by one cause alone. . . . It would be equally wrong to maintain that all romantic writers and artists were revolutionaries, who were aware of being so or at times unaware of these tendencies within them. Many of them were apolitical (like A. de Musset) or respectful of the established order (like Mérimée or Tocqueville). Nevertheless, in almost all of them could be detected a feeling of revolt, either political or social, or else inspired by passion and directed against morals which were considered too constraining, or literary in nature and directed against former proprieties and rules. But it was during the period when romanticism was asserting itself and more particularly around 1830, when it seemed to be on the verge of winning its battles, that there appeared in France what the English historian Alfred Cobban, using Napoleon's phrase, called "the myth of the French Revolution," a myth which, according to the Emperor who always considered himself as the successor and the consolidator of the Revolution, people wanted to believe and consequently did believe. The expression was commonly used at that time, even by those who, like Chateaubriand, did not really wish for a new Apocalypse, but who felt that the future held something new in store for them (*Etudes historiques,* Preface of 1831). Joseph de Maistre, whose inconsistent and impassioned ideas influenced Vigny and later Baudelaire had himself, like the Englishman Burke, been very impressed by the diabolical or perhaps divine greatness of the Revolution, which inspired in him feelings of terror mingled with admiration. He regarded it, not as a series of events controlled by men, but rather as a mighty force, perhaps even a monstrous one, which made use of men. He very nearly celebrated it as being of divine origin, by a *Te*

Deum, as he had done for the war. Ballanche, who reasoned less rigorously, aspired, like so many other romantics who believed in mystical phenomena, to a great regeneration, and proclaimed a law of human progress and the continuing development of mankind, but, unlike Turgot and Condorcet, not in a perspective of rationalistic agnosticism. He welcomed suffering as a unique distinction, but not restricted only to individuals; Providence can inflict great ills on entire nations as well, in order that some good may result from it. De Bonald imparted some of these views to his young admirer, Lamartine, who was, however, optimistic in nature. Lamennais, after his revolt against the Roman hierarchy, which had been startled by his *Paroles d'un croyant* in 1834, and even earlier in his journal that was aptly entitled *L'Avenir,* had also perceived and acclaimed the hand of God in such historical catastrophes as revolutions. In his words, they are a shining proof of the presence of God in worldly affairs (and this God is not a God who protects the established order and authorizes injustice embedded in orthodoxy).[2]

THE REVOLUTION EXTOLLED BY LAMARTINE

No one has written a history of the theme of revolution in general, and of the French Revolution in particular, in the romantic novel, theater, and poetry. The Reign of Terror, the capture of the Bastille, the imprisonment of the king and Marie-Antoinette provided an ideal background for melodramas and historical novels. But what is really more romantic is the way in which poetry has viewed the subject from its epic and philosophical points of view. Among the great romantic writers, Lamartine is undoubtedly the one with the keenest political sense and the most prophetic ideas which are also the noblest and the most imaginative. Like Michelet, Daumier, and many others, he was deeply impressed by the days of the July Revolution of 1830, and even more by the workers' riots in Lyons and Paris of 1832 and the Transnonain Street massacre. One was able to visualise oneself on the brink of a great upheaval and view it without apprehension. Lamartine foresaw this in his letters; and in 1831, he stated his foreboding openly, in a remarkably lucid and forceful pamphlet, *La Politique rationnelle.* He gave a stern warning to his compatriots: the hour was struck; the world has been shaken; the reorganization of the social structure is imperative. In 1831, he composed a very eloquent poem on *Les Révolutions* which he included in his collection entitled *Harmonies poétiques et religieuses.* In it he lashed out against timid conservatives,

> The quiescent peoples of the stupid West,
> Men paralyzed by your stupid pride,

incapable of understanding that change is the principle of life, laid down by God himself, who never stops telling nature and man to "progress." It is fruitless and cowardly to complain because a nation suffers greatly and a throne totters!

> Move forward! Man does not live by a single
> guiding principle,
> Each night he blows out the light which guided
> him that day,
> And he lights another candle from the immortal
> torch.

The poet had not read Hegel's works and probably he had scarcely heard his name. But the noble idea of the perpetual growth and unceasing development of humanity, which had already been formulated by various Encyclopedists, appealed to his imagination. The man who owed his initial success as a poet to his religiosity and who had again sung abundant praise of the Lord omnipresent in nature in his *Harmonies,* which Veuillot laughed at and characterized as "your *gloria patri* drawn out over two volumes," no longer hesitated to take a diametrically opposite view to that of the Catholic orthodoxy. Church tradition is not unalterable; an eternal Gospel is presented to us and it renews dogmas. Let us know how to bury what is dead and gone without weeping over the past that is done with.

> Your centuries little by little spell out the Gospel,
> You only read one word in it, and you will read a
> thousand.
> Your more daring children will read more deeply into it!

Lamartine's apparent nonchalance, which at times makes us think of that of La Fontaine, whom the romantic poet did not like very much, only partly concealed the fact that he had very firm intentions and an unshakeable determination not to become an adherent of any orthodoxy, literary, religious, or political. In the very beautiful and often profound second "epoch" of *Jocelyn,* the young man who had taken refuge in his Alpine grotto during the period of the Convention reveals in very vivid verses his thoughts on "this blood-stained abyss of revolutions." He sees in these often bloody events a message from God himself. He has not confided his secrets to any government or ruling body, nor has he promised them power that lasts forever, proof against all upheavals. Empires totter and collapse, as Bossuet and Volney had often repeated; laws become obsolete. With calm presumption, Lamartine alleges that churches and gods also pass away. For man, the eternal traveller, all that is only

Baggage that we leave behind as we flee,
Baggage that the future holds in contempt and does not bother
with.

To be sure, the seminarist who expresses in this case the views of the poet does not vindicate the crimes and injustices which accompany these historical cataclysms. The blood of innocent victims is shed; Lamartine does not accept, any more than Vigny does, the idea of the reversibility of afflictions, acclaimed by Joseph de Maistre, nor the concept that the innocent suffer for the guilty according to a cruel law of atonement. These great crises are the will of God since they take place and contribute in the last resort to the progress of "the human caravan." But men who serve as tools of the unfathomable divine will are fallible and often misguided. Some day, their descendants will enjoy the beneficial results of the reforms brought about by means of blood and fire; but those who had planned these revolutions, often with noble intentions, would be submerged by the tide of violence, maybe even put to death. The line that concludes the very fine development of this idea had impressed Renan, who witnessed with sympathy the events of February and June 1848, and later with far more terror the Commune:

Woe betide those who make them!
Fortunate are those who inherit them![3]

When he began to participate actively in politics and while he was preparing by his *Histoire des Girondins,* the 1848 Revolution, Lamartine did not hesitate to praise the Revolution openly and fearlessly from the tribune of the Chamber of Deputies and at a banquet given in his honor in July 1847. If the Revolution has left behind as a legacy some ruins, it has also bequeathed us with "a doctrine . . . , a spirit which will last and endure as long as man's reasoning powers will survive." Michelet, who also helped to bring about the Revolution of 1848 and prepared men for a new upheaval by ardently narrating the incidents of 1789, said likewise to those who bemoaned the Reign of Terror: "You tenderhearted men who weep over the afflictions of the Revolution, shed some tears as well for the afflictions which brought it to pass." But in a way it took more courage on the part of Lamartine, who was an aristocrat by origin and by affinity, to understand the common people with whom he had not really associated. He had dared to say in his *Voyage en Orient,* that those crazy rightwingers, the royalists, who had been the most foolish of all the parties since 1789, represented stupidity multiplied by a thousand!

THE INCONSISTENCY OF HUGO
AT THE BEGINNING OF HIS CAREER

Lamartine, who had a sentimental admiration for Rousseau to begin
with, reached the point where he professed the cult of Voltaire.
Napoleon, who, according to him, would have fought fiercely for
Rousseau in his youth, after having observed man "in the natural
state" in the Orient, had also abandoned his first love in favor of
Voltaire, whom he described to Roederer on January 12, 1803, as "a
man who was always reasonable and appealing to mature minds."
Victor Hugo, like other Frenchmen of Catholic upbringing, began by
mistrusting Voltaire and his century.

> Oh, eighteenth century, impious and chastised! . . .
> May your writers be shamed before all nations! . . .
> As smoke rises from a boiler,
> From Revolutions their baneful glory emerges!

He railed thus in a poem, really very mediocre in quality, which is
included in the collection *Les Rayons et les Ombres* (1840): "Regard jeté
dans une mansarde."

He later changed his way of thinking; but already, in the famous
poem "Napoléon II" of *Chants du crépuscule* (1835), he had ended an
ode, epic in inspiration, by a very declamatory meditation on revolution: an unfathomable mystery which defies human understanding,
but perhaps an indispensable element in the great divine plan, as
necessary as thunder and lightning are "à la perle que font les mers"
("to the pearl produced by the sea"). His own development to the
point where he could adopt a revolutionary attitude was impeded by
the fact that he became a peer. At times, there was an affinity between
the socialists and himself; at other times, he was distrustful of these
para-religions, especially of Saint-Simonism; did he know at that point
(before having meditated upon the unfathomed deep of "la Bouche
d'Ombre") that he himself would one day be venerated by some as a
founder of a religion? He was more himself when he expressed his
deep pity for the lowly and the unfortunate, stood up for childhood
and the right to education, and upheld his hatred of oppression of any
kind. In the fifth book of *Contemplations,* he inserted a wearisomely
protracted epistle in verse form, *Ecrit en 1846,* which retraced his
political evolution with some irony. As a child, he had grown up
among aristocrats. After that, he lived and thought by himself, and he
learned to recognize that through the fires of revolutions glows the
dawn of a more glorious future:

Revolutions, which come to avenge all things,
Do eternal good, in spite of the momentary suffering
they inflict . . .
Through all the uproar, the corpses, and bereavement,
The dregs and the pinnacles which become dangers,
The preceding centuries, driven to despair,
Impel Revolutions, monstrous tides,
Oceans made up of the tears of all mankind.

These are not Victor Hugo's best verses. But he too acknowledged how fascinated he was by the Revolution of 1789 and the eternal revolution about which Malraux would write a century later: "Revolution! Everything that is not Revolution is worse than it."

THE INFLUENCE OF SAINT-SIMONISM

We have no intention of outlining in this work the history of the role of the two Revolutions of 1830 and 1848 in romantic literature; many less important writers, poets who were at one time popular throughout Europe, such as Béranger, or the working class poets of 1848–1850, would figure in a history of literature which was more interested in the sociological point of view than in aesthetic values. The influence of Saint-Simonism on literature has not been studied in depth with its complex ramifications, and the greatness of these men who were ahead of their times, true Fausts of their age, has not been sufficiently recognized because it was not depicted in the novels or poems of romanticism. George Sand and Michelet showed little interest in this organizing socialism, which, however, was inspired by far more sentiment and passion than was apparent; the interest that Vigny showed in their doctrine, at the time when he was writing his poem *Paris* (1831), was short-lived. Sainte-Beuve understood the Saint-Simonians, but no doctrine ever held his attention for long. It would have taken a Balzac, a Dickens, or a Zola to interpret them effectively. Curiously enough, Fourier's ideas were more appealing to Leconte de Lisle when he was young, and also to Dostoyevsky for a short while during his youth, and some of his less chimerical ideas were restored to favor when André Breton, a descendant of the romantics, whose style was not at all sans-culotte, and Herbert Marcuse, who was anxious to restore to a position of importance the principle of pleasure and to make Eros one of the gods of a modern revolution, paid homage to him.

THE INDUSTRIAL REVOLUTION AND ROMANTICISM

Literary historians, anxious to explain by analogies and by causing a movement as multiform as romanticism, have tried to compare it with the Industrial Revolution. Unfortunately, the second of these vast concepts is no easier to define or understand than the first. And the cause-effect relationship between great economic or social phenomena and literary or artistic works has never been established in a satisfactory fashion, much less a scientific one. The most systematic attempt to do this has been made by an American literary historian, Albert J. George, author of works on Lamartine and Ballanche and a discriminating connoisseur of romantic literature, in his book: *The Development of French Romanticism: The Impact of the Industrial Revolution on Literature* (Syracuse University Press, 1955). In it, he maintained the thesis that "the Industrial Revolution had been one of the major causes of Romanticism and, at the same time, had become a powerful force that had transformed the initial character of this literature." The second point will be more readily conceded than the first; moreover, it is less novel. Jules Marsan and many others had pointed out in great detail that the cohesion of what is called "the romantic school," a cohesiveness that was in any case short-lived and limited, had not lasted beyond its victories of 1830 and the effects of the July Revolution. With the exception of Musset, Nerval, and Gautier, the poets were attracted by politics; they wished to appeal to the common people. They sympathized with the troubles that the newly developing mechanization and the migration of laborers to the big cities created for the working man. They denounced the inhumanity of great proprietors and of those whom Saint-Simon called "entrepreneurs," and also crimes, thefts, and prostitution. Several of these poets and artists considered art for art's sake as something egotistical and atrocious which threatened to dry up their well of inspiration as it would isolate them from the commoners.

Furthermore, some of these romantic writers were also attracted by another result of mechanization and of democracy that was growing, threatening but inevitable, as Tocqueville had noted in America as early as 1831: a public of a few thousand connoisseurs was going to be extended by an increasing number of people who would know how to read and would be eager for serial stories, thrilling dramas, sentimentality, and even songs about political events. The press aimed at printing in large quantities; the romantic publishers (Renduel, Ladvocat, Barba—the second and third of whom were ruined in 1830) cherished great ambitions and promoted effusively the works of the young authors. For a long time women had undoubtedly constituted at least half of the admirers of *Manon Lescaut, La Nouvelle Héloïse,* and *Paul et Virginie.* But Balzac—as Sainte-Beuve, envious of his success, had not failed to emphasize—won their hearts; and novelists became their confessors, to the same extent that their priests were and to a greater degree than their husbands. They preferred the romantic nature of Balzac's works, his moralistic discourses, his courtesans and his semi-saints or martyrs in the cause of conjugal fidelity, and even his impractical realism, to Stendhal, who recommended the accumulation of "small true facts."

All that, however, brings us back to the same conclusion: the atmosphere had changed after the first third of the nineteenth century and no one could remain unaware any longer of the social and economic movement which enriched one section of society while it eradicated another. Those who claimed to be ignorant of it (Gautier, Leconte de Lisle, Flaubert) nevertheless felt its after-effects. But neither romanticism as it was before 1830, nor preromanticism with its despair, its passionate cries, its complaints about the ennui of life, nor the outbursts of admiration for Young, Ossian and *Werther* could be explained by the influence exercised by the Industrial Revolution (which had not yet taken place on the continent), and most certainly this could not explain German romanticism, since Germany underwent its Industrial Revolution still later than France, a long time after Novalis, Schiller, the Schlegels, and even Goethe had died. It is a very risky undertaking to discover cleverly a precise relationship between the birth of a literature and art on the one hand, and the reign of a great sovereign, military victories, and economic prosperity on the other. There are many clichés on this subject in literary histories and the great collective histories of a country or continent edited by Cambridge, by French, Italian, and German historians, or by Unesco. The floraison of the English literature called Elizabethan is thus attributed to the national excitement brought about by the victory against the Armada (1588). But it was after the humiliating defeat of the same Armada that Spain had its great literary and artistic period—that of Lope, Cervantes, Calderon, Guillen de Castro, Tirso de Molina, Gongora, and painters of great talent. Germany had its richest period of philosophy and literature after it had been carved up and trampled underfoot by the Napoleonic cavalry; and it had another such period after its defeat in 1918, when the political regime seemed unstable and there was the threat of unemployment.

The best characterized industrial revolution began in England around 1760–1780, especially in the textile industry. It rapidly increased the population of the country, which was only six million in 1720, to nine million in 1801, while France in 1801 had about twenty million inhabitants. British superiority over the industries of other countries undoubtedly reached its peak in 1851, with the Crystal Palace Exhibition. A population that was still less than half of that of France produced more than half the cotton, coal, and iron of the entire world. There were very varied reasons to account for the slowness of the French industrial development and they did not result only from the isolation of Europe during the Napoleonic wars, the relative scarcity of coal, or the delay in the construction of railways in France. Germany's development lagged behind that of even France and the Netherlands until the last decades of the nineteenth century.[4] But since the days of Turgot and even more during the Napoleonic era and the Restoration, some superior men had perceived or had a presentiment of the consequences of these changes which substituted machines for men and speeded up the importation of raw materials and the distribution of manufactured goods. Napoleon I did not suspect or understand either Fulton and his steamboat project, or Ampère or Fresnel. But although his continental blockade prevented the French from discovering and studying British techniques, it contributed to the development of several industries on the continent (at Roubaix and Mulhouse). Karl Marx has even praised him for having established on the continent conditions which allowed competition to exist and exploit the lands resulting from the division of large estates. It was apparently during the First Empire that the expression "industrial revolution" was used for the first time in Europe; in any case, that is the conclusion which an English historian, Anna Bezanson, has drawn.[5] In 1806, the Elboeuf Chamber of Commerce linked together the two words "revolution" and "industry." In 1827, another Frenchman made a similar association, and in 1837 Adolphe Blanqui noted in his *Histoire de l'économie politique:* "The industrial revolution (that of Watt and Arkwright) took over England." John Stuart Mill adopted the expression in 1848 and his *Principles of Political Economy.*

SOCIALISM AND ROMANTICISM AFTER 1830

But the industrial revolution, British in origin or at least carried out first in Great Britain, and the political revolution, accompanied by barricades and the uprising of the commoners, are not on a par. The first, which was the work of the middle classes and resulted in strengthening the power of the bourgeoisie, short of actually preventing the second, perhaps made it unnecessary. The millenarian messianism of political and social revolution, dreaming of spreading happiness, "a new concept in Europe," according to Saint-Just, but one which had already been celebrated by the American Declaration of Rights, set little store, at the beginning, by the development of mechanization and certainly did not recommend renouncing the agrarian myth in order to attract the peasants to urban factories. Saint-Simon, and even Michelet, who did not like this doctrine very much, soon realized that Christian messianism, which encouraged passivity in man, should be opposed by another type of messianism which would require man to assert his liberty in the face of all misfortunes and to take his destiny in hand. From the very beginning, the new science extolled by a former disciple of Saint-Simon, Auguste Comte, who gave it the name of "sociologie," was to resist, in France, the mere study and description of collective facts and was to refuse to lay claim to an objectivity which is beneficial to an established order that is justified by the very fact of its existence. It professed to be normative. The other key word of the nineteenth century, "socialism," appeared independently, it seems, in Italy (in 1803, in *L'Antisocialismo confutato* of Giacomo Giuliana); then in the work of Pierre Leroux, who claimed to have invented the term in France before 1830, and who used it in writing in 1833; and a little later, in 1835, in Robert Owen's work in England. And the word crystallized aspirations which till then had been diffuse and vague. In any case, no romanticism in Europe was more intimately and more widely associated with socialism than French romanticism.[6] The few poems by Shelley or Thomas Hood, in England, are of little significance compared to the socially inspired works of Lamartine and Hugo, George Sand and Balzac. The social novels of Disraeli, Charles Kingsley, and Dickens certainly surpass in quality the French or German novels which attempted to describe the fate of workers. But the writings of Fourier, Considérant, and Cabet, the mystical works of Pierre Leroux and Jean Reynaud, and later those of Louis Blanc and Proudhon were read by more people and impressed writers and artists.

Should these utopian reformers be called romantics? To be sure, not many of them were distinguished writers, even though in the works of every one of them, from Saint-Simon's famous parable to Proudhon, can be found some very impressive pages. There is a confused mass of ideas in the works of Fourier and Pierre Leroux, commoners who had spirit enough to want to remain so. But the French, too fond of rhetoric and elegant style, did not appreciate the vigorous prose of those two graduates of the "Ecole polytechnique," Auguste Comte and Jean Reynaud, both of whom were mystics in their scientific logic. A text by Jean Reynaud, "De la société saint-simonienne," which appeared in the January-March issue of the *Revue Encyclopédique* and was followed in the next issue of that same year by an essay that was just as noteworthy, "De la nécessité d'une représentation spéciale des prolétaries," is very lyrical and as romantic as many pages written by Victor Hugo, Michelet, and Quinet, who had undoubtedly read it.[7] It was Pierre Leroux who, more clearly than Ballanche or Joseph de Maistre, called upon the romantic poets to go beyond appearances to what was invisible, to thus be boldly in keeping with their times and to proclaim that "the principle of art is the symbol" (*Revue Encylopédique,* "Aux artistes," November and December, 1831).

The socialists were deeply romantic in the sense that they studied
the past and observed around them the first upheavals caused by
industry, but they did this in order to have an effect upon the future.
Like the young romantics, with an arrogance that was equally com-
mendable, (but running much greater risks, as they were not spared
the trials of lawsuits, exile, and imprisonment), they realized that they
had to convert the world and change it in order to triumph. Few
sayings are more noble than that of Duveyprier, as he defended the
Saint-Simonian doctrines at the time of the trial of 1832: "If we
convert the world, we are in the right. If we do not convert it, we are in
the wrong."[8] Karl Marx was unappreciative of these utopians, whom
he was bent on ousting and whose place he wanted to take, and
undoubtedly this was inevitable. However, both Engles and he owed
them a great deal. It was Bazard, the most political-minded of the
Saint-Simonians, who had initiated the expression "the exploitation of
man by man." Many of the statements of the Communist Manifesto of
1848 are those of the Fourierist Considérant, who was inept enough
to try to form utopian groups in the wilds of North America and failed
in the process. But he is worth reading. In fact, the reaction against the
over-analytical philosophy of the Age of Enlightenment and the
"laissez-faire" policy of the economic liberalism of Turgot and the
Encylopedists, with which German and French romanticism have
been credited, was far more deliberately willed by the socialists of the
romantic period. Foreign historians of the cultural history of France,
less traditionally inclined to separate literary works from their historical and social background, have, more readily than the French, tried to
see in this pre-Marxist, socialism (and, it may be added, the socialism
of Proudhon, Jaurès, Péguy and even Blum later on) a movement akin
to romanticism.[9] Both movements were inspired by a similar sensibility, an analogous feeling of revolt against the condition of the lowly,
"the damned of the earth," but also against the human condition.
Romantic poets, novelists, and historians took a close look at the
world around them, the world of the insurgent silk-weavers of Lyon,
the destitute painted by Daumier, and criminals of the "barricades" of
Paris, like the abandoned Claude Gueux, Jean Valjean, and Gavroche.
At the end of a very scholarly sociological-historical study, Louis
Chevalier, who himself specialized in statistics, in the thousands of
"petits faits vrais" ("small true facts") dear to Stendhal and in police
reports, concluded his long work, *Classes laborieuses et classes
dangereuses à Paris pendant la première moitié du XIXe siècle* (Plon,
1958), by praising the novelists (Hugo, Balzac, Eugène Sue, Jules
Janin) who were more clearsighted than all the sociologists and politi-
cans of that same period. The sympathy of the artist for those whom he
observes and recreates in his work, his vast imagination which lets him

identify with other beings, and even the tenderness of his responsive nature are sometimes better than objective justice. Dostoyevsky, an admirer of Balzac, Eugène Sue, and George Sand, speaking to the privileged classes of his age, exclaimed: "Justice you have, but tenderness you have not, and that is why you are unjust."

5 "Mal du Siècle" and Romantic Pessimism

ALFRED DE MUSSET AND THE "MAL DU SIECLE"

Alfred de Musset, the most tragically "damned" of all the French romantic poets and the one who, more than Nerval and even Baudelaire, stubbornly persisted in bringing down malediction upon his own head, has left us some dramatic or rather melodramatic pages dealing with the malady which, according to him, afflicted his entire generation of followers of romanticism. Unquestionably, the moral of his *Confession d'un enfant du siècle* (1836) is unskilfully presented. The author himself admitted to Franz Liszt that these types of works "are not nearly authentic enough to be memoirs, nor are they make-believe enough to be novels." But the grandiloquent introduction, evoking those children conceived between two battles during the wars of the Empire, who were suddenly in great trouble due to the fall of the master who had for a long time been crowned with glory, and who were even more deceived by the mediocrity of the Restoration, affirmed peremptorily:

> All that afflicts the present century results from two causes: the nation which has suffered through the period of '93 and of 1814 bears the scars of two mortal wounds.
> All that existed before exists no longer; all that will come into being one day is not yet in existence. There is no need to look further for the cause of our afflictions.

Rarely had there been such an abrupt break in history, or at least it had hardly ever seemed so abrupt to contemporaries. It was all very well for future historians, supported by statistics and able to see events in their proper perspective half a century later, to show that a great deal of continuity persisted if one loked beyond superficial upheavals, and that already widespread reforms in the allocation of property and economic progress had been accomplished in France before 1789 or in Russia before 1917. The psychological shock experienced after political revolution leaves, nonetheless, a mark on sensibilities. Posterity has acknowledged that the "mal du siècle", which the romantics gloried in or complained about, retained the importance of a great myth; and it is likely that, in the future, at the beginning of every new century, men will feel that they are afflicted by the same malady and will display their restlessness as their privilege and as a sign of being special, just as at the end of every century (from 1970 onwards, the twentieth century has begun to use these terms lavishly), men will think that their times are characterized by decay and will analyse with secret pride their own decline. Actually, like so many other aspects of romanticism, the one characterized by wailing, cursing existence, making a show of anguish, and continually wishing, quite sincerely moreover, for death—the prelude perhaps to a desired revival—did not disappear from Europe, and especially not from France, once the so-called romantic period was over. The generation of Flaubert, Leconte de Lisle, Jean Lahor, then that of Laforgue, Elémir Bourges, Suarès, of Gissing and A. E. Housman in England, still later that of Roger Martin du Gard, Mauriac, Ribemont-Dessaignes, and Pierre-Jean Jouve, and finally in our times, those pessimists contemptuous of their age and fostering little hope in man, men like Montherlant, Green, Céline, and Cioran, are no less imbued with disillusioned romanticism, inspired by pride or melancholy pity, depending on the individual case.

It is obvious that this "mal du siècle", felt most acutely by Aloysius Bertrand, Nerval, Musset, Maurice de Guérin, Gautier, and Mme Ackermann (all born between 1807 and 1812), was nothing radically new or unique. We recalled earlier that the obsession of suicide, discussed at length by Saint-Preux and Milord Edouard in Rousseau's novel, had troubled a great many suffering souls and weak-willed people in France between 1760 and 1789. The theme of death had become predominant at that time in the poetry of several nations of Europe, but it was treated more skilfully and with more stirring and colorful rhetoric by Young and Gray, and then by Novalis and Foscolo, in languages other than French. The role played by fashion in literature and art is considerable, even if our minds, craving for rational explanations, revolt at attributing too much to chance or the contagion of a rather ineffectual mimesis. There are feelings that our parents had undoubtedly experienced before us (pantheistic impulses inspired by landscapes, delight in solitude, contemplation of a moonlit night, a desire for death or revolt against it), feelings that it had not been fashionable to express; or else they did not have the necessary vocabulary, the gift of inventing images, or the lack of modesty needed to display one's inner self. The literary, musical, or pictorial expression of a feeling makes us suddenly aware of its intensity. Finding it thus magnificently expressed or boldly orchestrated in the art of our period, we feel this mood more intensely, we analyze it in our letters or our private diary, and we, in our turn, help to spread it.

POSSIBLE CAUSES OF THIS MORAL EPIDEMIC AMONG THE PREROMANTICS

The historian may pursue his inquiry into the more general causes which helped to infect a great number of "preromantic" souls during 1775–1785, and later the romantics, during 1815–1830, with the contagion of this collective fashionable malady, which sometimes reached epidemic proportions, or which prepared the way for it. But it is very difficult to specify the effect of these causes in each individual case. One of the causes most often alleged by the victims of this malady of the century, for it is convenient and ennobling to use this as an excuse, is the loss of religious faith by them and those around them. As a matter of fact, there were very few people after 1789 who considered themselves "delighted atheists" or felt an unbridled joy in attacking Christianity head on after having received an ecclesiastical education like Boulanger, Mably, Morellet, or Toussaint. The weakening of the power of traditional religion inevitably made many social institutions totter and shook the framework of daily life. Those who craved most for a firm faith found it easy to transfer their need to believe in something to an anticlerical or revolutionary doctrine. Those whose religious faith was based on emotional needs or who, according to the words of Ninon de Lenclos, had never had enough of it to want to change it, were perhaps more at a loss. But it would be useless to try to explain a great variety of temperaments by a single category of causes. These romantics who reached their thirties around 1800—Sénancour, Constant, Chateaubriand, and Napoleon—and whose melancholy is best revealed to us through their writings and letters, were not really religious people. The clever remark made by the émigré Chateaubriand, on the death of his mother, "I wept and I believed," is perhaps a sincere statement by this man who was sincere about many things successively (or even simultaneously), but his religion was above all a source of literary inspiration, and it did not form an integral part of the lives of even his characters such as Atala, Amélie, the Bianca of *Le Dernier Abencérage,* or Eudora, but only served to stimulate conflicts which we do not take very seriously.

Benjamin Constant, throughout his life, through all the troubles he endured as lover of several women at the same time, through his debauchery and his betrayals, dreamed of writing a work in which he would show, without having any more faith than Bourget, Barrès, or Maurras would have later on, that it was necessary to believe, and he would support his arguments by erudition. He finally wrote this work in five volumes in the autumn of his troubled life and published the five volumes between 1824 and 1830. It did not reveal at any point the kind of heartbreak that breaking away from their religious faith caused Jouffroy or even Renan. In any event, the "mal du siècle" certainly did not affect only unbelievers suffering from the loss of their intellectual or emotional comfort: Shelley, Keats, Leopardi, and the Goethe of *Werther* did not regret for a minute the fact that they no longer believed or that they had never believed. On the other hand, neither Lamartine, at the time when his faith was still intact, nor Lamennais, saying over and over again that "his soul had been born with a gaping wound," nor even Kierkegaard owed the sadness that they expressed and felt to a lessening of their religious beliefs. The Danish philosopher, torn at the same time by anguish and irony, noted at the age of thirty-five, in 1847, in his *Journal:* "From my earliest youth on, an arrow of grief has been stuck in my heart. As long as it stays there, I am ironical. If it is pulled out, I will die."

The feeling of political and social insecurity has undoubtedly affected more those men who, with the downfall of the monarchy, the imprisonment of the king, civil war in many French towns, and the abruptly revealed class hatreds, had witnessed the collapse of the relative order in which they had grown up. The sight of the massacres perpetrated by the enraged crowd in August and September 1792, the news of the "noyades" in the Loire at Nantes, mass executions at Lyons, the atrocities of the civil war in the Vendée could not help but upset well-balanced people who, only a few decades before, had admired Voltaire's hymns to tolerance and had stigmatized the persecutions attributed to "Intolerance." Strangely enough, however, contemporary writers reveal little trace of indignant condemnation of these massacres, just as the writers of 1670 or 1685 did not criticize the havoc wrought in the Palatinate or the repeal of the Edict of Nantes, nor did the non-Jewish Germans of 1933–1943 protest against the Nazi crimes. Benjamin Constant survived these political upheavals by remaining more preoccupied with his love affairs than with the misfortunes of the country. He lashed out against the spirit of acquisition and usurpation in firm and strong language, but he had few qualms about abandoning first one regime and then another in 1814–1815 and, after Waterloo, in noting cynically as he rushed for the spoils: "Time is pressing if I want to be in at the death." Sénancour preferred to live in seclusion and remain uninvolved, and he undoubtedly showed the most nobility of all these semi-sick souls. Chateaubriand showed very little remorse for having fought along with the princes against his own country; his attitude towards Napoleon varied considerably from being fascinated by the genius of the First Consul, to being envious of him and wishing to have the same glory as the warrior and politican, and to being vexed as a nobleman by the off-hand manner in which the upstart Corsican treated certain aristocrats. But several others were excited about the overthrow of the old order, and Talleyrand was among the very first of them, even though he deeply regretted the end of "the pleasant life." The insecurity of the times helped especially to increase their desire for power and their ambition. In 1800 and again in 1830, love of money, position, and power were found side by side with the spiritual vacuum felt by certain people and complaints about the ennui of life and the weakening of wills, and this has been brought out very well in *La Comédie humaine*.

For quite some time, social classes had no longer been separated by the watertight bulkheads which have been too often ascribed to French society under the monarchy. Saint-Simon had already expressed several complaints about the rise of the newly rich and the conferring of titles on commoners. People from the provinces and foreigners (Law, Abbé Galiani, Casanova, Cagliostro) met with little opposition when they ventured to beguile the Courts of the Regency, of Louis XV, and of Louis XVI. But the less ambitious individual was still fairly closely tied to his family, his social and political group, and the district of Paris in which he lived; or else he found without too much difficulty a new social life, a literary circle with which he could identify himself. With the breakdown of social life brought about by the Revolution and the political rather than literary or philosophical nature of the clubs which soon multiplied rapidly in Paris, many writers felt estranged from their class, cut off from their provincial or family ties. The feeling of moral solitude that the romantic poets and moralists were to express so often, has rarely been experienced as intensely as by Sénancour, Chateaubriand in his *René* and his *Mémoires*, and that romantic Bonaparte, a man of letters who soon became a man of action. At the age of seventeen, on May 3, 1786, the young officer wrote: "Always alone as I am in the midst of men, I retire within myself to dream alone and to indulge in the vividness of my melancholy." He avidly read Ossian and *La Nouvelle Héloïse*. From Egypt, where he was victorious and fawned upon, he confided to his brother Joseph, in 1799: "I need solitude. I am tired of greatness and bored by glory. At the age of twenty-nine, I have nothing more to look forward to." The thought of suicide had obsessed him since his adolescence, just as, according to Goethe, such an idea must have crossed the mind of every man worthy of the name, at least once in his life. In May 1786, when he was still unknown, he had exclaimed: "What is to be done in this world? Since I must die, is it not as well to kill myself?" Indeed, he was as familiar with *Werther* as with Ossian, and he liked it just as much.

THE TEMPTATION TO COMMIT SUICIDE

Romantic suicide or the literary theme of suicide (for the dramatic element was inextricably blended with what might have been sincere in the confessions written by men who were already old and were reliving their turbulent adolescence) was actually omnipresent in literature, from Preromanticism to Flaubert, Maxime du Camp, and Baudelaire. It would be a worthy subject of a monograph which ought not to be uniquely sociological or medical. A specialist in mental illnesses and psychiatrist of the nineteenth century, Brière de Boismont, studied this phenomenon as early as 1865 in his book *Du Suicide et de la folie suicide;* and E. Caro, a moralist with considerable insight, wrote an essay of about a hundred pages about this book, which he included in his *Nouvelles Etudes morales sur le temps présent* (Hachette, 1869). Goethe, in recollections in which poetry and truth are intertwined, has brought out the intense feeling of the futility of everything—studies, future careers, joys of nature—which had overpowered him when he was an adolescent and knew deep down within him that he was destined for great fortunes, which, however, were too slow in coming for his liking. The monotony and absurdity of existence overwhelmed him. He thought admiringly of the Emperor Othon, who had stabbed himself to death. He himself placed the point of a dagger against his chest, but shrank from the deed and preferred to rid himself of the temptation of suicide by writing *Werther.* The novel, inspired by the actual suicide of a young man in love, by the name of Jerusalem, led, it is said, a few readers too quickly affected by literature to kill themselves, while Goethe marched on to conquer serenity.

Threats or promises to commit suicide, made to himself or various confidants, abounded in Benjamin Constant's *Journal intime.* At the very time when he was reading *Adolphe* to his friends and was finally going to publish, in 1816, this short novel on which his reputation is based today, he was courting without success Juliette Récamier and, frustrated and jealous, he solemnly wrote (as he had previously done during many other lover's intrigues): "Made up my mind to die . . . I will not reverse my decision to die" (September 5, 1815 or October 9, 1815): "Spent the night writing to Mme de Krudener that I want to kill myself." He was at the time almost a quinquagenarian, but he took pleasure in feeling and acting inconsistently and in believing that he was eccentric and an enigma to himself. Many romantics, after this keen analyst of passions who could not live without them, gazed at themselves in like manner in a mirror, astonished and naively proud of their duality. He confided in his *Journal,* with the self-conceit of one of Molière's aristocratic fops (April 11, 1804): "I have excellent qualities of pride, generosity, and devotion." He added however this strange statement that a seventeenth century Frenchman would never have made: "But I am not a completely real person." And his novel of transparent cruelty, like that of Laclos, seemed to have frightened him to the point where he wrote a fictitious letter to the publisher assigning to it a moral aim and he made every effort elsewhere to generalize this particular case which had been more or less his own (the inability to love along with an invincible need to love) and to present it, long before Musset, as a malady of the new century:

> I wanted to describe in *Adolphe* one of the chief moral maladies of our century: that stress, that uncertainty, that lack of strength, that constant analysis which makes mental reservations about all sentiments and thereby spoils them from the beginning.

Chapter 14 of the third part of *Mémoires d'outre-tombe,* entitled "Temptation", evokes once again the romantic childhood of Chateaubriand, his intense fear of his strange father, the joy he felt in scouring the countryside in autumn, "the season of storms," his reveries about some woman being at hand, a Sylph, the fallen Eve or Phryne, and his anguished questions about the significance of life. He alternated between self-contempt and the pride of knowing that he was so exceptional that no one would ever appreciate him. He related that finally one day he loaded an old shotgun and placed its muzzle in his mouth. By chance it did not fire. He added in a more modest tone than that of other similar reflections recalling the *qualis artifex pereo* of Nero: "If I had killed myself, all that I have been would have been buried with me. . . . I would have increased the number of nameless unfortunate people; people would not have followed the trail of my sorrows like a wounded man can be tracked by the trail of blood he leaves behind."[1]

There is undoubtedly some affectation in the awe-inspiring attitude of melancholy which Chateaubriand took pleasure in adopting, as he listened to the secrets whispered to him by the sea or the forest. But it is too easy to accuse the enchanter of insincerity. In his work, as in that of so many other writers who were in his line of descendants, from Barrès to Malraux, Drieu, and Camus, there was a blend of sincerity and love of verbal ostentation which made the writer exaggerate the expression of an impression. Several avowals found in the *Mémoires* confessed this ambiguity which always affected his personality, and, he maintained, that of superior men since the advent of Christianity. Already, in the last pages of *René,* when his sister confessed to the hero "her guilty passion" and when true sorrow took the place of his vague, languishing sadness, which until then had been without cause the traveller to the country of the Natchez remarked: "What is odd is that from the moment I was really unhappy, I no longer wanted to die." Instead of killing himself, he traveled across the ocean to the New World. A similar duality filled him with pride for having been the first in France to have analyzed the "mal du siècle" with complacency and communicated it to his successors; then, irritated by them or jealous of the French admirers of Byron who made these vague yearnings and this obsession of death commonplace, he maintained that he wanted to stigmatize "this new type of vice and present the fatal consequences of love exaggerated by solitude."[2] Chactas nonetheless consoled the querulous René by assuring him that "a great soul must contain more grief than one less great" and that suffering from a malady mainly imaginary and without a precise cause brings a pleasure unknown to the majority of men.

Certainly none of these sentiments, which caused deep distress to Chateaubriand or the young men of 1820 to whom he communicated the contagion of his moral malady, were very new; it is as difficult to invent new sentiments as new sensation. Even before the advent of Christianity, the ancients had bewailed the instability of all things, the passing of time *(eheu! fugaces labuntur anni)* and the slow and sure death of all the affections of the heart. Pascal, whom the author of *Le Génie du christianisme* greatly admired, had denounced, after Montaigne, the need for new obstacles, or goals that are no longer desired once they are attained, a need on the basis of which Chateaubriand modulated so many of his best orchestrated sentences: a difference of religious or civilization, a suspicion of incest were not enough for him; even women, fascinated by him although they detected his self-centeredness (or perhaps captivated by that very element), readily succumbed to him. His own wife, neglected, waited and suffered, almost uncomplainingly. He discerned in advance the vanity of everything that he pursued, but he did not go to the point of making the Pascalian wager which would make him reject these fleeting or illusory pleasures for an immortality in which he just could not really believe. The feeling of the eternal haunted him, as it later haunted Lamartine and Musset: human destiny is to leave us with this gloomy fact that our existence—our pleasures as well as our afflictions—is short-lived, and therefore spoiled in advance by the presentiment of their end; human beings are incurably incomplete and dream of a plenitude which they declare impossible to achieve or of a joy which they know, deep down within them, cannot be lasting without becoming insipid. Jean-Pierre Richard and other recent critics of Chateaubriand have stressed how constant the obsession of death was in his work. The word '"death" was the *leitmotiv* of his *Mémoires,* just as it was later in the *Anti-Mémoires* of Malraux. Death for him, however, was not, as it was for Hugo, the gateway to a true life ("Do not say die; say be born"—Sixth book of *Contemplations*) or a vision of paradisal felicity like that of Dante at the end of his long tour. In one of his magnificent sentences, he has evoked the gracious end our life can have:

> On our death, the earth opens its bowels to us and throws over our remains a covering of plants and flowers, while it transforms us secretly into its own substance, in order to reproduce us in some graceful form.

At other times, he has evoked in a more gloomy manner, forestalling Gautier, Hugo, and Baudelaire, worms feeding on the carcass in the tomb, the body of Talleyrand eaten away by gangrene, or Rancé, that Ninon, who "devoured by time, was only left with a few intertwined bones, such as one sees in Roman crypts."

The symptoms of this moral malady, so often condemned by moralists but analyzed with complacency by the very people who suffered from it and thus intensified their suffering, are well-known; however, each case was a specific one and the depth of anguish felt varied depending on the temperament of the individual. The accusation of charlatanism made against them by men, during the romantic period itself (almost unanimously by critics and by doctrinaire and bourgeois politicians), and later during the anti-romantic reaction of 1900–1925, was most unjust. To be sure, Balzac and Hugo were also extremely ambitious men and they were plagued by financial troubles and worry about their reputation. The notes they exchanged were often typical of men of letters, heedful of the most likely strategy to advance their success or attentive to the minute questions of language, versification, and technique that writers raise, just as painters and musicians exchange views on their own professional dodges. But the grimace of sorrow frozen on their face, doubts about the significance and goal of life which beset them, formed nevertheless a new psychological phenomenon in Western Europe. Almost all creative geniuses who have followed them have inherited this malady.

An acute state of nerves was undoubtedly at the root of this greater capacity for suffering. From Virgil to Pascal, Racine, and Marivaux, there had always been vulnerable, susceptible, and sensitive souls; but never had so many sick souls or excessively touchy people been affected this way before. Rétif, Laclos, and Sade, who had placed this cultivation of feelings in the forefront of literature, nonetheless lived long lives, perhaps because they were stimulated by the obstacles and dangers which they had faced: poverty at times, revolution and political upheavals, imprisonment. They had rarely been prostrated by a dismal sluggishness or apathy. The chasm that separated the ideal that they dreamed about and dull reality had not made them despair. They had not transfigured the woman of their dreams into an inaccessible goddess, as Stendhal, Nerval or, in other countries, Novalis or Shelley did later. According to the famous little statement—supposedly by Thucydides—that Stendhal presents in *Lucien Leuwen,* the romantics "will spread their nets too high." Even in art their ideal seemed inaccessible to them as it was so far above them, and the deficiencies of linguistic or pictorial resources in relation to their dream led them to despair. La Fontaine or Voltaire had not bewailed thus the inadequacy of expression with respect to the conception of ideas. It was after enthusiasm was considered as the surest sign of genius in art that the men of the new century felt threatened by these repercussions of enthusiasm which undermine creativeness.

There were many individual cases of the dire consequences of the "mal du siècle" in several European countries. Goethe did not succumb to it, and Schiller died young; but there were several others in Germany who were most distressed by the impossibility of fulfilling their dream and became neurasthenic or mad or resorted to suicide. Soon after he was thirty, Hoelderlin's mind became unhinged, and, in a few brilliant flashes of lucidity, he uttered cries of revolt like the following: "Like a man buried alive, my spirit revolts against the darkness in which it is fettered." Heinrich von Kleist committed suicide with Henriette Vogel, after having once again shrunk from consummating his love. Caroline de Gunderode killed herself at the age of twenty-six, for love of a professor (Creuzer); Charlotte Stieglitz did the same, in order to inspire her husband to genius; Lentz failed in his suicide attempt, but became mad. Novalis died before reaching the age of thirty, after the most chimerical, and in the opinion of the wise, the most foolish of impossible loves for a young girl. Jean Paul wrote to a friend: "Man reaches out toward the infinite; all our desires are only fragments of a great boundless desire." Wilhelm Schlegel, however learned he might have been, was no more sensible in matters concerning his love life; at least, he deceived himself with complete awareness of what he was doing and a little of what Baudelaire later called "love of lying" in one of his strangest poems. "I first pretended a passion which I soon came to feel," he confided in his singular and gauche novel, Lucinde, which toyed often with the idea of suicide.

Wackenroder died at the age of twenty-five, not quite right in his mind. Much later, not long after Nerval's suicide in a Parisian alley, the musician Schumann died in an insane asylum (1856), after having failed in an attempt to drown himself in the Rhine to put an end to his anguish.

Among the English romantics there were fewer unhappy souls who considered suicide as an alternative to their over-ardent dreams: the painter Haydon, the poet and dramatist Beddoes (in 1849). But De Quincey and Coleridge sought salvation in opium; Charles Lamb, who lived in close proximity to madness (his sister who was mad had murdered their mother), succeeded in taking his mind off it by humor. Many others, from the second half of the eighteenth century onwards, had lapsed into neurasthenia. Cries of despair echoed in the verses of Byron and Shelley and sometimes even in those of Keats, who was to die of tuberculosis at the age of twenty-five. It is a well-known fact that, in France, Hugo dreaded intensely becoming insane as one of his brothers, Eugène, had done, on the very day of the marriage of the poet, and as his daughter did later. Balzac was also afraid of the same thing. Antoni Deschamps, who was more gifted than his brother Emile, lived at Dr. Blanche's place in order to receive treatment for his mental crises, and tried to find deliverance through poetry and the translation of Dante. Musset went through crises which made him seem half mad to George Sand and later to his brother Paul de Musset. The minor romantics in France, with the exception of Nerval, were more easily engulfed in the abyss within them than the more richly talented poets who found in their more successful creativeness a distraction from their malady; their psychology was nevertheless peculiar and it is through them that we have an inkling of how deeply romantic moods distressed Frenchmen steeped in literature around 1825–1850 and even later: Charles Lassailly, author of the peculiar work *Roueries de Trialph,* who in 1843, at the age of thirty-seven, killed himself; Charles Dovalle, who died in a foolish duel in 1829, at the age of twenty-two, after having believed that he was dogged by a dismal fate[3]; Alphonse Rabbe, author of *Album d'un Pessimiste,* committed suicide in 1829, and Victor Hugo evoked him in a long poem of *Chants du crépuscule* (XVII):

> Oh Rabbe, my friend,
> Rigorous historian asleep in the tomb

the eloquence and the passion of the Provençal who was secretly fed up with living. Esquiros, another Southerner, lived longer, wretched, exiled under the Second Empire for his political views, unbalanced, without any will. In 1942, Desnos, who was already marked down by the German police, who were responsible for his death in a concentration camp in 1945, asked the question which will undoubtedly remain unanswered: "What Baudelaire scholar will be able to enlighten us about the relationship between the author of *Les Fleurs du mal* and Esquiros? . . . [Can it be] that his tone, muffled in the verses of Pétrus Borel or Esquiros, had preceded him and was awaiting him to be finally articulated by him alone, in a loud and clear voice?"[4]

DELACROIX AND THE HAUNTING MEMORY OF FAUST AND HAMLET

It was not only the failures and the unproductive writers who were adversely affected by the discrepancy that existed between their ambitious dreams and what life offered them during a period which they considered completely materialistic and callous as far as human relations were concerned. Hugo and Lamartine, who wondered in verse "why is my soul so grieved?," Balzac, and of course Napoleon and Chateaubriand before them had been, or became men of action. Delacroix represented one of the most typical examples of the domination exercised throughout his life by this destructive "mal du siècle" over a prolific artist who was unceasingly inspired. His letters and the notes in his diary always praised reason, restraint, Poussin more than the painters of his time, Racine more than Balzac and Hugo; in them, he defined inspiration as "reason itself embellished by genius, but following a requisite course and controlled by superior laws" (*Journal,* I, 365). He warmly praised Boileau in his diary. Elsewhere, it must be admitted, he declared he was guided only by instinct and aspired after "happy negligences" which, it seems, restore improvisation into the execution of a picture, premeditated for a long while. But these contradictions themselves revealed his vacillating nature.[5] It is well known that Hamlet haunted him, perhaps more than any French romantic: he has left us lithographs of Shakespeare which Baudelaire and many others after him in France have gazed upon. Perhaps he suffered from the romantic malady in spite of his silence on this subject, on account of some resentment against his mother for his being the son of Talleyrand and not of his putative father, which disposed him to identify with the Danish prince; but he blamed even more nature's indifference towards man, the constant presence of nothingness close by us, the solitude which persists even in love. Like so many other romantics, he fostered a secret anger against himself, because "his cowardly heart does not dare to prefer the peace of an indifferent soul to the delightful and distressing torment of a stormy passion." Some of his letters to his friend Soulier numbered among the most romantically sorrowful of the period. In them, he repeated

that he found himself in front of a terrible abyss" (the word kept
recurring), in moments of insomnia or serious reflection about his
actions, when he fully faced "the horror of his profound misery . . . ,
this cruel nothingness for which there is no consolation possible." The
thought of death haunted him then. "It takes courage for a man
endowed with imagination not to go to meet the spectre and embrace
the skeleton." Without having read Vigny's *Moïse,* he was sure at least
that this despair was the sign of great men who were misunderstood.
He certainly was unappreciated and vilified for having painted *La
Barque du Dante* with a "tipsy brush." But he resisted combining
forces with Hugo or Balzac, who were fighting a similar battle at this
time, and later with Baudelaire, whom he treated coldly, disgusted
even by the translation of Poe that his young admirer had offered him.

A weakening of will, which was itself due to physiological or
psychosomatic causes, was perhaps at the root of the "mal du siècle" of
certain romantics of 1800–1830—although that was to become more
pronounced in Baudelaire or Leconte de Lisle, later in the Pierre Loti
of *Fleurs d'ennui* or the neurotic Maupassant of *Sur l'eau,* or in Proust.
But it was the habit of ruthless self-analysis, at the very moment when
one felt intensely the aggravation of feeling and sensation by this
mental self-contemplation, ultimately a strange delight in believing
that one was unhappy through stubbornly choosing to be so, which
constituted the true originality of the romantic "mal du siècle." It is as
easy to make fun of these afflictions that are partly imaginary as it is to
laugh at the despair of certain children. Works such as those of Louis
Maigron on *Le Romantisme et la mode* (1911) have found it easy to
gather together anecdotes and stigmatize this shrivelling of the heart
and this weakening of the will to which has been imputed what Ernest
Seillière had already condemned as *le Mal romantique* (the romantic
malady). To be sure, Musset and particularly Berlioz expressed at
times melodramatically the trembling of their limbs, the spasms the
musician felt in his chest when he heard Harriet Smithson playing
Shakespeare (he did not know English) or the feeling that there was "a
crater in his heart" and that he was on the verge of fainting from
giddiness when he listened to Beethoven. But it was precisely the
characteristic of romanticism and later of surrealism and modern
writers, who found oblivion from their anguish and revolt in drugs or
soporifics, not to separate literature or art from life. Modern writers,
who are victims of a moral malady which saves them from a much
more serious ill (resignation to apathy or to the egotistical acceptance
of the established order of things), should feel pity and perhaps
gratitude towards those pitiful victims such as Larra or Zorilla in
Spain, Leopardi on the other side of the Alps, Kleist or Lenau in
Germany or Austria, Nerval, Gros (who also committed suicide),

Géricault, Berlioz, or Musset in France. Mingling oratorical questions with verses of a more sorrowful and profound inspiration, Alfred de Musset, evoking at the age of twenty-six, when he was barely over his first great crisis, the death at twenty-eight of the Spanish singer Malibran, recalled at the same time Léopold Robert (who committed suicide at forty), Bellini, and Carrel the artist who was killed in a duel. "The threshold of our century is paved with tombs." The only worthwhile thing in this world is to love, he concluded; and as love dies or is forgotten, it is nobler to die for a more exalted love: that of art.

Still, one has to be able to love. But it was the inability to love which aggravated this malady in the romantics who were most affected by it; Paul Bourget pointed this out later in connection with Baudelaire and Amiel, in his *Essais de psychologie contemporaine,* which remains one of the masterpieces of literary criticism of the last century, written by a moralist who suffered greatly from this malady himself, was fascinated by the victims of a belated and exacerbated romanticism, and was passionately keen to be cured and to cure his successors of it. Like Swann or Marcel later, or Stendhal, their precursor in the art of crystallization, the only antidote they could find for ennui was love. Although, at certain times, Benjamin Constant, Chateaubriand, George Sand, Flaubert, Gautier, and even Baudelaire during his years of solid activity (1845–1857) tried indefatigably, they could not overcome their ennui with the *labor improbus omnia vincit* recommended by the publishing house Lemerre. On the first page of his *Journal,* Constant presented clearly the refrain of his entire life: "Fear of ennui is my most powerful motivating force; and my great risk in changing positions is precisely ennui." According to Constant, complacent self-analysis is a form of narcissism which takes one's mind off one's boredom for a while. It adds value to love since one creates an illusory image of the other, which one pursues. The celebration of sexuality prepares it, extends it, embellishes it with anticipation and regret, aggravates disagreements which are sometimes followed by remorse and a more harmonious agreement. And then Constant adds the revealing little sentence: "My attachment was increased by the pain that I had inflicted on it." There quickly slips into these intellectual loves a certain element of cruelty and the delight of a remorse which justifies us in our own eyes and purifies us. If one can only love another intermittently, at least one loves oneself. The famous remark made by Constant's cousin, Pauline de Beaumont, about him was as sad as it was witty: 'He cannot even manage to love himself."

THE MELANCHOLY OF ASTOLPHE DE CUSTINE

There were contemporaries of the romantic writers who were more seriously affected by the "mal du siècle": for example, Astolphe de

Custine, born in 1790. His father had been guillotined, after outstanding service in the army, in January 1794; his grandfather a year later;
his mother Delphine almost suffered the same fate, but was liberated
in October 1794. She had an intimate relationship, which aroused
great interest, with Chateaubriand from 1802 onwards. Astolphe
almost married the daughter of Mme de Staël, then that of the
Duchess of Duras; but although he got married in 1821 and had a son
(and became a widower as early as 1823), he had homosexual inclinations. He felt he was overflowing with the capacity to love, but was
incapable of expending it freely. He could not be classed among the
romantic writers, although he knew Balzac quite well and inspired him
perhaps to depict Vautrin's feelings for Lucien de Rubempré. Much
later, just before he died, he praised (with some reservations) *Les
Fleurs du mal* and wrote to Baudelaire: "You have brought something
new into a declining literature." The analysis that he did of Russian
nature in *La Russie en 1839* was the most discerning as well as the most
severe of the last century. But from the age of twenty-one, with his
soul, according to him, brimming over with a profound sadness, he
affirmed:

> At the age of eighteen, I felt that everything was over for me in this
> world. I am condemned to languish in the world, without plans and
> without illusions. . . . If I do not give myself up entirely to a feeling
> which absorbs me completely, I will become mad and die before the year
> is out.

There were many follies and imprudent acts in the life of this
ostentatious aristocrat, enormously rich like William Beckford, the
author of *Vathek* and a homosexual who carried his afflictions and his
quest around with him to various countries. Long before he could be
affected by the literary trends of romanticism, the Marquis de Custine
made profuse complaints to young friends about the enigma of his
nature and the abyss in his heart:

> Since I was born, my nature has been an enigma that no one has
> fathomed or probed, and which I can understand less than anybody
> else. . . . I live like a torrent which, instead of flowing along its
> stream-bed, carves a deep hollow at its source and spins around in a
> whirlpool.

GEORGE SAND'S DEFENSE OF THIS YOUTHFUL MALADY

The facility which Lamartine has called "the grace of genius" and
which at times seems more to be something that prevents talent from
rising to the level of genius, had not been bestowed on the "minor
romantics" as we call them today, or on Custine, who had more of a

bent for personal writings or travel narratives than fiction-writing. It had, however, been meted out, and too liberally, to George Sand, who was fourteen years younger than him. Her ancestors had had just as stormy and as irregular an existence as had those of Custine, during those times which we would like to picture as more stable and wiser than our own. Disgracefully treated by a brutal husband, she sought other consolations. But she expected too much from sensual satisfactions and, in the first version of *Lélia,* she did not conceal this incapacity for fully experiencing sensual love which she arrogated to herself: "My heart remains detached even in the most intimate situations," Lélia confessed to Sténio, whom she loved in a motherly fashion and who loved her madly and ended up by drowning himself out of unrequited love for her. The former convict Tremor later strangled Lélia to punish her. The strange priest Magnus fascinated her but he passed judgment on her. "I could not be anyone's equal in love. My frigidity made me inferior to the most despicable women; the exaltation of my thoughts made me superior to the most passionate men." She was the counterpart of the heroes of Byron of the opposite sex, attracted by other women more than by male lovers to whom she would have liked to be able to yield but whom she ended up looking after like a motherly nurse. No work depicted more unwisely and more faithfully the exacerbations of the "mal du siècle" than this novel of 1833. The author toned it down later and produced a less revealing version of it in 1839. It is well known that she transferred her intellectual passion to socialist reformers, wrote innocuous but charming pastoral novels, a strange epical and mystical novel, *Spiridion* (1838), which was perhaps her masterpiece, and she confessed one day to Juliette Adam: "If I had to begin my life over again, I would be chaste." But she did not regret having suffered pangs of this "mal du siècle" which had been the prerogative of her generation. In 1865, she confessed to Flaubert, who showed her affectionate respect: "Grief is not unhealthy; it prevents us from becoming insensitive." The following year, responding to those who made fun of the earlier victims of the "mal du siècle" of 1830, she replied boldly and proudly:

> Perhaps our malady was better than the reaction that followed it, that craving for money, pleasures without ideals, and unbridled ambitions, which does not seem to characterize very nobly the "moral well-being of our century."

Along with all that the anguish of these first generations of romantics contained that was dramatic and immoderate in expression, ridiculous at times in its excesses, it also included genuine grief, impatience with limits imposed on the ambitions and dreams of man, dissatisfaction with the present and a desire to change it after having analyzed its defects. Without these romantics who were discontented with themselves and who ruthlessly analyzed their aboulia or their passion that was never completely satisfied, mankind would be poorer and duller. Lamartine, George Sand, Delacroix, Quinet[6], Michelet, Hugo and many others were, after all, men of action and reformers of their art and often of the society around them. Like the young eagles in a sentence of *Fantasio* which Taine liked to quote, they shot out of their nest with the indignation of the young generation which hopes to change life. They failed only partially in their endeavor.

6 The Obsession of the
Past and Other Places

THE ROMANTICS' GREAT DESIRE "TO BE OF THEIR TIME"
AND "TO WRITE FOR THEIR ERA"

From a hasty look at French romanticism, it would be easy to believe that the classical-romantic dispute, to which an exaggerated importance is attached in our literary histories, was a sort of revival of the old quarrel between the ancients and moderns, to which, according to the comparatist Joseph Texte, the entire history of French culture amounts in one sense. The victory of the young romantics, between 1816 and 1930, represented an almost unanimous and definitive acceptance of the precept: "One must write for one's time," which Sartre proclaimed later with even more conviction as he started his magazine *Les Temps modernes* and, as the Deschamps brothers had first formulated it, "one must be of one's time." In 1828, in their *Préface des études francaises et étrangères,* these very curious forerunners of the new school of poetry affirmed that "men of true talent are always endowed with an instinct which impels them towards the new".

Certainly this originality might be based on something which had been engulfed in oblivion, and it was the Spanish romances, "that *Iliad* without a Homer" translated as early as 1822 by Abel Hugo, and, particularly in Germany, Lope de Vega and Calderon that the first romantics had tried to revive. Spanish literature, too hastily designated as classical by Mme de Staël because it was a literature of the South, definitely had something that fired the enthusiasm of the Schlegel brothers and even of Shelley, who successfully tried his hand at translating Calderon, of Hugo and the Deschamps brothers. It was rooted in the soil and history of the nation; in it were found, shamelessly mixed, the evil and the sacred, the gross and the sublime;

and love seemed to justify everything, including murder. So, one was of one's time by drawing one's inspiration from this literature if one could, or by translating it if one lacked creative genius. The same important preface of 1828 clearly stated: "The time of imitation is over; one must create or translate." Five years earlier, in his slap-dash and unmethodical *Racine et Shakespeare,* Stendhal had proposed even more dogmatically his famous paradox on romanticism as "the art of presenting to people literary works which, in the existing state of their customs and beliefs, are likely to give them the maximum amount of pleasure possible." Classicism, on the other hand, would have given the greatest possible pleasure to our great-grandfathers—what Stendhal was forgetting was that they, however, had underrated or disparaged the majority of these "classicists" and derived greater pleasure from Benserade, Quinault, Thomas Corneille, Pradon, or Bourdaloue. A formula which would identify romanticism with modernity, or come close to doing so, would make a fortune. In his *Salon de 1846,* Baudelaire defined twice in this way romanticism, of which he knew he was a grateful heir and acknowledged himself to be one: "When one speaks of romanticism, one talks of modern art." and "Romanticism is the most recent and most timely expression of beauty." Banville, in *Mes Souvenirs,* borrowed this statement word for word, as he declared himself an opponent of the wretched school of common sense; according to him, both Asselineau and he, great friends of Baudelaire, were and had remained "romantics"; that is to say, they strove after "the most recent expression of beauty."

REALISTIC DESCRIPTION OF DAILY LIFE

Certainly the characteristics of this multiform movement that was romanticism included this desire to be of one's time and this wish to be or to try to be original. From the time of the intimate, familiar poems of Sainte-Beuve, which approached prose, as much by a lack of imagination as by intent, and later when *Les Feuilles d'automne* and *Jocelyn* were written, the poets revealed a distrust of outbursts that were too exalted or unnatural, a fear of eloquence that was too ostentatious, and a sort of realism. There was no less a desire to adhere to the most commonplace reality, at times to reproduce it graphically even to the language and conversation of the most ordinary people, in Balzac's work and in perhaps the most realistic nineteenth century work, Henry Monnier's *Scènes populaires* which appeared in 1830, the same year as *Hernani* and *Harmonies poétiques et religieuses.* Moreover, breaking with the outmoded poetic style of their century, Goethe, in *Hermann und Dorthea,* and Wordsworth, in the *Lyrical Ballads* of 1798 and its preface which followed two years later, had already endeavored to use everyday language and to embellish scenes, banal in appearance, with poetic intensity in order to bring out some tragic aspect of it without grandiloquence. It was a cold, basically rational realism, deliberately objective and avoiding emotion, by which the author wanted to do away with anthropomorphism, not let himself be beguiled by the celebrated "pathetic fallacy" of Ruskin, preserve the integrity of objects, and advocate concretism. This realism was by no means absent from the novels of Charles Sorel and Scarron, the poetry of Théophile, Saint-Amant, and Boileau, of Pope or John Gay, the English author of *Trivia*. When writing their descriptions of Tours, Saumur, or the Vauquer boarding house, or presenting vividly the swan that escaped from its cage during a Parisian summer, or evoking little old women, Balzac and Baudelaire were fully aware of the fact that they were heirs to a long line of predecessors. But there is also a realism of imagination and intense emotion. A sensibility that is deeply stirred, an imagination in its most ambitious flight, often penetrate the cover of the object, laying bare what is hidden behind the surface, and discerning an almost Swedenborgian correspondence between the exterior accessible to all and the secrets concealed in the subconscious or in the soul, whose outward manifestation is the symbol. The basically imaginative or affective realism, which is perhaps the only real kind, was present in Coleridge's poetry (for example, *This Limetree Bower my prison,* 1797) and even in the works of the most obviously ethereal and the vaguest of the English Romantics, Shelley, the Ariel of romanticism (*Letters to Maria Gisborne,* 1820, and *Julian and Maddalo,* 1818). In the earlier poems of Lamartine, this realism was more uncommon, but it was used with great success in several of the "Epoques" of *Jocelyn* and later in *La Vigne et la Maison.* The systematic realism of 1855–1870, of Courbet and Zola, and even of Champfleury and Duranty, despite their lack of imagination, or that realism on the subject of which Baudelaire later wrote his most forceful pages on aesthetics in *Le Peintre de la vie moderne,* was only in many respects the pursuit of one of the veins of romanticism. Zola was well aware of this when he wrote the articles which he submitted to a Russian newspaper and which, when published in book-form, were entitled *Documents littéraires;* for, along with Taine, he was one of the most perceptive and understanding of the writers of his generation in his brilliant homage to Stendhal and Balzac. In demanding that the painter and poet stick to the characteristic detail of fashion or costume in order to extract what is beautiful and perhaps eternal from the real and the intangible, Baudelaire was evoking an aspect of romanticism which had been overshadowed by clichés, particularly in painting (with the academism of the Salons and the students of Ingres): mythology used as embellishment, pseudonobility and pretentious frigidity in style.

REHABILITATION OF THE PAST

But the watchword "to be of one's time" lends itself to many interpretations, and those who have inscribed it on their standard have not defined it any more precisely than Boileau, Molière, Diderot, or Hugo had done for the noble precept "nature and truth". For that can mean you conform to the most superficial of styles, to please the reader of the evening paper or the spectator who only wants to amuse himself after his dinner; or you can borrow from contemporary jargon, whether it be that of the symbolists, existentialists, disputers of language, or pseudophilosophers who undertake at every turn to "reveal the being". Sartre demanded that one forget the myth of posterity and address only the living; the younger generation, twenty-five years later, repudiated him and wanted to find elsewhere what was "relevant" and the situation in which it would feel involved. But Stendhal was not any less "of his time" when he recalled the intrigues of the Parmesan court and the dreamy loves of Fabrice than when he was dealing with politics under the Restoration or the petty provincial vanities of the garrison and salons of Nancy in *Lucien Leuwen*. Victor Hugo was no less of his time when he evoked Booz, Cain, or the Satyr considered as the symbol of the rebirth of paganism in the sixteenth century, than when he wrote his poems on the men who had died for the motherland or on poor people. Thinkers and artists have often been the most "modern" and have survived the wreck of the past by swimming against the current, and not allowing themselves to be submerged by the alleged tide of history which carries us away towards the future. Indeed it has often happened that many creators have become aware of their originality by going back and rediscovering certain periods of the past, poorly understood up to that point, in the light of the present and by plunging into the *hic et nunc*. In the cultural history of the twentieth century, the discovery or rediscovery of Egyptian art or archaic Greek art, that of the Incas or the blacks of Benin, of medieval music or Romanesque fresco, have been more significant landmarks than many of the modernistic contributions by Marinetti and Apollinaire to "Lettrism" and neo-Marxism.

ATTITUDE OF WRITERS AND ARTISTS
TOWARDS THE MIDDLE AGES

Taking into account this rehabilitation of the past, one of the most enriching elements that we have attained, thanks to romanticism, is a tremendous increase in our taste and cultural enjoyment by its revival of the past or rather the multiple pasts which preceding centuries had neglected, perhaps in reaction against the extreme zeal that the Renaissance had shown in this respect. The former definitions of romanticism, which had often paid particular attention to the obvious characteristics of that great agitation of European sensibility, had laid too much stress on its exoticism, the English and German romantic poets' fondness for travel or that of the French writers (Vigny, Hugo, Musset, later Leconte de Lisle and Baudelaire) for armchair travel, and finally their enthusiasm for the Middle Ages. Most certainly, a notable event was Chateaubriand's rediscovery or near rediscovery of the Gothic cathedral, its bold style and its resplendence; it inspired Augustin Thierry to follow his vocation as a historian. Hugo received from it the first impetus to produce, soon after, *Notre-Dame de Paris,* which, in spite of all its faults, is a grandiose historical novel and one of the few, perhaps the first in France chronologically, to move and stir the souls of the masses.

Michelet, who has contributed more than any Frenchman in inspiring a revival and a love of the era of cathedrals and Joan of Arc, noted how much he had been influenced, at an age when his mind was most receptive, by a visit to the Museum of French Monuments which Alexandre Lenoir had succeeded in establishing in the former "Couvent des Petits-Augustins," now the site of the "Ecole des Beaux-Arts." The Middle Ages had certainly not been totally neglected in the seventeenth century, much less in the eighteenth century.[1] In various parts of France they had continued to build in the Gothic style long after the alleged break with the Renaissance; for example, Saint-Etienne du Mont, Saint-Gervais, the cathedral of Orléans. Many clerical historians or Jansenist laymen, such as Lenain de Tillemont, not to mention the commentators of St. Augustine or the Church Fathers, lived in spirit in the first ten or twelve centuries of the Christian era. But the impact on their sensibility appears to have been feeble. In any case, they had not communicated this to the general public, as Walter Scott and Chateaubriand did later. Although a certain amount of confusion was involved, Lenoir accumulated all kinds of sculpture, fragments of architecture, and tombstones in his Museum. He has been accused of faking, at times of mutilation and of showing very poor taste. Nevertheless, the budding romanticism saw its love of the Middle Ages developing as a living thing in this jumble of stones that attracted many enemies until 1816, the date of the dispersal of this medieval museum. However, this did not give rise to great romantic sculpture. Rude and Carpeaux only appeared later. The example set by Canova was too prestigious. Théophile Gautier observed later, in his *Histoire du romantisme,* that "of all the arts, the one which lends itself the least to expression of the romantic imagination is undoubtedly sculpture"). He was forgetting architecture, for which the last century did not succeed in creating a new style. But once the love of the Middle Ages was stimulated, the discovery of the *Chanson de Roland* and other "chansons de geste," the cult of Villon, *Tristan et Iseut,* and Celtic culture were to follow.

ENTHUSIASM FOR THE SIXTEENTH CENTURY AND THE AGE OF LOUIS XIII

Furthermore, interest spread rapidly from the Middle Ages to the Renaissance and the reign of Louis XIII. The pioneer work of Sainte-Beuve, who wrote a *Tableau de la poésie française au XVIe siècle,* is well-known. Actually, his "description" was very incomplete, and the sentiment which inspired it was very cold in comparison with the warm enthusiasm which prompted Coleridge, Lamb, and Hazlitt in England to reinterpret Shakespeare and other dramatists or the Elizabethan lyricists. It would still be a long time before people would fully appreciate the subtle mysticism of Maurice Scève, the Platonism of Marguerite de Navarre and Du Bellay, the cosmic and philosophical poetry of Ronsard, and the grandiose lyrical satire of d'Aubigné. But at least the novelists who used the disparaged genre of the historical novel—which, however, can have a lasting effect on the imagination—gave to the public of the romantic period some idea of the seething cruel, and tragic life during the reign of Charles IX (Mérimée), the plots of Catherine de Medici and the horrors of Saint-Barthélemy (Alexandre Dumas, *Marguerite de Valois,* or Balzac, *Cathérine de Médicis* and *Contes drolatiques*). Among the most curious aspects of French romanticism were its fascination with the "place des Vosges", the "brick châteaux with cornerstones," evoked in a pleasing "fantaisie" by Nerval, in which he presented a dark-eyed blonde at the window[2], and the great animation and independence of those whom Gautier called, using the word in a good sense, the "grotesques", whom we have since appreciated once again along with the baroque style. There is a profound affinity between the baroque writers of 1620–1650, at least in France, and romantic baroque writers, in spite of the evident differences between them in range and tone. It was perhaps in some of Hugo's poems and in Baudelaire's extraordinary "ex-voto in the Spanish style" offered "To a Madonna," that the baroque style, which had developed somewhat imperfectly in France during the time of Richelieu and Saint-Amant, found its most faithful expression.

EVOCATION OF THE ORIENT AND THE MEDITERRANEAN COUNTRIES

In the years when it was considered good form by the partisans of a nostalgic neo-classicism to disparage romanticism, one could make fun of what was superficial and showy about the romantic love of local color which was artificially imposed in *Les Orientales* or in *Contes d'Espagne et d'Italie*. This facile irony moreover was not at all justified so far as these two collections were concerned. The second is filled with youthful playfulness, spirit, and a mixture of impudence and great imaginative charm that Byron has not equalled and Pushkin has not surpassed. It is regrettable that the story in verse, a form which Verlaine still used, no longer tempts modern poets, who have taken their role of seers and decipherers of the invisible so seriously. As for Hugo, his inspiration was undoubtedly heightened when he was tested by life and contemplated the abysses. But already in the third book of *Odes*, "L'Ame", which was preceded by a quotation from the Pythagorean *Vers dorés*, and "Le Cauchemar" in the fifth book, in which Hugo recalled the terrors of dreams, were not lacking in appeal. And much earlier still, as long ago as 1822 when he wrote his preface to *Odes*, the twenty-year-old poet had declared in terms that later the Swedenborgians or Baudelaire might have recalled:

> Moreover, the domain of poetry is unlimited. Beneath the real world exists an ideal world which appears resplendent to those who, through serious meditation, are accustomed to seeing more in things than the things themselves.

Traced with a rhythmic virtuosity then unprecedented in France, the evocation of glowing colors and Moorish architecture stood out sharply on a blue sky in *Les Orientales*, and reestablished in poetry a needed debauch of imagination—even if critics of other countries prefer to call it "fancy" or ornamental fancy. It was Leconte de Lisle, who has often been considered to have been in revolt against romanticism, who rendered the most moving homage to *Les Orientales*, upon succeeding Hugo to the "Académie française" on March 31, 1887. This collection of poems had brought to de Lisle, on his native island, the revelation of poetry; it had even opened his eyes to the grandiose beauty of the tropical nature in the midst of which he had grown up without sensing its strange magnificence.

This liking for a theme in poetry, treated in a descriptive and narrative fashion, has momentarily disappeared in our times, just as has the fondness for the descriptive or suggestive music of "Gardens in the Rain" or "The Fountains of Rome" and for theme in painting. Historically, however, it was beneficial for the arts to return to the concrete and for poetry in particular, which had produced innumerable odes to enthusiasm and spirit and other abstractions, once again to take root in reality. Relativism, that increase of curiosity in Western man which made the contemporaries of romanticism come out of themselves, opened their dazzled and tolerant eyes to the differences in human experience and even to the anomalies that natural history was studying at that time. The conception that theologians and poets had formed of the "eternal" and abstract man, presented by the French classicists and Pope, was suddenly broadened. One guessed that in order to understand this king of the universe, one must first closely observe animals, as the philosopher Max Scheler later asked his disciples to do. The animal was not of much interest to French poets, after Baudelaire's sonnets and those of Taine, which were less poetic but more touching, on cats, and the celebrated descriptive meditations of Leconte de Lisle at the "Botanical Gardens." They became too enamored with their role as thinker in verse or short verse to divert their attention from themselves.

THE LITERATURE OF TRAVEL

The poetry of travel too has suffered from the fact that the romantics had often made use of it with excessive complaisance. We have detached ourselves from it just at the time when it is rare to find men of letters who are not also ardent travelers, harassed like Montherlant, amused like Morand or Giraudoux, sentimental according to a title of Pierre-Jean Jouve, or simply seeking a renewal of their inspiration like Gide, Duhamel, or Butor. In one of the attacks which Sartre has spiritedly launched against his predecessors in the Parisian literary world with *Qu'est-ce que la littérature?,* he has dealt scornfully with romantic travel, on which Gobineau has certainly contributed the masterpieces:

> The traveler is a perpetual spectator, who goes from one society to another, never living in any, and, as a foreign consumer in a hardworking community, he is the picture of parasitism.

Certainly there is a detestable kind of travel literature, and there is a great deal of it today. But it is not certain that its documentary, and even anthropological, interest will not one day seem greater than that of most of our novels. We treat with respect Herodotus' pages on the Egyptians, those of Pausanius, or the travel poem of a later Latin writer, Rutilius Numatianus, and Joinville's narratives, which are devoid, however, of the picturesque and even of psychology. Stendhal established the stereotyped theme of touring in literature at the same time that Mérimée was preserving Romanesque frescos and opening the eyes of posterity to a neglected art. Like Chateaubriand, Victor Hugo had a knack for using the stories of former travelers; he has nevertheless betrayed, in *Le Rhin,* some of the most precious secrets for us about his manner of seeing and transfiguring what he had discerned with a keen eye. If travel during the romantic era is a form of evasion, one begins to regret that the era of hothouses in literature, the period of Maeterlinck and Mallarmé, or of the diverting puns and witticisms of *Le Voyage d'Urien* and *Paludes* of Gide, has not used more often this flight from its closed world. Man depicted in *La Maison du berger* as "tortured by self-love and self-study", and the romantic poet symbolized by "the ignorant Lamartine who only understands his soul", have profited by escaping from the prison of their ego and by observing that others in other places have also suffered, loved, and diverted their melancholy on other shores and before other ruins.

A NEED TO LOSE ONESELF IN THE FOREIGN AND STRANGE, A CRAVING FOR THE HEREAFTER

Behind these dreams of exotic travel to the land of Ossian, to "dreamy Germany" as Lamartine called it, to Andalusia, Greece, or Palestine, can be detected again the sentiment which, more than any other perhaps, characterized romanticism: the impossibility for the romantics to be satisfied with the present and with their surroundings. The romantics of subsequent generations, as we insist on calling them in this book, men like Baudelaire or Mallarmé, understood better the great sadness which had often driven their elders of 1800–1850 far from home. They chose to shut themselves up in their study and to only travel from one house to another in Paris. This was the case with Flaubert after his tour of the Orient (except for his trip in search of the local color of Carthage), with the Goncourt brothers, with Zola, with Baudelaire, who described those people who were crazy about traveling as dissatisfied soul—"Their longing always made them anxious"— whom death alone would satisfy with its great unknown, and with Mallarmé, who, miserable in his flesh and believing that he had read all the books, characterized Rimbuad, the wanderer of the unfathomable depths, as "that eminent passer-by." Shelley, in the poem in which he mourned the death of Keats, called Byron "the Pilgrim of Eternity." Childe Harold, and the Alastor of Shelley himself, and Keats' Endymion were in fact all pilgrims in search of an almost mystical unity with nature, with a female self which would make them complete, or with the divine.

Undoubtedly there had been people who craved for the infinite in other ages, and more genuine mystics than these writers of the nineteenth century who, in the wake of the solitary dreamer Rousseau, secularized mysticism. One may question Pascal's mysticism on his night of enthusiasm and tears of joy or in the tender imploration of his *Mystère de Jésus;* but the romantics were not very much mistaken when they considered him one of their predecessors or intercessors, yearning for the One behind the multiplicity of our vain diversions and an infinity beyond the world of appearances and disappointments. In general, however, the period of La Rochefoucauld or La Bruyère, the era of Pope in England, had not bothered about probing the mysteries of the next world. To make life more pleasant by abiding by a reasonable prudence seemed an attractive ideal at this time when Tibullus and Horace were greatly read. *Hoc erat in votis,* one could say again; and wishes restricted to the sphere of the possible were fairly easily fulfilled. With Blake, Novalis, Lamartine who rediscovered Platonic accents, Coleridge, even Poe who inspired Baudelaire with the formula of his *Notes nouvelles,* "the insatiable craving for what lies beyond" was the sign of the true poet, and dissatisfaction prevailed. In their enthusiasm for the ocean, the Alpine peaks, rivers, and trees, the most ardent of the romantics dreamed of nothing less than obliterating all dividing lines between the self and the non-self. Shelley referred many times to this yearning for the impossible, which was similar to the "desire of the moth for the star." Never did a poet, who had turned to the most vehement atheism because of his discontentment with a hidebound, organized, and despiritualized religion, have a more naturally Platonic soul, which wanted to blend multiplicity into oneness and find the stable and durable behind the changeable. Coleridge craved idealism just as much, and the Germans in whose works he had found the philosophical basis of his aesthetics had also dreamed of a unity between the self and the nonself, the terrestrial and the divine; the words Eternity (*Ewigkeit*) and Infinity (*Unendlichkeit*) were the refrain of their cogitations and their dreams, whether they were orthodox and sometimes mystical believers or, much later, like Nietzsche, declared themselves to be deniers of God. The last lines of his poem *Zarathustra,* "Glory and eternity," are famous:

> Most exalted star in existence
> Which no wish ever reaches,
> Which no sound ever troubles,
> Yes, eternity of being!
> I will forever say yes to you,
> For I love you, Eternity!

Unlike their predecessors of the Age of Enlightenment, it was not really happiness which the romantics dreamed about, at least not in their period of youth and creativeness. Wordsworth no longer wrote poetry when he took refuge in the prosaic serenity that happiness involves. The other English romantics never experienced happiness. Only Goethe could retain his background of Faustian restlessness, his passionate impulses of the *Elegy of Marienbad,* his scientific curiosity, and reconcile that with his absurd pursuits as organizer of fête

provincial court, and his naive satisfaction at having been decorated by
Napoleon. The romantics declared themselves to be and were in
reality unhappy because their aspirations were too idealistic; they
never achieved total satisfaction of their desires. Lamartine himself
was prevented from experiencing this complete satisfaction by the
obstacles of his political career, his setbacks, his debts and, later in life,
the pressure of his literary work; and Hugo, by the death of his
daughter and the anguished existence he led in exile. It was the
English poets who, even better than the French, with the exception of
Musset and Baudelaire, had analyzed and written about that stagger-
ing letdown that followed their upsurge of joy; for it was joy, much
more than happiness, that was the object of their desires. Coleridge, in
the most beautiful of his poems, *Dejection: an Ode,* written in a moment
of psychological distress, exclaimed: "Joy . . . , joy that ne'er was
given, save to the pure, and in their purest hour . . . It is the spirit and
the power which wedding nature to us, give in dower a new earth and a
new heaven." He had lost this joy forever, after having become
addicted to opium and having seen his willpower disappear.
Wordsworth had thought he had experienced this joy in childhood,
even though everything for a child is surrounded by a halo and he
seems to bring into the world the vague recollection of a previous
existence. The term "Delight" was one of William Blake's key words:
its source was "energy." "Energy is eternal delight." Shelley uttered
his most moving laments when he deeply regretted, once his earliest
youth was over, that the "spirit of delight" was absent or only came
upon him on rare occasions. ("Song," which begins with the words
"Rarely, rarely, comest thou, Spirit of Delight", and "A Lament.")
When one rereads their poems of despair and nostalgia, it seems very
wrong to say, as some have done, that the "mal du siècle" was above all
an exhibitionism of egotists who loved verbal rhetoric. Almost all of
them had aspired after what was beyond the realm of the possible;
they had wanted to stop the flight of time, achieve a unity with the
exterior world and with the divine or angelic which they felt was above
them. They broke down from despair; or they took refuge in the
golden myths of former ages or in those which they managed to
imagine.

REDISCOVERY OF DANTE, THE BIBLE, AND THE ANCIENTS

This escape from themselves, accompanied by the secret awareness
that they would find their self in the artists of other periods and other
places, this painful pursuit of dreams, brought to the Romantics a
tremendous widening of their horizons, and consequently of our own.
It was they who discovered Dante, so badly misinterpreted in France

by the five preceding centuries. Ampère, Ozanam, Antony Deschamps, Auguste Barbier, Hugo, who brought renown to the *Divine Comedy,* finally naturalized among us the most personal and passionate of the great poets. They awakened the sensibility of their compatriots to the grandeur of the Bible—although d'Aubigné, du Bartas, and Bossuet had certainly not failed to appreciate it, nor had the French translators of Milton, in spite of their prosaic and limited taste. But it was Chateaubriand who was the true initiator of it. From that time onwards, the romanticism of France, a Catholic country in which the reading of sacred texts had only rarely been held in high honor, became the one which drew the most constant inspiration from the Old and New Testaments. The German poets, after Klopstock, did not bother very much about drawing inspiration from Cain, Job, Esther, and Ruth; they drived a little more of it from Christ on the Mount of Olives with Jean Paul, whose not very brilliant poem was distorted in meaning by Mme de Staël and by Nerval after her. Byron, the most profane of the English romantics, but whose Scottish Calvinism had left a mark on him in his childhood, was the only one who composed dramas on themes from the Old Testament (it must be added that this was done to find in them reasons for denial and revolt), and his more sentimental and soft-spoken friend, Thomas Moore, also wrote about the love affairs of the angels. Wordsworth, whose faith was more orthodox, Coleridge, Shelley, and Keats were not tempted by themes from the Scriptures.

On the contrary, all the French poets were greatly attracted by such themes, with the exception perhaps of Musset—the very same Musset whose vituperation against Voltaire and the Philosophes is unfortunately famous and who, in his *Espoir en Dieu,* condemned Kant for having declared heaven deserted and having concluded in favor of nothingness! Various scholars, Abbé Claudius Grillet in particular, have studied Lamartine's fascination with Lamennais for a while and with Genoude, the translator of the Bible, who was his friend and literary advisor. Job, the hero of revolt preceding resignation, impressed him especially, as well as the Solomon of the *Song of Songs* and the David of the *Psalms.* His most biblical collection of poems, *Harmonies,* which an opponent (Barthélemy) made fun of by calling it "Your *gloria patri* drawn out over two volumes," is perhaps the most sincere volume of biblical inspiration in French. Two or three years after its publication in 1830, Lamartine broke away from orthodoxy. But *La Chute d'un ange,* which he wrote later, was an ambitious and, in parts, an admirable religious epic. Vigny had read *Paradise Lost* a great deal in his youth, and he later recalled the greatest biblical drama of English literature, Milton's *Samson Agonistes.* Four or five of his famous poems were inspired by the Old Testament and *Le Mont des*

Oliviers by the Gospels. In them, the most reflective and serious of the romantic poets also proved himself to be the most personal, not hesitating to describe his own revolt against the Christian faith under the cover of biblical revolts. But it was Hugo who, of all the romantic poets, was most justified in saying, as he did: "The Bible is my book". Grillet, who later used this statement as an epigraph to his work *La Bible dans Victor Hugo* (Hachette, 1910), has studied the poet's evolution in this respect: at first a good Catholic and a staunch royalist, he used a few Bible stories as a source of a Christian supernatural element which was too obviously superadded. Later, he identified himself, like several other French romantics, with the great rebel, Job, uttering complaints and blasphemy; the English and German poets had preferred Prometheus. This was followed by the use of the prophets of Israel announcing the fall of Jericho or the punishment of tyrants in the imprecations of *Les Châtiments,* the apocalypticism of St. John at Patmos, adapted by the poet, and the great role of the two Testaments in the narratives of *La Légende des siècles.* But Hugo did much more than merely use suitable themes. There was nothing extrinsic in these poems inspired by the legend or history of Israel or by the resurrection. There was nothing adroitly personal, either, for Hugo did not hide himself, nor did he try to make himself important, by evoking Isaiah or St. John. But there was a strong, imaginative impulse which allowed him to relive with "supernatural"[3] intensity the most grandiose visions of the Scriptures. In our opinion, no literary evocation of human grief equals, in tragic force, the finale of *Les Malheureux,* in *Les Contemplations:* Adam and Eve, after the murder of Abel by his brother, lugubrious types worthy of the Florentine fresco of Masaccio or Michelangelo, are the prototypes of all unhappy people who have existed since their time. We will quote about forty lines of verse from this poem to show the novelty and Miltonian grandeur of French romanticism at their height of formal perfection and tragicality. Rarely have ease of versification, virtuosity in the division of lines of verse, force of antithesis, the evocative surprise produced by these copious moral adjectives conveying a concrete sculptural vision, better served a creative talent which assumed responsibility for the entire burden of lugubrious human sorrow.

> Aux premiers jours du monde, alors que la nuée,
> Surprise, contemplait chaque chose créée,
> Alors que sur le globe où le mal avait crû,
> Flottait une lueur de l'Eden disparu,
> Quand tout encor semblait être rempli d'aurore,
> Quand sur l'arbre du temps les ans venaient d'éclore,
> Sur la terre où la chair avec l'esprit se fond,
> Il se faisait le soir un silence profond,

Et le désert, les bois, l'onde aux vastes rivages,
Et les herbes des champs et les bêtes sauvages,
Emus, et les rochers, ces ténébreux cachots,
Voyaient, d'un antre obscur couvert d'arbres si hauts
Que nos chênes auprès sembleraient des arbustes,
Sortir deux grands vieillards, nus, sinistres, augustes.
C'étaient Eve aux cheveux blanchis et son mari,
Le pâle Adam, pensif, par le travail meurtri,
Ayant la vision de Dieu sous sa paupière.
Ils venaient tous les deux s'asseoir sur une pierre,
En présence des monts fauves et soucieux,
Et de l'éternité formidable des cieux.
Leur œil triste rendait la nature farouche;
Et là, sans qu'il sortît un souffle de leur bouche,
Les mains sur leurs genoux, et se tournant le dos,
Accablés comme ceux qui portent des fardeux!
Sans autre mouvement de vie extérieure
Que de baisser plus bas la tête d'heure en heure,
Dans une stupeur morne et fatale absorbés,
Froids, livides, hagards, ils regardaient, courbés
Sous l'être illimité sans figure et sans nombre,
L'un, décroître le jour, et l'autre, grandir l'ombre.
Et, tandis que montaient les constellations
Et que la première onde aux premiers alcyons
Donnait sous l'infini le long baiser nocturne,
Et qu'ainsi que des fleurs tombant à flots d'une urne,
Les astres fourmillants emplissaient le ciel noir,
Ils songeaient, et, rêveurs, sans entendre, sans voir,
Sourds aux rumeurs des mers d'où l'ouragan s'élance,
Toute la nuit, dans l'ombre, ils pleuraient en silence;
Ils pleuraient tous les deux, aïeux du genre humain,
Le père sur Abel, la mère sur Caïn.

MODERNIZED INTERPRETATION OF ANTIQUITY

The rehabilitation of the literature and art of the Dantean Middle Ages and of the poetry of the Bible took more audacity in a country which, for the last three centuries, had expressed its distrust of the Christian supernatural element and had failed in the epic genre. The eighteenth century, in a few intuitions of Fontenelle *(Essai sur l'origine des fables)* and of Président de Brosses *(Dissertation sur les dieux fétiches,* 1757), had tried to understand the frame of mind of the primitive people who had formerly created myths which seem to defy reason. Voltaire himself, in at least one article of his *Dictionnaire philosophique,* has perceived more reason in Greek polytheism than in the puerile stories of the Old Testament, which he fiercely mocked in the *Sermon des Cinquante.* Diderot had guessed correctly what was lacking in the poetry of his time, when he declared *(De la Poésie dramatique):* "Poetry needs something extraordinary, barbaric and primitive." There were many allusions to the thinkers and writers of antiquity in the works of the authors of the eighteenth century; the ancients provided a rich arsenal of weapons that could be used against Christianity. Like so many of our writers, from Jean-Louis de Balzac and La Mothe Le Vayer to Bossuet and, much later, to Simone Weil, those of the period of the *Encyclopedia,* however little attachment they may have felt toward Christianity, were internally divided. They had been raised almost exclusively on Homer, Sophocles, Plato, Virgil, and Tacitus, had admired the ethics of the Stoics and the nobility of Socrates in his prison, and had only read very little of the Scriptures or of the Church Fathers. Yet, Christian orthodoxy called upon them to condemn to limbo, if not to eternal hell, all those who had not had the good fortune to come into the world after the Redeemer or who had known nothing of his message.

The opposition of these men of the eighteenth century to a superstitious and hidebound faith had at least some effect, even on the romantics who were Catholic for a time. The vehement logic of *Soirées de Saint-Pétersbourg* impressed and perhaps convinced for a short while the romantics of the generation subsequent to that of the great pioneers: Baudelaire hailed Joseph de Maistre as his "maître à penser" and Barbey d'Aurevilly expressed "the indescribable delight which he felt on reading this man" whose work "took his breath away by its abundance of ideas and images." The others preferred either a frank esoterism going beyond the inhuman logic of the Jacobins of theology, or a sweetness and charm in their religiosity which they found in the works of Homer or Virgil even more than in the Gospels. Chateaubriand had presented the model; and, if Stendhal was exasperated by the images, the color and, above all, the attitudes of the man whom he mockingly called "Monsieur de Castelfulgens," the dream of Victor Hugo, Lamartine, and Gautier was to equal this precursor who looked upon them with gracious condescension, refusing to recognize in them the offspring of René.

PAGANISM AND HELLENISM IN ROMANTICISM

Chateaubriand's entire work was obsessed by the desire to reconcile "two empires in opposition": paganism and Christianity. When he was young, he had startled his strange father by the passionate tone with which he had recited the invocation to *Aeneadum Genitrix,* sensual pleasure of men and gods, and to Venus, with which the poem of Lucretius opens. The reading of the fourth book of the *Aeneid* was for him, as for many other romantics, the first revelation of love leading to death, *amor che a nullo amato amar perdona* of the one who had chosen Virgil as a guide and master. Tibullus excited him almost as much. In the preface which he wrote to *Atala* in the 1804 edition of *Le Génie du christianisme,* he already claimed that his principal merit was to have tried "to restore in literature this love of antiquity which has been lost in our times." He later left out this passage from his works. In the preface to the first edition of *Les Martyrs* and often elsewhere in his many statements about himself, he revealed the antique sources on which he had drawn. Sainte-Beuve was not wrong to affirm that in his *Itinéraire,* Chateaubriand was "Greek and pagan in spite of himself"; however, the "in spite of himself" is superfluous. The evocations of the Sylph, in the third book of *Les Mémoires d'outre-tombe,* which exposes humorously the phenomenon of romantic love created out of nothing by the imagination, invoke Aphrodite, Diana, Thalia, and Hebe. Marcellus, a distinguished Hellenist, who knew Chateaubriand well and spoke of him without the spiteful digs which Sainte-Beuve slipped into his studies, reported that the young traveler did not set off for the New World, in 1791, without taking along with him "a little Homer in Greek." Werther, the preeminent romantic, reread his Homer in the same way before the serenity he sought deserted him completely. In 1859, in his long work *Chateaubriand et son temps* which commented on the posthumous memoirs of the great man, Marcellus declared: "He was surprised at having presided over the birth of the modern romantic school, when, according to him, no human heart had ever been consumed by a greater love of the classics and noble antiquity." A literary historian, René Canat, rightly affirmed: "There is a hellenic inspiration in *Le Génie du christianisme.*"

On one point however, carried away by the thesis that he was bent on developing with opportunism in apologetic work, Chateaubriand misunderstood the originality of this Greece which the Breton wanted to make his second motherland: he had to and tried to maintain that mythology belittled nature and "Christ had to come finally to drive out this nation of fauns, satyrs, and nymphs, to restore silence to the grottos and reverie to the woods." Likewise, in Athens, Lamartine remained insensitive to the temples which were too small for his liking and were erected for "assumed or imagined gods." He is, however, the only French poet, after the sixteenth century, who has translated, in beautiful, flowing, and vague verse, Platonic aspirations and impulses. very few other French romantics besides Quinet and Nerval, none of the German poets and, with the exception of Byron, no English romantic undertook the trip to Greece. The material difficulties were undoubtedly great. But it can be surmised that they preferred not to have to shatter, by contact with modern Greece, the image they had formed of ancient Greece through ancient literature or their philhellenic impulse. To be sure, Béranger said that he was Greek once: "Pythagoras is right"; and it seems he declared to Jouffroy in 1830: "Homer is romantic," which means a great deal but at the same time very little. The imaginary journey to Argos, Péléon, beautiful Titarèse, and two towns with melodious names that a fantastic geography could imagine bathed by the same bay, was evoked by the Muse of May, who tried to soothe the sick poet. But Alfred de Musset who, moreover, in certain respects, approached, more than any other romanticist, the ironic and decorative grace which is at least as Greek as the Dionysian tragic style, was less concerned with Greece than with Florence or Venice.

The ardent, heart-rending nostalgia for Greece never reached, among the French romantics, the degree of intensity found among several Nordic writers. Historians of the romantic Hellenism of Schiller, Hoelderlin, Heine, Platen and, later, Nietzsche, have maintained with just a trace of amused exaggeration, that it had been nothing less than a sort of sacred mania, a mystical impulse of escape to an impossible Eden, imagined through the hypotheses of Winckelmann and through Roman imitations of Greek works of art. No Frenchman at that time dreamed of life in ancient Greece, glimpsed through paintings on a Greek urn, as Keats did, or built like him an imaginary temple to Psyche, the last addition to the goddesses of paganism. None of the Frenchmen identified themselves with a worshiper of the gods of Plato or a hierophant inspired by Diotima, as Hoelderlin did in his *Hyperion* and in several hymns. There is always more prudence in French folly; this was noted by Heine who, even when he was paralysed and afflicted with pains in the autumn of his life, dragged himself to the feet of Venus de Milo and wept bitterly *(Nachwort zum Romanzero)*. As early as 1788 Schiller had extolled the divinities of polytheism in a hymn entitled *Die Götter Griechenlands,* in which these gods were somewhat depersonalized and presided over a neoclassical aesthetics of harmonious order and slightly frigid nobility of style. The French romantics, forced to revolt against the doctrines of the "ideal of beauty" dear to the neoclassicists whom they opposed, did not like to recommend an aesthetics of symmetry, serenity, and the apparent restraint that prompts the author not to reveal himself in his work. Later, Leconte de Lisle and Flaubert, in reaction against some defects in the works of the rebels of 1830, assumed the role of arrogant critics. Hoelderlin himself, who was most passionately nostalgic about an imaginary Greece, a few years before becoming the victim of the madness that engulfed him for thirty years, had prudently observed in a letter to Böhlendorff on December 4, 1801: "It is dangerous to deduce rules of art solely from Greek excellence." Goethe had realized this, for he had had to give up his ambition to write an epic,

Achilles, because his extremely precise knowledge of ancient models prevented him in advance from giving full scope to his genius. His Iphigenia and even his Helen, victims of nostalgia, were in fact neither Greek nor even really alive. It was when he gave up these pastiches of a beauty too austere, that had been elevated to a grandeur too composed—the sort of beauty that had been praised by Winckelmann—that he succeeded in discovering the sensual joy of the *Anthology* and the charming invitations to sensual pleasure without remorse, which he had not found in his adoration of Frau von Stein. It was an insignificant artificial flower maker of Weimar who inspired the *Roman Elegies,* written on his return from the voyage that liberated him in 1788, and published only in 1795. Antiquity had educated him, to be sure; but the nights of love, free from philosophy and erudition, had done so even more. "Am I not acquiring knowledge by following the contours of a charming bosom and passing my hand over the curves of hips?" (*Elegy,* V). And this group of undisguisedly pagan poems concluded with the opinion that it is by remaining young and by loving youth that one most truly becomes part of the Greek school. "Live happily, and let the past thus live in you!"

SYMBOLICS OF RELIGIONS
AND RELIGIOUS SYNCRETISM

The great German work to which the first half of the nineteenth century owed its reinterpretation of mythology, *La Symbolique et la Mythologie des peuples anciens* by Friedrich Creuzer (1810–1812), was not translated in France (and adapted and published) until between 1825 and 1851, in ten volumes, by Guigniaut. Of course, there were few French romantic writers who read these involved accounts. But reports and discussions brought about by the explanation of Greek religion presented by Creuzer were passed on to the poets termed "Parnassian" and to Flaubert and his friends, thanks to Guigniaut, Maury, and Louis Ménard. Hugo's intermediaries were rather Pierre Leroux, Alexandre Weill, and perhaps even Jean Reynaud's work, *Philosophie religieuse, Terre et Ciel,* published in 1854. He guessed or created anew the ancient myths without needing mythographers. Moreover, Creuzer's thesis, opposed from the time it appeared, contained too many traces of the explanation of religions by the deceit or the ingenious plans of priests, an explanation popular in the eighteenth century. These priests, who were in possession of transcendental truths, were supposed to have expressed them through symbols to make them comprehensible to the ordinary people. Mysteries alone had preserved the original, hidden truth.

Such a theory, which did not discern clearly the way in which primitive man and the poet create myths spontaneously, without the implausible planning attributed to the process by a scholar who confuses symbolic myth and artificial allegory, was lucidly criticized by the Germans (Otfried Müller, Voss), as well as by Renan and Ménard, and omitted by Michelet in his great and fervently romantic work, *La Bible de l'humanité*. The French romantics, even more than the German or English romantics, turned to the ancient myths from a need to draw on a fresher source of poetry; these men, who were weighted down by the past, and who considered themselves "as having come too late into a world that was too old," were attracted by the youth of humanity, which they had dreamed about. This was their form of primitivism, which certain critics, such as the American philosopher Lovejoy, considered the main characteristic of romanticism. What they loved above all in antiquity, Greek or even Roman, were not the virtues that the classical education of the time had extolled too much (order, clarity, moderation), but lack of moderation, force and passion: everything that we have called Dionysian since Nietzsche's time. They were quite aware of the grace, the picturesque fantasy, at times the affectation of the Greeks, revealed in the Tanagra figurines and vases, even if none of them personally saw the Cariatids or the young girls in the little Acropolis Museum whose smile "like that of Chinese women" irritated Charles Maurras. Hugo inserted in the second book of *Contemplations,* a poem, "Le Rouet d'Omphale", which is at the same time graceful and vehement, and would not seem out of place among the works of Chénier or Henri de Régnier. On October 4, 1844, he had written proudly to Théophile Gautier: "You prove that what they call romanticism has all the forms of genius, Greek as well as others." The same year, two authors who were closely connected with Hugo, Paul Meurice and Auguste Vacquerie, presented a freely translated form of Sophocles' *Antigone;* they prefaced the publication of the tragedy by maintaining that the Greek theater is romantic through and through, blending the tragic and comic, and piling up corpses: there are only five corpses in *Lucrèce Borgia,* but seven in *The Suppliants;* there are three suicides in *Antigone,* not to mention the dead bodies which remain on the stage for half an hour.

Reference has been made to the great shock experienced by the sensual imagination of several romantics, on reading the song of victorious and destructive love presented by a chorus in *Antigone,* the odes of Horace, and particularly the loves of Dido and Aeneas and lamentations of the Queen of Carthage who, abandoned by her lover, kills herself for love on the funeral pyre and, at this great moment, seeks once again with her wandering eyes the light of heaven, only to wail as she sees it:

oculisque errantibus alto
Quaesivit caelo lucem ingemuitque reperta.

Berlioz in his *Mémoires,* Hugo, and Michelet have mentioned how
shaken they were on reading these lines. But contact with antiquity on
the part of these very imaginative persons was not only the action of
impressionable nervous sensibilities. Hugo, in particular, had a
mythopoeic talent given to very few other modern poets; Shelley and
Claudel were the only others to possess it.

The philosophy of Hugo did not form a coherent ensemble, any
more than that of any other poet. He declared himself to be more sure
of the existence of God than of his own, to have implicit confidence in
another life, to be opposed to the narrow-mindedness of several of the
Christian dogmas, and to be fascinated by the transmigration of souls
and by a sequence of regeneration more satifying from the moral point
of view than eternal hell. He identified with this or that biblical
prophet, as a sculptor of cathedral porches might have done. But he
was no less aware of the force of polytheism and of the grandiose fights
between Gods and Titans, Centaurs and Lapithae, of the accords
resulting from the antagonism of opposed forces. "Polytheism is a
phantasm to which man is a prey," states an aphorism of *Promontorium
Somnïi.* The laughter of the ancient gods and the irreverence with
which they were treated by Euripides, Aristophanes, and later Lucian,
amused Hugo, who was a great humorist in spite of statements to the
contrary, just like Claudel himself. For there is fun and laughter in
these gatherings of the Olympians, not only in the works of Offenbach
and Giraudoux, but long before that in Homer's work. In his "Youth
Theatre," Hugo made fun of one of the most beautiful ancient myths,
which has haunted Cocteau and Stravinski in our times, that of Or-
pheus:

> The honorable Orpheus about whom Pluto said:
> He is the first husband wanting his wife back.

Besides the gods, Hercules and Prometheus appeared in his poetry.
But the masterpiece of mythopoeic poetry in French, and perhaps in
any modern literature, is *Le Satyre* of *La Légende des Siècles,* unquestionably the most grandiose French poem. This little pagan spirit embodied for Hugo the Renaissance and the rediscovery at that time of
antiquity. In 1912, there was a debate between Eugène Rigal and Paul
Berret about whether the poem and its author were pantheistic. One
of these two scholars, Rigal, maintained that Hugo could not be a
pantheist, since he believed in a personal God who was separated from

the world: he cited Schopenhauer's sarcastic remark according to which "pantheism is only a polite form of atheism . . . , a courteous roundabout way of giving the Lord notice of dismissal." But a poet does not have to worry about defining his terms rigorously or classifying himself with a label which he always keeps pinned to his writing desk. The feeling behind many of Victor Hugo's poems was pantheistic in that everything contained a particle or germ of the divine. According to Thibaudet in his work *Le Bergsonisme,* "the Satyr," that poor humiliated creature who was going to overthrow Olympus and bring Jupiter himself to his knees, embodied "Creative Evolution, no longer devised by the reasoning powers of a philosopher, but experienced by the unconscious of a poet, expressed in an almost miraculous state of verbal tension." The poem, multiform and resisting any narrow interpretation, is in fact carried away by a great life force beyond all poorly conceived gods of human form, to an eloquent affirmation of the liberation of humanity. It plunges into a state of chaos to soar towards a divine element which does not despise matter, but rather considers it sacred. In 1863, Hugo had written: "For the pagan, God is multitude. His entire religion is protean. The pagan holds his breath all through life." The tone of this great poem in which Hugo appeared, as Péguy said later, "younger than the ancients before the ancients," is indeed "breathless" and inspired. Going beyond the unchanging antiquity presented by textbooks, the Greece of statues and museums, more daring than the second *Eclogue* of Virgil which inspired it, familiar and disrespectful like a Greek satyric drama, Hugo recreated, because he relived them in spirit, the greatest myths of Greece.

He also modernized them; but to do that, he did not need facile anachronisms, nor did he feel the need to vulgarize what was great, even with a familiar note added. More than the writers of the seventeenth century, romantics like Vigny, Hugo, and Michelet turned to the past and other places; but unlike the Humanists of the fifteenth and sixteenth centuries, or the disappointed and embittered romantics of the Parnassian school, they were not obsessed by the heritage of the Hellenic past, revering every scrap that was found written by some ancient voluminous writer and inclined to be contemptuous of the science, philosophy, and civilization of their time, like the damned in the twentieth song of Dante's *Hell,* with their necks and heads screwed down so that they could only look back. By an imaginative understanding of other times and other places in which they would have liked to live, the most fervent romanticists gained new energy to leap into the future and make it part of the present.[4]

7 Romanticism, Religion, and Religions

Saint-Beuve, who himself toyed several times with the idea of stabilizing his inconsistent nature by clinging to faith, has noted in one of the essays of the fourth volume of *Nouveaux Lundis:* "The nineteenth century opened with a religious revival." In spite of *Le Génie du christianisme,* Joseph de Maistre, or Mme de Krudener, that statement holds less true for the first two decades of the century than the period 1820–1848.

To be sure, mocking agnostics and those indifferent to religion did not hold their peace, by any means, at this time. Béranger popularized his God of good people, who was so prosaic and devoid of Christian sentiment; Paul-Louis Courier, Mérimée, and Stendhal did not even try to understand the religious phenomenon. A rather hasty generalization has led people to say that the bourgeoisie was Voltairian under Louis XVIII as well as in the reign of Louis-Philippe and again during Napoleon III's time. But it also included many admirers of Montalembert, Lacordaire, and even of Falloux and Veuillot. However, judging by writers that bourgeois read, Voltaire had just as many admirers in the so-called middle classes as Rousseau. Chateaubriand, who was not adverse to some contradiction, often reread Voltaire and praised him. He declared in a letter to *Le Mercure:* "You are quite aware of the fact that my personal faith consists of seeing Jesus Christ in everything." In actual fact, the person of Christ did not haunt him any more than it did other Catholics: Montaigne, Descartes, or Baudelaire. Denier though he was, Théophile Gautier, especially in his *Comédie de la mort* ("Les Venduers du temple," "Magdalena," "La

Vie dans la mort," "La Mort dans la vie"), or Leconte de Lisle ("Le Nazaréen") gave more prominence to the Redeemer in their work, even if they did this to deny his undertaking to redeem souls or to declare that it was a failure.

GOD, CHRIST, AND ANGELS IN FRENCH
ROMANTIC LITERATURE

No facile formula is acceptable in these matters. It has been asserted that in France and even in Germany (with Novalis and Wilhelm Schlegel, who became a Roman Catholic like his wife Caroline) romanticism was synonymous with Catholicism. This opinion certainly cannot be upheld, even in the case of Lamartine or Hugo at the start of their career, for they never sided with those who passed for typical Catholics around 1815–1830: the extremists. Others, equally suspicious of the reformed religion and the new literature, affirmed just as forcefully that romanticism, which was the offspring of the Reformation and was developing, like it, an increasing number of sects and cliques, was Protestantism in literature: Mme de Duras, Vitet, and several others, particularly in the Catholic reviews of 1824 which Pierre Moreau has studied.[1] In a dogmatic and uncompromising book, written during his youth, entitled *Le Catholicisme chez les romantiques* (de Boccard, 1922), Auguste Viatte criticized the French romantic poets for having taken delight in an extremely vague and totally superficial religiosity. Lamartine wrote many hymns to the Creator between 1820 and 1830, but with a facility which makes us suspect the sincerity and intensity of his faith. A friend of Genoude, one of the worst French translators of the Old Testament, he transformed the Psalms into eloquent and tender poetry. In his earliest odes, Victor Hugo introduced the name of Christ even more frequently; then, he broke away from him and from faith and made the Savior a more vivid and dramatic character in *Le Gibet* and in his first experience with death. Musset never discussed very much what religious faith he had left, but his spokesman in *Rolla* had repudiated "the holy word" and declared that God and morals were dead. Vigny, in one of his strangest poems, *Paris,* impressed like many romanticists by the revolt and misfortune of Rabelais, presented him holding up "as he weeps" the "ousted Cross." The great, impious town, guilty of a "second deicide," has "wiped Jesus Christ out of its heart as well as its mind." Traditional religion was dying. Chateaubriand had boldly asked the resultant question in his *Essai sur les Révolutions,* which he did not hesitate to republish in 1826, in the chapter entitled: "What religion will take the place of Christianity?" There were numerous laments everywhere, in the works of novelists, historians, and poets:

man could no longer believe; he needed a new faith which could make him understand the presence of evil and let him forsee the disappearance of this evil even in our earthly existence. It was no longer his personal, perhaps egoistical salvation that he desired, but the salvation of others along with his own, possibly in another existence, but first of all in this life. After the vague and youthful effusions of their early works, (which, however, were less vague than the many expressed by their romantic predecessors beyond the Rhine—Wackenroder, Novalis and the Schlegels), the romanticists soon returned to a sort of deism which satisfied them more.[2] The most original among them were tempted by a pantheism which was undoubtedly more poetic, or by an esoterism that was even stranger. In any event, far and wide, as the remote consequences of the Age of Enlightenment's attacks against religion were more deeply felt, the men of 1820–1850 (and even more so, those of the Second Empire, who turned more unmistakably still to Voltaire and Diderot) sensed that the traditional faith was wavering. God must grow, according to Diderot's wish, to satisfy yearnings after the great and the whole. The ways in which this confused trend began were manifold, almost as varied as the number of individuals. They led either to a horizontal extension of faith that was spreading to other men, to the lowly and working classes to whom the lyric poets themselves paid some attention, or to a syncretism that was just as vague, which dreamed of combining more ancient religions with a revitalized Christianity. Moreover, through the exploration of dreams and the unconscious that philosophers and psychologists were rediscovering at that time, romanticism felt drawn to every sort of esoteric and semimystical belief. One of the favorite forms of these romantic religions was a diffused pantheism, an impetus to go beyond man in the epic genre and find the superman. "From the sub-human to the superman" could be the title of this twofold romantic aspiration: one aspired after the chaos and the troubled inner depths of being or after the heroic fancies of an Icarus and the heights, hazardous in more than one sense, of the epic.

EGOISM AND EGOCENTRISM

A great deal—perhaps too much—has been said about the egoism of the romanticists and their individualism, which had taken the place of the search for the eternal essence of man, which partisans of classicism attributed to classical works, aiming at the universal. The artificial opposition of the two ages and their literature has encumbered education with old clichés for too long. It is only too evident that La Rochefoucauld, Retz, Mme de Sévigné, and even the satirist Boileau, as well as many other writers of 1660–1690, did not conceal their ego very much. There were as many, if not more, memoirs written by the participants of the Fronde and the nobles who flocked to Versailles as by the subjects of Charles X or Louis-Philippe. As a matter of fact, it would be puerile to try and judge which men in which period were most preoccupied with their ego, just as it would be to estimate which men loved the most or the best. To put it simply, the expression of sentiments depends to a large extent on what is fashionable, and a new terminology helps to identify, and probably to communicate to others, moods or attitudes poorly described until that point.

This was undoubtedly the case of egotism, which Stendhal loved, at the very time when Maine de Biran and a few other philosophers were trying to perceive in effort the essence of the self, or of the soul as they preferred to call it. Other thinkers, heirs to the sensualism of the eighteenth century, denied, like Taine, the existence of this autonomous self, distinct from sensations, impressions, and fleeting ideas which only are and make of the self "events." Auguste Comte had upheld before that one cannot reach this self by withdrawal into oneself, that is, by introspection. Neither Comte nor even Stendhal or Taine can be called romantics in the narrow sense of the term, since they did not belong to a group or accept the aesthetic and literary views of romanticism. But while laughing at the pretensions of the ego to know itself only by inner analysis, or speaking ironically but pleasantly about the word "egotism," borrowed from English, like the author of *Henri Brulard,* they felt nonetheless that the current of confession and introspection, which had begun with Montaigne and Rousseau, was going to become a great river in their century. Nietzsche and Max Stirner deified this ego even more in their philosophical outbursts of exasperated individualism. Barrès popularized the expression "Culte du moi," before reversing his views and laughing at it as he preached attachment to the soil, ancestors, and the motherland. Malraux, inspired by Barrès at the start of his career, like so many other romantics of the twentieth century (Montherlant, Mauriac, or de Gaulle, for example), tried, in his imaginary correspondence with a Chinese, to shake himself free of this extremely complicated cultivation of the ego, which is a malady of Western men. Writers who died young, like Jules Laforgue, or who found it difficult to mature, like Musset, could not go beyond their obsession with themselves and sacrifice their ego to a religious quest or expand it by identifying themselves with a large number of their fellow creatures. Nevertheless, Musset tried to come out of himself and get over his fondness for unhappiness in some prose works[3], even if he could not do this in his poems; and he attained this end in his theater. In *La Fanfarlo,* Baudelaire succeeded in describing himself humorously through his counterpart, Samuel Kramer; and in his *Tableaux Parisiens* and some of his prose poems, he dealt sympathetically (and also with some of a dandy's cruelty) with the afflictions of little old women or an unfortunate person shattered in mind and body like Mlle Bistouri. Victor Hugo, who, even before the age of thirty, had wanted to be the sonorous echo of his century, and whose ego was more hypertrophied than all other romantic egos, had the least trouble in expanding his inspiration and faith to celebrate the gods, or the idols, of the people. His cry, in the preface of *Les Contemplations,* after he had isolated himself in solitude and a personal mystical experience which was perhaps incommunicable, has remained famous; he said to his reader: "Oh foolish reader who thinks that I am not you." The most striking example of this evolution away from the narrowness of the ego lamenting or, as Michelet said in another context, "stroking its wounds to inflame them more," and toward the fraternity of mankind and social preoccupations, was that of Lamartine. This writer who had seemed "to know only his soul," who knew only how to complain or praise Heaven, and who, after *La Chute d'un ange,* had been severely reproached by the public for wandering in the clouds in an atmosphere in which he alone could breathe, repented nobly. In a beautiful poem, "A M. Félix Guillemardet", written in September 1837 and included in a volume which deserves better than the mediocre reputation that it has enjoyed, *Recueillements poétiques,* Lamartine did not hesitate to disown his past:

> My personality filled nature,
> One would have thought that before it no creature
> Had ever lived, suffered, loved, lost and moaned,
> That I alone was the key to the great mystery,
> And that all the pity of heaven and earth
> Had to shine on my ant! . . . . .

Then he had understood how narrow this egoism was and, once his youth was over, he learned to suffer with others and to exchange his religion, based on the relations of an individual with the divine, for a more noble faith:

> Then my heart, insensitive to its own miseries
> Later extended to the griefs of my brothers:
> All their afflictions flowed into the lake of my tears,
> And, like a great shroud which pity unfolds,
> The soul of an individual, receptive to the complaints of the crowd,
> Wept for all woes.

Inevitably, such preoccupations, which aimed at nothing less than giving a new orientation to Christianity, by leading it back to its origins and by reducing the role of organization and rites in favor of the fraternity of mankind, were to lead both Lamartine and Hugo to political action, and tempt Vigny for a while and even Leconte de Lisle during his youth. As long ago as 1831, in *Les Feuilles d'automne,* Hugo had been vocal about his hatred of all oppression of the less fortunate by the powerful: "I hate oppression profoundly." The following year, he had expressed his pity and anger, in prose, in *Le Dernier jour d'un condamné.* He clearly discerned in the Saint-Simonists a desire to found a new religion, and not to build up an intellectual structure; he did not hesitate to consider them romantics in their own way. "Romanticism and socialism are really the same," he proclaimed in *William Shakespeare.* And in a passionate poem of *Les Châtiments,* "Joyeuse vie," he stigmatized the revelry of the rich which formed a contrast to "the dismal hell" which he had observed in the cellars of Lille: child-labour, prostitution of young girls, much iniquity and poverty. In notes which he scribbled for *Les Misérables*[4], he repeated that, although one can certainly not do away with suffering, one can at least put an end to poverty and misery.

The entire century, or at least that part of it which can be called romantic in a broad sense, was carried away by this religion impetus. No other century had been as carried away by it since the Middle Ages and the poetic sermons of men like St. Francis or Joachim of Floris. But this religious sentiment extends beyond the dogmas and all orthodoxy. "Humanity has a religious future. The religion of the future will be greater, more powerful than that of the past . . . it will be the synthesis of all conceptions of humanity." Thus affirmed the Saint-Simonian doctrine, as it was published in 1854 at the Librairie Nouvelle. Fourierism was even more religious, even in some of its follies, and our age, since 1940, tends to give credit on this score to Fourier the prophet, through its poets (Andé Breton) and economists (like Bertrand de Jouvenel in *Arcadie,* 1969). Even Leconte de Lisle, who was strongly influenced by the Fourierist ideas, interpreted in his early poems, in serious and passionate verse, his anticipation of a new faith devised by man to satisfy his nostalgia of the past and desire for a happier future ("Dies irae," 1952):

> But to us who are consumed by an impossible desire,
> A prey to the evil of believing and loving forever,
> Tell us, days of the future, will you restore us life?
> Tell us, oh days of the past, will you restore us love?

ROMANTICISM AND LAMENNAIS

The relations between Lamennais and the writers of romanticism have been the subject of numerous studies. Lamartine and Sainte-

Beuve for a while, and, even more, Maurice de Guérin were disturbed by the passionate nature of the Breton priest. One cannot say that he himself was, in the strict sense of the term, either a socialist or a romantic, since he remained aloof from all groups. But he was a rebel and an unhappy man who loved his unhappiness. He almost considered it the sign of being the chosen one, like the heroes of Byron or of *Hernani*. He noted: "What am I good for? For suffering. That must be my way of glorifying God." And in a turn of phrase that was even more Chateaubriand-like, he observed: "My soul was born with a wound." His ordination at the age of thirty-four, which was literally forced on him by his brother who was already a priest and who thought he would thus make him more stable, was undoubtedly at the root of his troubles. He suffered terrible pangs of hesitation and remorse before daring to celebrate his first mass. He tried, however, to revive apologetics with his first work, which created a great stir in 1817: *Essai sur l'indifférence*. Then he became enamored of liberty, tried to assimilate the religion of the common people, and was condemned by the Vatican. In the long run, he was vindicated, if not officially rehabilitated, by the rise in Catholicism of trends aiming at putting an end to the divorce between religion and the working classes. The workmen-priests could have claimed kinship with him. The people loved him dearly as a democrat and advocate of fraternity, and in 1854 they gave him a touching funeral. The stilted, apocalyptic, and frequently tedious eloquence of his *Paroles d'un croyant* (1834) is certainly romantic in the worst sense of the word.[5] His very superior pages on aesthetics, in the third volume of *Esquisse d'une philosophie,* show that he was a thinker of some authority, conversant with the French and German philosophy of his time. He alone could probably have drawn the romanticists to a rejuvenated, sentimental, and democratic Christianity. Michelet, in *Le Peuple,* expressed almost the same opinion, and he approached Lamennais' ideas even more in 1831 when he wrote the curious pages of his *Introduction à l'historie universelle.*

Lamennais and Michelet had in common a hyper-acute sensitivity which made them at the same time wavering and contradictory. Once they had made up their minds, they became suddenly and aggressively implacable. Lamennais, the unfrocked priest and helpless prophet, even compared himself, like the unhappy Coleridge trying to find his lost willpower in opium, to an Aeolian harp which sounds with every passing breath of wind. He encouraged in his contemporaries a fondness for a vague religiosity and helped to give the Revolution of 1848 that characteristic of romantic messianism, removed from the reality of the working-classes, which Marx later ridiculed. Like Lamartine, Hugo, and Balzac, he had felt that a hidden instinct led nations to look for a new religion and that Catholicism, behind the times and sclerosed in its structure, was very strong in not recognizing this fact.

THE GREAT ROLE OF ESOTERIC MYSTICISM
IN FRENCH ROMANTICISM

The adjective "mystical" includes so many different moods and has been so smirched that its use should be even more severely forbidden than that of the word "romantic." The term "illuminé" is tainted with a pejorative meaning which risks holding up beforehand to ridicule those to whom it is applied. The search for some mystical esoterism was nevertheless one of the aspirations of the so-called romantic period. Still it is curious to note that the same liking for heresies claiming to communicate with the divine without an intermediary had been no less widespread in the century which is thought to be rational, the seventeenth century, if one can believe the great history of Abbé Brèmond. And it was in the century supposedly rationalist par excellence, the eighteenth century, that Auguste Viatte discovered the greatest number and the strangest of the "illuminés". Swedenborg himself, Saint-Martin, Fabre d'Olivet were after all contemporaries of Voltaire and Helvetius. They were still read during the time of Balzac and Nerval. The indulgence of the romantic period toward the expression of the most personal individual sentiments perhaps caused the men of 1820–1850 not to be tempted to immerse themselves in misleading doctrines. Nerval, Balzac, and perhaps even Gautier, who were Swedenborgians at certain times (attracted more often than we would think by spiritualistic themes), or Baudelaire, retained a curious rational restraint in their lives as well as their works. Their mysticism, if one can use this term for some of them, scared them, just as table-tapping finally terrified Hugo and the derangement brought about by artifical paradises frightened Baudelaire in the long run. Even Nerval, in *Aurélia,* drew a moral and almost a didactic lesson useful to science, from his descents into the hell of insanity.

HANKERING AFTER THE HEIGHTS
AND DESCENT INTO THE DARK REGIONS

The first half of the century which followed the Revolution and which recalled how easy it was for the cult of reason and the outburst of base and cruel passions to be juxtaposed in the same persons at the same time, plunged much further down into the depths than previous epochs; it also wanted to rise higher. In this respect the poet of *Les Fleurs du mal* was indeed the heir to romanticism, and he proclaimed this; Flaubert and Verlaine were no less so. The frequent presence of angels in the works of the French poets of that time has been pointed out in preceding pages, as has been the importance given to Christ. A broadminded and ingenious philosophy professor, Adolphe Franck, attracted by the whirl of strange ideas of the "illuminés" of the preceding century who continued to be read in his time, published in 1866 a work on *La Philosophie mystique en France à la fin du XVIIIe siècle*. In this work, which dealt particularly with Saint-Martin and his teacher Martinez Pasqualis, Franck quoted this significant statement of the unknown "Philosophe": "Every man, since the coming of Jesus Christ, has a gift which allows him to go beyond Christ." Some of these mystics who were contemporaries of Mme de Staël and Lamartine hid their thoughts in such confusion that the prejudice of French clarity wreaked vengeance on them by burying them in semi-oblivion; this was the case with Ballanche, who, however, was found at so many crossroads throughout the first half of the century. Others have been the subject of more accurate studies only much later and quite recently: Pierre Leroux, Jean Reynaud, Alexandre Weill, Elophas Lévi.[6]

To be sure, this twofold movement towards the depths and the heights has always characterized the nature of man, who is both angel and animal; and Saint Paul, after Ovid, had been one of the first to note this conflict within himself. The originality of the nineteenth century consists in having accepted this conflict and in having derived from it the means for a more complete knowledge of oneself and a source of pride. Kierkegaard was disturbed by it, but he did not really try to cure himself. Novalis asserted that "no one knows himself if he is nothing but himself and if he is not at the same time another." Hoffmann and those who are considered the minor romanticists of Germany were fascinated by the theme of the double, as was also the Russian Lermontov in his strange poem, "Demon," and later Dostoyesky. Goethe, who did not really like the peculiarities of the young romantics of his country, did, all the same, dabble in alchemy; and he left works of a mystical symbolism like the curious *Das Märchen,* written in 1795, which could be interpreted in a religious sense.

In almost all of them, the divine element to which they aspired in their fervor of rehabilitating a Christianity whose downfall they deplored, required as a counterpart the diabolic. Only a few basically noble and good utopians among them, like Pierre Leroux (who had, moreover, led a difficult life from the materialistic point of view), avoided this temptation of the demoniac. Leroux, in the foreword to the first volume of his *Oeuvres* in 1850, affirmed forcefully that he was not an author, but a believer.. He thus acknowledged the glaring defects of his books considered as literature, and dreamed of linking romanticism, the machine that recreated gods, with the best of eighteenth-century philosophy, which he did not want to renounce. As a matter of fact, it was thanks to it that it had been possible to place God, not outside the world, but in humanity. The abundant and confused ideas of Leroux impressed in different ways (on the social or metaphysical level) George Sand, Hugo, Sainte-Beuve for a brief period, as well as less important figures.

The other writers and philosophers of this period understood that the regeneration of man as a spiritual animal taking over the spiritual future of humanity had to take into account all the elements of an animal and even a monster in a person. Their angels shed tears over the condemnation of the Prince of Darkness. Shelley, in many a poem, rehabilitated the serpent, exiled from paradise. Hugo reserved his poetic tenderness for the worm, the toad, and the donkey: he punished the wicked by a metempsychosis which turned Verrès into a wolf and another criminal into a strange carnivorous beast. In the long chain of creatures, the human being is connected with the animal kingdom; his merit will be all the greater then in reaching out for the divine. Delacroix was fascinated by lions and tigers. Géricault by horses and some wild animals. "I begin by portraying a man: he ends up as a lion," he confessed one day in one of the most beautiful romantic turns of phrase. The plunges into ecstasy or lethargy brought on by drugs, the flights into the world of dream, cultivated as a second life and opening the gates of the subconscious, brought into the literature of Coleridge and De Quincey, Nerval, Baudelaire, Novalis, and Hoelderlin a dimension unknown to poets and novelists up to that point. Marivaux, Prévost, and even Laclos suddenly seemed tame and plain compared with *La Peau de chagrin or La Cousine Bette.* Jacques Bousquet, the author of a long book *Les Thèmes du rêve dans la littérature romantique* (Didier, 1964), goes to the point of saying that men have been dreaming only since 1780. This is undoubtedly reducing too much the imaginative and subconscious life of humanity to its very occasional literary expression. Goethe had rightly observed that literature is only one fragment of many and that only a very small part of all that was experienced has passed into history or written literature. But it remains true that it was only with romanticism (Blake, Novalis, Hugo, Nerval) that, in different literatures, dream—and reverie, cleverly analyzed by Bachelard as being even more poetic than the dream of the sleeper—poured out in the imagination of writers. The very rigorous logic of the premonitory dreams in Greek tragedy, the dreams of Pauline and Athalie, were then jeered at. The extremes met instead of opposing each other. "To destroy the principle of contradiction is perhaps the most important task of the greatest logic," declared Novalis, in fragment No. 578 of his book *Fragmente.* With instinctive foresight, this same German poet, with whom the French romanticists were barely familiar and whom Carlyle tried hard to naturalize in England, shortly after the death of Shelley and Byron, had announced that many unknown territories remained to be discovered in our study of ourselves, provided one dared to plunge deep down to rise again as a result of this probing. "The mysterious path leads to one's own inner nature. . . . Every descent into oneself, every inward glance, is at the same time as ascent."[7]

PANTHEISM, THE GREAT TEMPTATION OF THE ROMANTICS

If the romantics often mentioned abysses and chasms, and the romantics of the second half of the century did this as much as their predecessors, they tried even more often to climb to the heights, sometimes to some empyrean where the atmosphere was rare and very pure. No other generation in France had wanted to leap towards what is called "the infinite" as much as the one which followed *René* and constantly dreamed of its hero. Even Musset exclaimed: "The infinite haunts me in spite of myself." Several times Lamartine addressed his hymns to "the Infinite one in the heavens." Maurice de Guérin used the word quite naturally in his *Journal* and felt himself imbued with this sentiment of the infinite, which is a source of melancholy since nothing in this world is perfect, but also a privilege for those who cannot be satisfied with the ephemeral and the changing. Such a vague aspiration could not long be limited by a traditional and organized religion. It was inevitable for romanticism to want to combine religions in an unparalleled synthesis and find in Catholicism itself the multiplicity of pagan gods who had survived in spite of Christian theologies. Also quite naturally, this refusal to be limited by all dogmas and by a unique being who was supposed to have separated this world from himself to give it life, drove many Romantics to a diffused pantheism.

Much fun has been made of the so-called local color, often not very authentic, of landscapes and romantic evocations, which presented a curious image of Andalusia, Venice, Greece, or the Arab world. Furthermore, not everything, by any means, was artificial in Delacroix' *Femmes d'Alger* or later in the less dazzling paintings of Fromentin or Matisse, in *Les Orientales,* or in Musset's stories in verse. The stirring of the imagination by Bonaparte's epic in Egypt or his visit to the plague-stricken people of Jaffa found expression in more than pictures commemorating these scenes after the event. Along with the war of Greek independence, almost thirty years later, this powerful impact on the imagination prompted renowned travelers to go to the Orient. It was not so much monuments as men with their beliefs and customs that they went there to find.

The broadening of horizons brought about by this rediscovery of the Orient and its beliefs, similar to that caused by the reinterpretation of ancient mythology and Hellenism, led men, from Joseph de Maistre to Victor Hugo the visionary during his years in exile, to want to go beyond Christianity while rejuvenating it. Joseph de Maistre himself had noted that a new revelation was by no means impossible and that the new century seemed to expect it, just as Virgil had seemed to anticipate it in his fourth *Eclogue* when he spoke of *novus ordo saeclorum*. German and English poets, Shelley in particular, in a beautiful chorus of his drama *Hellas* which stated that "the world's great age begins anew," had appointed themselves heralds of this rejuvenated faith. Saint-Simon had not been afraid to use the title *Le Nouveau Christianisme,* and it was a strange misapprehension which caused Comte's positivism to be considered for a while as an antireligious undertaking; in spite of the law of the three stages, or by virtue of this law, a messianism promised men of the century a broader faith in humanity, which would find the divine in itself. The works and letters of the Saint-Simonians such as Rodrigues, Enfantin, and Comte himself vibrate with an enthusiasm for a God who extends beyond sects and theological formulae and becomes all that is and will be. Neither Schelling nor even Herder were much read in France. But they were not needed to introduce the great idea of gradual development in the reflection of thinkers and in the imagination of poets. For some, the vision of other civilizations, based on another religion, that of Mohammed in particular, crystallized their impatience with a Catholicism that was too withdrawn within itself.

Henri Guillemin, in his important thesis on *Le Jocelyn de Lamartine* (1935), has drawn attention to the religious atmosphere of the period 1820–1835 during which Lamartine's Catholicism became progressively less orthodox until it reached the point of heresy. In 1832, while traveling in the Orient, he was not afraid to announce the appearance of a new Messiah who would succeed Christ. More and more, he made human reason the repository, and even the equivalent, of the Divine Word, according to the formulae presented by Lamennais. He reported that his visit to Christ's tomb projected in him "a great light of reason"; actually, it helped to complete his conversion to a kind of pantheistic deism. He contrasted with the petty quarrels of Christian sects about the entombment of Christ, the nobility of attitude of the Mohammedans, "the only tolerant people," whose cult, which has no priests, "is only a philosophical cult." He placed Mohammed on the same footing as Christ, and perhaps even ranked him slightly higher.

The other classic text which tactfully evoked the nostalgia for a religious syncretism comprising beliefs which Christianity had but lately tried to oppose was the preface to *Sylvie* (1853). In it, Gérard de Nerval evoked his youth during the years which preceded and followed 1830; at the time, he and his friends were obsessed "by philosophical or religious aspirations, vague enthusiasm, mingled with certain instincts of rebirth." In their dreams, it was the goddess Isis who appeared before them and was to regenerate them. In 1845, in the Fourierist review *La Phalange,* Nerval had published a curious article on "Le Temple d'Isis," for this goddess and the symbol of the veil in her temple haunted him. Still earlier, at Victor Hugo's place, when he was being teased about his lack of religion, Gérard had exclaimed: "I have no religion? But I have at least seventeen of them!" And on the last page of his *Mémoires d'Orient,* he expressed his "successive admiration for the different religions of the countries he visited." It was equally possible for him to be a pagan in Greece, a Mohammedan in Egypt, and a pantheist elsewhere. But it was to the Turks and "the nobility of their universal toleration" that he paid the most ardent homage. Louis Ménard who, fourteen years younger than Nerval, professed a religious syncretism even more systematic than that of the older poet, presented in his poem entitled *Panthéon* the pagan gods side by side with the Blessed Virgin and Christ; moreover, he only truly believed in the first. Later, he wrote humorously in the preface to his *Rêveries d'un païen mystique:* "If it is good to have a religion, it cannot be bad to have several.

Such syncretism is of course a poetic attitude, sometimes even an intellectual pastime for those who like to reconcile the most diverse points of view, rather than a logical theory. It resembles at times, even in those who made fun of Victor Cousin, the eclecticism advocated during the Restoration period by this eloquent professor, whose influence over the first half of the century was greater, and probably more beneficial, than one likes to admit. This reconciliation of the gods of the West and East, of monotheism and polytheism in a symbolic pantheon, encouraged, moreover, a new interest in the history of religions. It was responsible for quite a number of poems, sometimes moving, on the theme of the death of the gods, written by Leconte de Lisle, Jean Lahor, and others. For it is easier for the mind to contemplate these gods in their tombs, all swathed in wrappings and not in a position to instigate religious wars and persecutions, than to hold them up as always true to the faithful who are to inclined to intolerance. Concurrently with this burial-ground for gods and religions which Renan took pleasure in contemplating, Théophile Gautier and Malraux, the private prophets of their idols, fervently professed another cult, no less characteristic of romanticism: that of "sovereign verses", which remain "stronger than bronze," of the "hard metal" of Heredia, who alone preserved in his medallions "the immortal beauty of the virgins of Sicily," evolving into the cult of the metamorphosis of the gods celebrated in the romantic prose of André Malraux, as it is preserved by the only true triumphant conqueror of fate, namely, art. Syncretism popularized by romanticism will become the attitude which characterizes modern man, an attitude respectful of every faith, tolerant and anxious to explain East and West to each other.

Strangely enough, the term "pantheism" has for a long time scared away the champions of orthodoxy and even the unbelievers and deists much more than the word "syncretism." It is a well-known fact that Spinoza was greatly feared during his lifetime in Holland and not appreciated for a long while still after his death by Bayle and Diderot.[8] It was the Romantics—Goethe, Schelling, Tieck, Jean Paul, and Novalis in Germany, Shelley in England—who rediscovered pantheism and personally experienced it, without having recourse moreover to Spinozistic theorems. "He who has once sought God ends up by finding him everywhere," Novalis noted. It was thanks to these poetic and ardent imaginations that the word finally stopped being considered a shameful and artful synonym of atheism, as the eighteenth century had believed it to be after the Englishman Toland had first used the term in 1709. Lamartine, who discussed many confused ideas in his prose works between 1830 and 1840 (*Les Destinées de la poésie* and particularly *Politique rationnelle*) and whose philosophy, which was not always spiritless and timorous, is too often belittled today, exclaimed in *La Chute d'un ange:*

> My works and I, we are not two separate things:
> Form, substance, spirit, what am I not?

God is in all creation, and the poet finds him there. It would take a whole volume to discuss Victor Hugo's pantheism, which was never doctrinal or systematized. As early as *Les Feuilles d'automne,* written before he was thirty, he was fascinated by the god Pan and the symbolic meaning of the Universe which he attributed to this word. "It is God who fills everything. The world is his temple" and "Get intoxicated by everything! Get intoxicated, poets!," he declared in a strange and already Dionysian poem, *Pan,* which Baudelaire may have recalled later on. Through the romanticism of several countries, of France and England in particular, perhaps on account of the famous anecdote related by Plutarch in his work on the oracles, and also on account of the symbolic meaning of the divine Universe which the Greek term included and which the Stoics and even Saint Paul had rendered mysterious and majestic, the good Pan, inviting men to get intoxicated and experience joy, filling nature and living beings even more with a strange thrill, has become a leading theme. Keats introduced in the first song of his *Endymion* a solemn "Hymn to Pan"; Shelley composed another, more bantering in tone and full of rhythm, in the last years of his short life.

This pantheism was seldom laid down as a philosophical doctrine and it did not have to be. Implicitly, it denied a creation *ex nihilo* by the *fiat* of a god, since active nature and passive nature (Spinoza's *naturans* and *naturata*) were considered as consubstantial and both equally eternal. It was like a great being in movement in the universe, aspiring always to more life and more consciousness. Among the romantic writers and artists, this instinctive and sentimental pantheism expressed impatience with all barriers, the energy of the creator who wants to live the life of things, to become them and let himself be imbued by them. Shelley's entreaty to the West Wind is famous: "Be thou me, impetuous one!"; and his desperate desire to be able to merge with the clouds or the waves is well known. Likewise, Beethoven had sighed in a letter: "I would like to embrace the world." More than a century later, accused of pantheism considered as an infamy which could exile him from Catholic orthodoxy, Reverend Teilhard de Chardin, having had recourse several times to the citation from St. Paul which he loved and which was to support the entire structure he had set up as a poet and scientist,[9] gave vent to his quasi-despair at not being able to "detach Catholic dogmas from the geocentricism where they originated." In a long passage, "Panthéisme et christianisme", included in *Comment je crois (Oeuvres,* Vol. X, 1969), he dismissed the charge of pantheism, but with some reservations, since "pantheism is a faulty explanation for a basic tendency: the religious preoccupation with everything." He added, and this could also be said of the romantics, whom he resembled moreover in spirit:

> Whether it is a question of poetic impulses or
> philosophical constructs, pantheism in a broad sense . . .
> that is, preoccupation with the Universe, always seems to
> us religious, fundamentally religious.

MAURICE DE GUERIN

No texts of the French writers of the first half of the nineteenth century, regarding pantheism, were so filled with emotion and so artistic, with so little rhetoric, as those of Maurice de Guérin. According to Sainte-Beuve, one of Guérin's friends called him "the André Chénier of pantheism." The critic himself had guessed that the pantheism of this young writer, brought up in a religious atmosphere, looked after by a sister who feared the excesses of his excitable nature, influenced by Lamennais, was more pagan than Christian. For a while, there was some fruitless debate, full of sophisms, as there was later in the case of Rimbaud or Jacques Rivière, on the question of whether he was a true believer or a Catholic moving towards a syncretism which gave preference to Centaurs and Bacchantes over Christ and the saints. His two famous long poems in prose, very superior to his verse, revealed by George Sand (whose earlier, passionate works Guérin himself had enjoyed; for he cited the character Sténio, who was madly in love with Lélia, in his private diary), are numbered among the very exceptional masterpieces in a genre which can boast very few of them. All the passion of his heart and senses, delighted by the ecstatic union with nature, has flowed into these rhythmical lines. Later, Laconte de Lisle did not forget these visions of a god or a half-man, half-animal, in the most romantic of his long poems, *Khirôn.* One could almost believe that Valery's young Parca herself, as she gambolled in the meadows, was reliving the ecstasies of these two mythological figures.

But it was in his *Journal,* which he wrote for about two years (1833–1834) and then gave up when he felt that it was disclosing the pursuit of the ideal to which he wanted to devote himself, that Maurice de Guérin expressed his urge to mingle with things and to fill his soul with them. "To delve into the soul of men and let nature fill his soul" was what he seemed to propose as a program for himself on March 15, 1833. The same year, at Easter (he was then twenty-three years old), he combined religious effusions with more passionate effusions which united him with wild and tempestuous nature, and with *René, Lucrèce Borgia, Han d'Islande*—all books that he dearly loved. His first sight of the sea shook him so much that he wanted to die: "The soul is not equal to this sight; it is bewildered by this great apparition." At the end of the same year 1833, on December 8, he translated into words the magnificence of a stormy ocean which had made him wild with delight. Two weeks later, scared by the hold that nature had over him, "beset in the darkness by a barbarous and wild harmony," he confessed that he experienced "a sensual pleasure in terror." Strangely enough, in a poem by Shelley which he could not have been familiar with, was found the no less revealing line, in connection with a picture of Medusa with which Leonardo da Vinci has been credited: " 'Tis the tempestuous loveliness of terror." As a matter of fact, Shelley, at times Hoelderlin and, later, Lautréamont and Verhaeren were among the few who were as excited by storms and who loved the ocean as passionately as Maurice de Guérin. Other notations (for example, that of August 20, 1834) described literally a pantheistic and semimystical ecstasy, such as the ecstasy analyzed and celebrated in poetry, after Rousseau, by Wordsworth in *Tintern Abbey* and Shelley in *Mont Blanc:* "The soul sees through dense darkness . . . understands certain mysteries . . . it converses with ghosts; the gates of a marvellous world are opened to it." God was not forgotten in these descriptions of delight in the presence of nature, but he was no longer a personal god. He was rather "the omega point" to which seeds, roots, animals, and man himself reached out. In terms which recalled again the pantheistic outbursts of a Shelley, de Guérin exclaimed, on September 29, 1834, in a curious notation:

I would like to be the insect which is lodged and lives
in the radicle. I would place myself at the extreme
tip of roots and contemplate the powerful effect of pores
which suck in life: I would look at all life passing from
the womb of the fruitful molecule into the pores which,
like mouths, rouse it and attract it by melodious calls.
I would witness the ineffable love with which it rushes
towards the being which invokes it, and the joy of the being.
I would watch their embraces.

There is no need to be a great scholar of psychoanalysis to guess
what advantage could be taken of these pages of Maurice de Guérin by
a psychiatrist who would like to expose in them a sexuality which had
not as yet become aware of itself, or which had restrained itself in
order to gush out more passionately later. Long after Maurice de
Guérin's death, at the age of twenty-nine, letters of his, which were
disclosed, revealed him to be impatient with the control that his sister
wanted to impose on this pantheistic paganism which, she thought,
jeopardized his piety. She considered him cruel. Guérin wrote a letter
of confession to Barbey d'Aurevilly which would have delighted the
young Flaubert; it was published in July 1957 in *La Nouvelle Revue
française* (pp. 168–169):

Could I dare to confess to her that in my soul I
have the whims of a very great cruelty? I remember
that, at a very tender age, I took a bitter pleasure
in beating the animals I loved. . . . When they cried out,
I felt a heartbreak, a certain sensual pleasure of
pity which I craved. If I were a Roman emperor,
I would perhaps have my friends tortured to satisfy
my longing to pity them.

ENTHUSIASM OF THE ROMANTICS FOR THE EPIC
MYSTIQUE OF THE SUPERMAN

The two successful works of Maurice de Guérin, apart from the
notations of his *Journals,* are epic extracts. It is a known fact that
Victor Hugo first thought of giving the name of "short epics" to the
poems with a narrative and indirect lyricism for which he finally
adopted the more appropriate title of *Légende des siècles.* Leconte de
Lisle, at the same time or before him, also included ancient and strange
civilizations in his melancholic series of poems on humanity presented
as a prey to its follies and sinking into decay. The individual poems of
an epic nature written by this proud denier described the history of
poor human beings through what has been called "a stream of gods."
Heredia and, with less success and a very cold pedantism, other poets

or prose poets, too influenced by the Parnassian school, followed their example and composed great, clumsy productions (André de Guerne, Pierre Quillard). Victor Hugo's warning in his preface to *Marie Tudor* was barely heeded by this nineteenth century with its tremendous romantic ambitions: "The danger of the great is the false." He added, besides as the second term of the antithesis: "The danger of the true is the petty." Alfred de Vigny, who knew his limitations better, had disclosed as early as 1832 in his *Journal* that he was an "epic moralist" and, a few days earlier, that he had "always felt the epic spirit." But since length seemed to be a condition of the epic and and he did not approve of it in poetry (or did not feel qualified to attempt it), he had had recourse to prose to manifest his "epic spirit."

The history of these romantic epics in France has been very competently traced. The book by Herbert J. Hunt, published in England at the very time when the country was writing its own epic pages in history, has patiently surveyed these epics in prose and verse, some Christian, mostly pagan, and almost all of them full of humanitarian or theosophical messages. With all due deference to Voltaire and the famous little statement in which he refused his compatriots "the epic mind," no country, not even that of Klopstock, Jean Paul, and the author of *Faust,* has numbered between 1775 and 1860 as many attempts to write an epic. Certainly there were many failures. Many of these emulators of Icarus have fallen pitifully into pools of pretentious tedium. One of those who tried his hand at it, and who was in other respects a fairly skilful verse writer, Charles Coran, has humorously confessed: "The one who conceives you is lucky, the one who writes you is very foolish." Much later, in America, Ernest Hemingway, who was enamored of violence, war, and his ego, remarked more concisely and maliciously that "all bad writers are always enamored of the epic." Ballanche, Quinet, and Laprade were not poor writers, and the first two at least had rich, courageous, and innovative ideas. But that was not sufficient for them to give new life to the themes of *Antigone* and *Prométhée,* or for Laprade to revive that of *Psyché. Eloa, Jocelyn,* more than twenty poems of *La Légende des siècles* and as many by Leconte de Lisle, *La Fin de Satan* and, to a lesser degree, *Dieu* are at all events splendid successes, only surpassed in European literature by the heroic-comic epic of Byron, *Don Juan,* the incomplete *Hyperion* of Keats, and Goethe's *Faust*—the last is of course an epic drama rather than a long poem, and thus there is less danger of monotony.

Perhaps the real romantic epic, although it does not have recourse to mythology and transposes into realistic and dramatic terms the search for the divine and the struggle with the devil or angel, is the one which novelists have written (Balzac, Tolstoi), even one which is a partial failure like *Salammbô,* or the lamentable epic of the artist considered as the rival of God. This last theme has fascinated the Goncourts, Zola in *L'Oeuvre,* Thomas Mann in *Doktor Faustus;* and Géricault or Delacroix, before Cézanne, could have been their hero. But this obsession of syncretism which wants to group all religious forces together, and that of pantheism which unites what is divine in man with a nature which is itself semidivine reveal one of the great ambitions of romanticism: to rise higher and drive man to surpass himself, while being fully aware of the abysses and plunging ecstatically into the chasms, "the fallen God who remembers the heavens." Such was the dream of Lamartine and other Romantics, aspiring to an impossible paradise or wishing to recreate this paradise in this world, "Which of us, which one is going to become a god?," Musset had asked in *Rolla.* This declamatory cry expressed something of the aspiration of the generation which reached manhood about 1830. From this time on, as a matter of fact, the century, which wanted to accomplish nothing less than the parareligious revival of humanity, was carried away by the mystique of the superman. One of the men who have been most aware of the grandiose ambitions of romanticism and have most successfully expressed them in words, the art critic Henri Focillon, has rightly said of this French romantic period: "No age has done more to enhance man."[10]

8 Eloquence, Imagination, Symbol, and Romanticism

Balzac, writing about himself under the pseudonym of Caliban in a minor review, *La Caricature,* on August 23, 1840, defined his method of criticism in the following way (he had just founded his *Revue parisienne*): "M. de Balzac works at the form to bring out the substance. This way of analyzing imparts life instead of devitalizing." We certainly no longer dare today to state so peremptorily such an opposition between form and substance. The cutting gibes of Valéry have made an impact: "What is called substance is only faulty form." Since then, it has often been repeated that language is not an outer cover or garment that one puts on and throws off nonchalantly, but a focal point of all our secret structures. Ideas, images, sensibility certainly cannot be expressed without language and style.

This work on French romanticism has been undertaken for the purpose of reacting against a prejudice, particularly prevalent among foreigners, based on the belief that form is what counts for our compatriots: ceremonial, ritual, polite, conventional phrases, rules of grammar and style. The Frenchman is generally portrayed as an individual who is not very concerned about content or meaning, thought or feeling, but much more about the correct and if possible striking manner of expressing what he has undoubtedly borrowed from other sources. As far as romanticism is concerned, books and chiefly school textbooks of literature have certainly confirmed this preconception. They have more than amply emphasized the importance of the debates on or against the rules of the dramatic unities, laughed at the handkerchief in Vigny's *Le More de Venise,* or the enjambments and

128

language, which at times was not very formal, of *Hernani*. To be sure, all that has been of great consequence. A writer works with words, images, and sounds, as a painter does with colors. The liberation of form was the very condition of everything else. The French, as much as the most ceremonious nations of the Far East, it is said, had, around 1820 or 1830, forgotten *Le Père Duchêne* and the crudeness of the revolutionary writings; they had become disaccustomed to the flexible and sometimes dislocated verse of Marot and Ronsard; they liked a style which had little color and was monotonously rhythmical in prose and even more so in poetry. Hugo could rightly boast about the red cap placed on the old dictionary and about speeding his winged verse on its way to heaven, where individual lines of poetry with their over-carefully planned rhymes were finally liberated and blended into a free poetic style.

But this aspect of romanticism is well-known and, if it struck contemporaries most forcefully, particularly the timorous academics fond at that time of Boileau's verse, it no longer appears daring to the modern reader. The latter has seen all the poetic forms renounced one after the other, the syntax expertly manipulated by Mallarmé, the old, excessively prudish moral standards upset by Céline or replaced by new mannerisms. It has often been repeated that our greatest surprise, when we study coldly and in historical perspective the revolutionaries of the past, is to note the ludicrous limits they had placed on their audacity. The creations of Hugo, Michelet, and to a lesser degree Balzac are astonishing from the point of view of the vividness and sensuality of the language and the abundance of images. In 1826, at the early age of twenty-four, after a conventional and clumsy start in poetry (only Nerval, in his earliest poems, equalled its old-fashioned insipidity), Hugo had formulated the warning which his contemporary Delacroix—who was, it must be added, so wary of him—proposed for himself in painting: "The writer will have to take care not to obliterate the particular characteristic by which his expression reveals the individuality of his mind." But there remained many traces of outdated stylistic ornamentation in the prose of *Les Martyrs* and *Les Natchez,* in the poems of Lamartine and Vigny. The troubadour and Empire styles took a long time to disappear. It is disconcerting to note once again that the adversaries, in the conflicts or debates between romanticists and classicists, from 1815 to 1825, borrowed a great deal from each other. As in political revolutions, our enemies influence us, or we exchange with them our quivers or swords. The young romanticists made use of the same jaded metaphors and trophes as Delille and Lebrun-Pindare. Until the middle of his life and even later, Vigny remained markedly influenced by his predecessors of the preceding century, as Lamartine was by Léonard, Thomas, and particularly

Parny; and in other countries, Wordsworth remained at times under
the influence of Thomson, and Shelley of Akenside. Sainte-Beuve
praised, at one time, the poetry of the sixteenth century, but his own
poetry resembled much more that of the eighteenth century with its
clumsiness and its platitudes; and the contemporaries of Baudelaire
who, maliciously, looked on him as a more anguished Boileau were
not entirely wrong. Fortunately, Vigny and Baudelaire succeeded in
attaining quite a different kind of grandeur in many poems. But it is
strange that Baudelaire was often more caught up in "outworn poetic
ideas," as Rimbaud called it, than Musset who, from his earliest
poems, broke away from this with ease.

THE MELODIOUS CHARM OF LAMARTINE'S POEMS

Moreover, it is not certain that recourse to "poetic diction", which
Wordsworth in England disparaged in the famous preface in which he
recommended the use of everyday language and considered the
spontaneous outburst of strong feelings as identical to poetry, was the
major force which stood in the way of the creation of great poetry in
the eighteenth century. Was it such an unpardonable crime to give the
moon names such as "Phoebe" and "queen of the darkness" (with her
vaporous chariot)? "Ischia,' in *Les Nouvelles Méditations,* is in our
opinion a very beautiful poem in spite of some jaded ornamentation.
A discreet sensuality is added to the poet's sensibility when he com-
pares the ocean which is in love with the shore to the lover who
embraces the virgin in his passion, or dies "like a heart oppressed by
the burden of sensual delight." The young woman's words to the
fisherman whose boat she has been watching are poetized in some of
the most musical and voluptuously tender stanzas of all French poetry:

> Maintenant sous le ciel tout repose ou tout aime:
> La vague en ondulant vient dormir sur le bord,
> La fleur dort sur sa tige, et la nature même
> Sous le dais de la nuit se recueille et s'endort. . .
>
> Vois: la mousse a pour nous tapissé la vallée:
> Le pampre s'y recourbe en replis tortueux,
> Et l'haleine de l'onde, à l'oranger mêlée,
> De ses fleurs qu'elle effeuille embaume mes cheveux.
>
> A la molle clarté de la voûte sereine
> Nous chanterons ensemble assis sous le jasmin,
> Jusqu'à l'heure où la lune, en glissant vers Miséne,
> Se perd en pâlissant dans les feux du matin. . .

Now under the sky everything rests or loves:

The wave comes rippling to the shore to sleep,
The flower sleeps on its stalk, and nature itself
Under the canopy of night retires within itself and
                          falls asleep. . .

Look: the moss has carpeted the valley for us:
The vine-branch bends in tortuous folds,
And the breath of the wave, mingled with the orange-tree,
With its flowers that it sheds makes my hair fragrant.

In the soft light of the serene canopy of the sky
We will sing together seated under the jasmine,
Until the moment when the moon, moving towards Misenus,
Becomes pale and disappears in the morning light. . .

In the past, a great injustice has been done to Lamartine by seeing in him only the poet perpetually pining and whining, endlessly rewriting his so-called last words, or *Novissima Verba,* which were followed by other words. Indeed he was a poet haunted by death and suffering, even if the macabre images of death were not those he preferred. Through the indiscretion of biographers, we have learned that he had got over the absence and death of Elvire in the arms of more robust beauties, and that Elvire herself, in her letters to her lover, was just as consumed with sensual passion as Juliette Drouet or Marie Dorval. Lamartine had not completely concealed this with the sentimental adornments that he added to his narratives. In his prose work, *Raphaël,* he put the following words into the mouth of Julie (her name in this narrative as well as in reality), whom he had just saved from being shipwrecked on the lake: "Eternity in a minute and infinity in a sensation." The "Chant d'amour" of *Les Nouvelles Méditations* is a very inspired poem: the Zephyr, the dinghy, the boughs shaken by the breeze, the carpets of moss and grass, the song of the nightingale, and the plaintive wave like a long kiss are found again here, a slightly hackneyed décor for love, but not much more artificial than the limpid mirrors and the flowers on the shelves which form the setting for Baudelairian love. The last two verses evoke love fulfilled in and by death, and the two spouses, lying side by side with languid grace, are hardly more ornamental than the two hearts of Baudelaire's "La Mort des amants", which become two torches and light up twin mirrors with two spirits.

There is no way that French romanticism can be cleared of all reproach, but one should not refuse to recognize its real charms solely because taste has changed, probably for the good, since 1840. The three most serious reproaches that can be levelled at it are that is was not sufficiently daring in its renovation of poetic vocabulary and imagery, that it made facile use of an excessively oratorical rhetoric, and lastly that it had too often allowed the expression of sensibility to degenerate into sentimentality or even sentimentalism.

THE LEGITIMATE PLACE OF SENTIMENT IN LITERATURE

Much could be said about each of the points listed above, not to vindicate romanticism, which has been subject to many failures, but to examine with a fresh outlook some of the rules by which literature was bound. In painting and poetry, we revolt at too direct an expression of sentiment and tears, whereas the novel, cinema, and music can sometimes allow themselves certain elements that we disapprove of in other arts, which risk being dehumanized through their restraint. Dickens, Tolstoi, Loti, and Proust, when the opportunity offered, did not think it necessary to have recourse to irony or sarcasm, as various lovers of dandyism or masters of malicious humour did. A smile shining through tears is more deeply touching, as old Homer was aware of a long time ago. A part of the public, and not the worst either, which should and could enjoy literature in our democratic societies, is forced to turn to bad literature or the worst romances and vulgar songs because of the refusal of talented authors to excite our emotions. It is no longer in poems that authors are trying to move their public: it is in their private diary that they now prefer to pour out their sentimentality, or their self-pity, by analyzing in a melancholic manner their ability to love and often their inability to write. By reopening, after the men of the eighteenth century—the century of sensibility—the floodgates of sentiment, by glorifying passion and its rights, by reacting against the unfeelingness of ideologists and over-analytical minds preceding them, the romanticists, who have been considered sick, restored health and equilibrium to human nature. They claimed the rights of emotion and passion and reminded the moderns, in the words of Hoelderlin, who was one of them, that man nevertheless lives poetically on this earth: "Doch dichterisch wohnet Der Mensch auf dieser Erde."

THE NEED FOR ELOQUENCE IN POETRY

The criticism of being excessively oratorical is the one most frequently levelled against one of the literary genres of romanticism in France: poetry. The novel and the theater have been no more tainted with rhetoric than in Germany or Great Britain. The painting of Gros or Delacroix is certainly no more declamatory than the art of Canova, the pictures of Haydon or, a little later, those of the Nazarene school of Germany. Michelet's style, from Le Tableau de la France to La Sorcierè, is intense, abrupt, broken by urgent imaginary dialogues, much less inclined to eloquence than that of Macaulay or Carlyle. But it has become commonplace to repeat that the French romantic poets were, in poetry, the true heirs of Bossuet or Bourdaloue, putting moral truths and didactic reflections into verse. The classicism with which they were imbued was supposed to have prevented them from relieving the burden of prose and abstraction which weighed them down. It has been affirmed rather casually that it was only with Symbolism that French poetry finally achieved the mystic strangeness which had formerly been the prerogative of the romanticists of the so-called Germanic countries.

The case against eloquence is a strange one! Verlaine, who claimed to have done away with eloquence and who has left us the cliché that poetry and eloquence are antithetical, has all the same made use of the art of logical development, coordinating conjunctions, interjections, and questions in his most beautiful poems, more moving than his little songs about "the pale Moon" or the sobs of the violins of autumn. One only has to reread the series of sonnets in *Sagesse* which opens with: "Mon Dieu m' a dit: Mon fils, il faut m'aimer" ("My God said to me: My Son, you must love me"); or the admirable, stately and solemn "Bournemouth" in twelve stanzas of five lines in the collection *Amour;* or even, in *Jadis et Naguère,* the heart-rending evocation of Rimbaud in the long demoniac poem in the form of an imaginary story entitled "Crimen amoris." Many admirers of Verlaine would give for these hundred lines of poetry the majority of the short poems composed of fleeting impressions and popular rhythms which have made Verlaine a poet loved by musicians and young girls who took up singing as a pleasurable art. Verlaine's friend, Rimbaud, repudiated, at a younger age and more fiercely, logic and the sequence of ideas or images in poetry. But the poem with which he won over the literary circles of Paris at the age of seventeen, and many readers of the two worlds ever since then, *Le Bateau ivre,* is one of the finest achievements in the genre of poetic eloquence in the century. Mallarmé's *Toast Funèbre* is perhaps not as distinctive as his last manner, which his true admirers prefer. But this dirge is as melodiously orchestrated as the most eloquent poems of Hugo, although slightly less pompous. Much could be said about the rhetoric which characterized the symbolist poets, trained in Latin discourse and in the well-ordered French dissertation just like their predecessors of 1800 or 1840. In Verhaeren's work, passion and eloquence combine to move the reader, just as much, if not more, as in Henri Régnier's fine short odes or even in Laforgue's witticisms and his presentation of sorrow with a bitter smile. Valéry denounced verbosity in poetry, and it is known that he has been praised for his search for purity. In the pungent aphorisms which he liked, he has cautioned amateurs of poetry against inflation of style, with reason and spirit. "You must choose the smaller of two words," this Southerner liked to say.[1] He has nevertheless made use of the kind of questions which expect no answer and to which only the interrogator answers back, almost as much as Musset and Baudelaire had done. The young Parca questions the wind from the very start of the long rhapsody of Valéry: "Who is crying there, besides the mere wind, at this time? She later entreats death to carry her off before spring stirs her senses and clouds her mind: "Don't you hear these airy names quivering,/Oh deaf one!" And she continues, surprised at her weakness: "What mortal could resist these currents?/What mortal being?" At another point the poet himself questions the sleeper on the secret of her radiance, knowing full well that he alone is in a position to respond if there is an answer:

> What secrets does my young friend hide in her heart,
> Soul by sweet disguise sniffing at the flower?
>
> With what vain ailment does her naive enthusiasm
> Create this radiance in a sleeping woman? . . .

Claudel, who was in so many respects the complete antithesis of Valéry, at least showed more frankness when he outlined various elements of poetics. He did not conceal the fact that whatever theories he produced were the indirect justification of his failings or commended his qualities. If he appreciated in the East the penetrating conciseness of certain Japanese or Chinese poems reduced to three or five very short lines, he has nonetheless proved in *Les Grandes Odes* that he was the master of an eloquence which envelops the reader in an ample cloak draped three times around him. Gérald Antoine has analyzed with finesse this art of repetition which Claudel used as a means of exercising an effective influence over the sensibility of the reader. Moreover, Claudel was not the only one to recognize how much taking possession of the whole man (reader or author), senses and soul, intellect and emotion, can depend on this abundance and these repetitions, just as a musical symphony can depend on ingenious variations and the recurrence of subtly varied themes. Apollinaire liked the revealing turn of phrase "Il y a" and Saint-John Perse the formula "Celui qui", which begins several of the enumerations which he is fond of. André Breton, who has remarked upon this in *La Clé des champs,* has himself not repudiated the effects of abundance and ritual enumeration in his longer poems, *L'Union libre,* or the rhetorical ode addressed to Charles Fourier, which is no less moving for being oratorical. The alleged revolution of poetry which, about 1857–1863, was supposed to have renovated everything in France, has not really done away with eloquence, which is always rising up from the dead, any more than Hugo had done in the passionate poem in which he cried "death to rhetoric and peace to syntax." Lamartine, at the end of "Ischia," had achieved fine effects by repeating "Celui qui" at the beginning of every stanza. In "A Villequier" or in "Paroles sur la dune," Hugo haunted the reader with his grief by multiplying the term "maintenant que." Musset had recourse on various occasions to "Puisque . . . puisque . . ." to prove, in verse that was quite haunting moreover, that "one must love again after having loved"). In his *Novissima Verba,* Lamartine launched into a vast and ardent hymn, of thirty lines, to love and woman, the idealizing sentimentality of which may provoke a smile, but which reveals that facility which is, by Lamartine's own confession, the "grace of genius," and also a bountiful power of inspiration which many poets, limited to the sonnet or the miniature, could have envied him.[2]

We could continue endlessly with this review of modern poets (Pierre-Jean Jouve, Pierre Emmanuel, Patrice de la Tour du Pin, Jean Grosjean, Claude Vigneé, et al.) and establish that at least a good half of the most successful poetry of the twentieth century owes its influence to the methods taught by rhetoric, for they constitute the surest and most honest way to convince, move, and communicate pleasure or joy. As soon as poetry wants to become oral once again, to be heard and to take (or take once again) from music some of its richness, and as soon as it is addressed to an audience which feels its emotions through ideas as well as through sensations or brilliant images, it is almost inevitable that it has recourse to certain processes which surround the listener with an exquisite network: amplifications, at times direct invocations to the reader, passionate queries, a continued pursuit of the effect to be created, surprise which interrupts and intensifies the hidden but spirited logic of the poem. Formerly, the Stoics used to praise rhetoric as a virtue as well as a science, and Bacon, in his *Advancement of Learning,* defined it as the application of "reason to imagination for the better moving of the will." Certainly there can also be something else in poetry: there are times when the unprofound song of "Un vanneur de blé au vent" by du Bellay or "La chanson de Barbertine" or "Jet d'eau" by Baudelaire delight minds that are weary of all the didacticism of the press, of television, and of the speeches of our rulers and masters. The poetry of nonsense and the doggerels and nursery rhymes of the British also have their place in poetry. But it has to be admitted that people who had not acquired the habit of eloquence, considered a virtue by the Stoics, regretted it when, beyond the Rhine, they let themselves be hypnotized by the first tirelessly eloquent leader in their history. Means of mass communication have, alas, caused the art of eloquence to be ranked highest among the tools of persuasion in our century. It is all very well for poetry to cultivate the recondite and refine emotions and ideas to reserve the enjoyment of them for a very few people. But there is nothing reprehensible either about it expressing and transmitting emotions to a larger number of persons who are conscious of a need for it, as we need music disseminated by records and the "imaginary gallery" of painting and sculpture. In our opinion, everywhere today young people, starved of emotion, yearn for more romanticism and crave poetry, the word being understood in a broad human sense.

Moreover, there is no need to leave the domain of literature to note, by observing French romantic poetry in comparison with other romantic poetry which has recently been praised as being less tainted with the vice of eloquence than our own, that the difference, if it exists, is slight. The first line of *Hymns to the Night* by Novalis (as also the first line of *Elegies of Duino,* written a century or more later by Rilke) begins with a completely oratorical question. Exclamation, questions, repetitions, and amplifications abound in the last of these hymns, "Sehnsucht nach dem Tode," and do not spoil its beauty at all. In "Der Archipelagus" of Hoelderlin, which Friedrich Gundolf has cleverly elucidated, or in his more tenderly elegiac poem, "Brot und Wein," and in many other prophetic hymns by him, like "Der Rhein" or "Patmos," there is as much recourse to rhetoric as there was in the works of Pindar or Hugo. Schiller, whose opinion was sought by Hoelderlin, and who did not really understand him, in a letter of November 24, 1796, cautioned the young poet against "the hereditary failing of German poets, this verbosity which often buries a very felicitous thought under an endless development and a deluge of stanzas." He recommended to him more clarity, simplicity, and artistic economy.

English language critics are those against whom French scholars of British literature, unqualified admirers of English romanticism,[3] were bent on protesting, because they insisted on refusing to acknowledge that the French poets before Baudelaire had the qualities of suggestion and imaginative intensity. Too often, Julius Caesar has been invoked as having characterized the Gauls as a people, or as a country, divided into three segments (and not into those two groups which, elsewhere, are supposed to relieve one another and assure political stability). The same Caesar had noted with gracious condescension their fondness for *argute loqui,* the eloquent ingeniosity of the lawyer. It is certainly true that the transformation of the hackneyed poetic diction of the eighteenth century, still present in Byron's works, took place on the other side of the English Channel much earlier than it did in our country. The best poets over there had more rapidly made evocative qualities and dreamy strangeness the essence of poetry. One can speculate about the reasons for this phenomenon indefinitely:

ancient Celtic heritage, a love of mystery and obscurity, superstition
of the supernatural mixed with daily life, belief in spirits considered as
real as the individuals who surround them, and perhaps even the more
concrete nature of the language.

But it is by no means belittling the force and originality of this
poetry to note that it very often had recourse to oratorical qualities
and that it comprised in fact more attempts at long, narrative, and
eloquent poems: *The Excursion, The Prelude, Don Juan, The Revolt of
Islam, Julian and Maddalo, Endymion, Lamia, Hyperion,* without men-
tioning those which were less successful (by Southey or, later, Tennyson). The superstition, spread by E. A. Poe, which decrees the long
poem an impossibility and a true contradiction in terms, has not been
accepted in Great Britain as a new Gospel (by Browning, Swinburne,
Morris, Arnold, Eliot, Yeats) as it was for a while in France, on the
strength of Baudelaire's authority. Furthermore, it would not be a
paradox to suggest that Baudelaire's best poems were, with the exception of the prosaic and fast-paced "Voyage," his longest. The magnificence of Elizabethan rhetoric was not absent from Shelley's *Cenci* or
the lyricodramatic poetry of that imperfect genius Thomas Lowell
Beddoes, much less later from the work of Dylan Thomas and Hart
Crane. Wordsworth's "Ode on Intimations of Immortality" and his
long poem on "Tintern Abbey," which was perhaps his masterpiece,
were logically and flawlessly rational, and were filled (at least the
second was) with formulae of orators and logicians: "if," "consequently," "and thus," "just as much, I think," "once again," "It is not
for that that . . . ," and almost untranslatable ones like "nor perchance if I were not thus taught," "nor perchance if I should be." Even
Corneille was less rationale. Keats adopted, in this respect as in others,
not only the grave and solemn diction of Milton, but the articulation of
his reasoning. There were in his most beautiful odes numerous purely
formal questions which orators like:

> Who are these coming to the sacrifice?
> What little town, by river or sea-shore   ?

asked the poet, as he gazed at the sides of the Greek urn. And, in his
masterpiece of condensation and unified structure, the "Ode to Autumn," he evoked, by questions with a very obvious answer, the
previous season of spring: "Where are the songs of Spring, ay, where
are they?" The most sensuous of his odes, addressed to Psyche, was
full of invocatory exclamations. It would be easy to collect twenty such
examples of recourse to oratorical processes and to the voluptuousness of the intellect in Coleridge's work ("Ode to the departing Year,"
"France: an Ode"), and in Shelley's purest poems ("Hymn to intellec-

tual Beauty," "Ode to the West Wind," "To Jane: The Invitation"). Actually, can there be an ode or hymn or any poem going beyond the limits of a brief song without eloquence and without appeal to intellectual values? A poet is no less good because he has thought as well as felt and enjoyed the beauty, that is also sensuous, which the ode calls for. Surprise itself, which the surrealists, those romantics of the twentieth century, have so cleverly used in their peoms, was not absent from the poetry of Hugo or Musset (whose *Nuits* were perhaps not his best works). But it is most deeply felt when it stands out abruptly against a steady continuity and suddenly delights the reader. Behind many of the criticisms made against the romanticists ever since the French thought they perceived in Nerval, Baudelaire, and Mallarmé, the masters of lyrical alchemy in their language and the only poets who equalled the romanticists of the "Northern literatures", there is perhaps some nonchalance as well as submissiveness to the changing fashions of taste. In fairly long poems (which does not necessarily mean epics of thousands of lines), animated by a vaster inspiration which is communicated to the reader willing to make a somewhat sustained effort of understanding and to relinquish temporarily his sensibility to the magician who wants to stir him totally, the author has been able to add one of the qualities of music, drama, and the novel which is denied to short poetry that rejects all eloquence: movement. A fine critic of modern poetry, Gabriel Bounoure, has rightly written: "Every poem is an itinerary for the soul. There is no motionless poem."

LITTLE AESTHETIC SPECULATION ON IMAGINATION IN ROMANTICISM

It is undoubtedly true that, in spite of so many complaints of the romanticists about their solitude and their pride in being all the more powerful because they were more solitary, like Childe Harold or Alastor, Vigny's Moses or his wolf, the first half of the nineteenth century had not yet broken off relations with its public. And eloquence, like wit, presupposes a public that can be raised to one's level, or with which one can identify. The poetry of the romanticists of France or other countries is not necessarily, because of that, a pose or posture. But, after all, it wished to be heard, and perhaps given attention. Several of the romantics, and not only those of France, were thus attracted to political prophecy: Lamartine, Hugo, Vigny until he recognized that he was unsuited to it, Baudelaire for a very brief while. Shelley wished that his hopes of reforming a world made bad by man could be spread throughout the universe like the ashes of a poorly extinguished fire scattered by the wind. Perhaps in this way he would kindle thousands of sparks to illuminate and excite other minds and become the worldwide herald of a prophecy. One may speculate about the similar evolution that the poetry of Keats might have followed, after his second version of *Hyperion,* if the poet had lived beyond the age of twenty-five. After the universal victory of the bourgeois class and the business world, between 1840 and 1860, and the failure of so many socialist utopias around 1848–1850, the concept of alienation took on a more carnal truth. It is still with us today and has become, a century later, one of our most well-worn clichés.

This insistence of the artist on isolating himself from his audience, which is, in our times, the exacerbation of a less anguished sentiment among the romantics, was accompanied by a fondness for esoterism, sometimes for a mysticism and a magic understanding of which Nerval already seemed to have provided examples, and especially by an increasing importance given to the imagination as the gift par excellence of the poet. It is undoubtedly the privilege of poets, if they do not become critics, not to define terms which they like most and to vary the meaning that they seem to give them, depending on the opportunities and the context. But the term "imagination" is the one which has suffered most from this confusion, or which has perhaps gained most in prestige by thus remaining inconsistent and mysterious. Neither Montaigne nor Pascal have used it with clarity, nor have they employed it to designate a gift which would be the prerogative of the poet. But we do not have a semantic history of the word and, to be sure, through the word, of the concept. For a word "imagination" is found much more frequently than one might think in the writings of the psychologists, moralists, and poets of the seventeenth and particularly eighteenth centuries in France. Certainly in the plural, "des imaginations," that is, whims or dreams of minds of minds which wander, and even in the singular when the word evokes "la folle du logis" ("imagination"), imagination is opposed to common sense, prudence, and wisdom; and it is called upon to yield or give priority to "the best apportioned thing in the world", Cartesian common sense.

Echoes of this discredit thrown upon the imagination were found again in the works of French critics who lived during the period of romanticism, against which they almost all vituperated. Désiré Nisard had said some good about the romantics, when he was young. In 1829, he had even dared to prophesy, with much circumlocution in order not to shock his public, that one day Victor Hugo would perhaps be "studied and commented on as a classic, and again as a classic . . . presented as a prize in competitive examinations." He quickly repented having been this rash. In the same volume, *Essais sur l'école romantique,* in which he replaced this article, he added another, "Victor Hugo en 1836," to criticize "this voluptuousness of imagination substituted for sentiment" (in *Les Chants du crépuscule*) and complain that "in Victor Hugo's work, imagination takes the place of everything else;" he sacrifices reason to this consuming imagination. Nisard repeated this idea the following year in connection with *Jocelyn:* "Every work in which reason has no part is still-born."

Nevertheless, Diderot, Rousseau, and many others had praised the ability to create a new reality by the imagination and, like the author of *Les Confessions,* lived mainly and loved in "the imaginary world" which was more real for them than the real world. But on the whole, under the influence of the psychologists La Mettrie and Condillac, who were moreover more original than has been admitted, the speculation of Frenchmen on the imagination had been marked by the analytical and associationist spirit of the period. This "faculty," as it was called for a long time, was principally a passive imagination, resembling memory, that was decorative and took pleasure in inventing ornamental and ingenious details. For a long time, it confined itself to forming images, which, according to Aristotle, are the main element of poetry. At the age of twenty-three, the English poet Akenside had published a long and very pedestrian poem, *The Pleasures of the Imagination,* which was typically pseudo-classical, and which he worked on again twenty years later without, however, being able to make it any more inspired. Towards the end of the century, Delille also composed a long epic-didactic poem in eight songs and two volumes, which was just as prosaic. In his preface to it, he confessed: "What took most effort in my work was avoiding the ill use of the subject's richness, and not sacrificing instruction to the vividness of paintings and the pomp of descriptions."

Philosophical tradition, which had for so long, from Descartes to Kant, given priority to intellect over instincts, was first attacked by German philosophy: by Schopenhauer, who rejected any intellectualistic explanation of the world and emphasized on the contrary the great role of the unconscious; by Schelling, from whom Coleridge borrowed and sometimes shamelessly plagiarized ideas on this subject. The English romanticists, whose original contribution was later defined by Watts-Dunton as "the renascence of wonder," thus rejoined Plato who in the *Theaetetus* had perceived in wonder "the philosophical sense par excellence." This amazement of poetic sensibilities before nature and life is in itself a state that is more passive than active. But it superseded reflection and analysis that dissects and destroys. And it led the creator to be satisfied no longer with "fancy," the pleasant and decorative fancy of the English, which remained analytical and combined details, but to recreate a whole, independent of the parts which may compose it. Descriptive realism, the rational, and the didactic were thus repudiated. As Delacroix said before Baudelaire, nature became a vast dictionary. The writer drew inspiration from it to create his own ensemble. He expressed himself quite spontaneously in images. And, above all, his imagination saw right through facades of the material order and detected the invisible behind the visible, the correspondences between the terrestial and the supernatural, and symbols. So this imagination which begot a new world was literally creative, and especially hieroglyphic as Baudelaire called it (after several Germans and even after various French prose-writers, illuminists or semi-mystics, Fabre d'Olivet, Ballanche, etc.).

The points which we are anxious to emphasize here are the following: chronologically, and if one leaves out the true romantics of the eighteenth century (Diderot and Rousseau, in particular), the preeminence of revolt over conceptual and rational values was mainly a characteristic of German philosophy and of a German criticism imbued with philosophy, and of a few Englishmen (Blake, Wordsworth) who, without any contact at the time with Germany, had rejected the idea that the universe can be understood rationally. Theories on the imagination, which was praised as an inner vision far superior to the observation of the real, were much more persistent in Germany than in France. In France, the works of the creators (Balzac, Delacroix, or Hugo) preceded their theory, and French literature and art can be pleased about this. Speculations on the imagination dried up Coleridge's poetic inspiration or, at least, it took the place, and not very well either, of the failure of the poet in him. Critics who take pleasure in seeing in literary works the application of abstract doctrines or even of a preexisting philosophy may regret it. In the last fifty years, they have written twenty times as much on Coleridge's ideas as on his poetry. Those who love poetry or those who, like us, persist in considering criticism as a derived and secondary intellectual activity, are happy that Balzac, Delacroix, and even Baudelaire have been satisfied with making a few, often contradictory, statements and have fought shy of any system "a type of damnation which leads us to perpetual abjuration," as Baudelaire said in his article on "L'Exposition Universelle de 1855."

But if anteriority can be a merit in the history of ideas, the thoroughness with which descendants, or simply scholars, rediscover and reinterpret what the initiators had said, or return to the views of their predecessors, deserves no less credit. The French, who only became familiar much later with Freud, Marx, and what "structuralist" elements already existed in the German romanticists' insistence on organicism and the work compared to a plant as a whole, have given a fresh richness and new life to views which had become sterile elsewhere: Bachelard, Ricoeur, Lacan, Althusser, Foucault, Lévi-Strauss. Baudelaire, in his observations on imagination (inspired by Delacroix, but also by Poe, and to a lesser degree by Coleridge and Catherine Crowe), seemed to have thought once again about what had been dimly perceived before him and to have transmitted it, twenty times more effective, to the symbolists and modern writers. A first-rate work on this subject, Frank Kermode's *Romantic Image,* gives great importance to Nerval, to the French symbolists as Arthur Symons and Yeats had interpreted them, and to Paul Valéry. What is curious is that a mind as Cartesian and intellectualistic as Valéry's in a rich and dense essay like *Poésie et pensée abstraite* (published first in England and addressed to a British public), helped primarily to diffuse ideas which deny the priority of the intellect, and rejoined mystics fascinated by the occult, like Yeats. He himself was by no means an extremely imaginative person. But neither was Baudelaire. Moreover, it was perhaps because of this that the poet of *Les Fleurs du mal,* aware of the fact that it was difficult for him to become the "architect of his enchanted world" and create "a suggestive magic containing at the same time the object and the subject," assiduously praised once again this imagination which he admired in Balzac and Delacroix, but which he felt he was himself devoid of. Vigny, the other French poet who, before Baudelaire, had spoken most often about the imagination, had the least powerful imagination among the romantics.[4]

One could have many reservations about those extravagant eulogies of imagination, such as those by Baudelaire in Sections III and IV of his *Salon de* 1859, in which he revered this sovereign quality as "queen of the faculties" and extolled the "control" that it must exercise, even on morals and the critical faculty; moreover, the critical faculty is part of imagination itself. This recalls the overexalted odes formerly addressed to enthusiasm by the most frigid poets, or to the "beautiful disorderly effect of art" by poets who were extremely prudent. Baudelaire himself, like his inspirer in these matters, Delacroix, had made a point of cautioning the reader prone to be taken in by fine words: "The more imagination one has, the more skill one should have to accompany the imagination in its adventures and surmount the difficulties that it avidly seeks" *(Salon de 1859, I).* The imagination also leads sometimes to a loss of contact with the real, as must occur at times in the case of those who come to grips with this chaotic reality and attempt to introduce it into a work of art, without, however, mutilating it or simplifying it excessively. "The chaos is the facade, the order is at the bottom," declared the most imaginative of French poets, Hugo. After Baudelaire and his eloquent developments on imagination, which his successors have failed to appreciate or to which they have paid little attention (although they were included in Volume II of the Michel Lévy edition of 1869), the more daring French poets, Rimbaud, Apollinaire, Michaux have ignored the timid advice of Baudelaire who, even through artificial paradises, did not want to lose his soul by changing the order of the world. On the contrary, they wanted to make the poet a magician who can interfere with this order as he pleases and, by strange visions and words which become divinities, get rid of the real and consider himself on a level with God. Compared with the innovations of avant-garde poetry after 1867, the prose poet of the imagination, Baudelaire, seems to resemble the romantics much more than his successors.[5]

THE RESPECTIVE ROLES OF THE METAPHOR AND THE SIMILE IN FRENCH POETRY

The creation of imagery is one of the functions of the imagination and, as August Wilhelm Schlegel had declared, images and symbols are the means by which the infinite can be explained and revealed. But on this aspect of the imagination as well, confusion has prevailed for a long time and continues to do so even today. In one of the many writings in which he praised the imagination, *De la Poésie dramatique,* Diderot had defined it as "the faculty of calling images to mind." Elsewhere, in more inspired fashion and emphasizing less the role of recollection, he portrayed the writer and especially the poet as following an inner model and making it tangible by colors and imagery. It would be quite naive to compare, from one language and poetry to another, the imagery of poets of several European nations. Certain poetry, like that of Leopardi for example, contains little imagery, and it is perhaps, because of that, denser but no less evocative. There is everything in Dante's work. But his ample and majestic similes move us more than the numerous metaphors of other great poets: that of the she-wolf, more hungry after her meal than before, or that of the shades of Semiramis, Cleopatra, Helen, Dido, and Francesca de Rimini, in the fifth song of *Hell;* similes which resemble long lines of cranes flying and singing or the more sensitive doves aroused by desire. Paul Valéry noted one day in his *Cahiers* that the profusion of imagery in Shakespeare's works offended him to the point of disgust. That is really the honest reaction, even if it is rarely expressed, of several of us when we read many of the Elizabethan dramatists or the surrealist poets. An American writer whose poetry and prose are among the most artistic of this century, Randall Jarrell, recalled, a few years before his death, that imagery in poetry is not an end in itself, but merely a means.

Lamartine and even Baudelaire preferred similes to the remarkable unexpectedness of metaphors, as Claudel did a hundred years later. The indexes of terms in *Les Fleurs du mal* add up today, for our information, the number of times the little word "comme" ("like, as") has been repeated in his work. The poet has managed to communicate just as forcefully with his reader by using the slower but no less surprising forms like "comme" ("like, as"), "ainsi que" ("just as"), "tu fais l'effet" ("you create the effect") or "sont l'embléme de . . ." ("are the symbol of . . .") rather than the more abrupt metaphor in his best known lines of poetry:

> Comme de longs échos. . .
> Like long echoes. . .
>
> Je suis comme le roi d'un pays pluvieux. . .
> I am like the king of a wet country. . .
>
> Comme ces longs serpents que les jongleurs sacrés. . .
> Like those long snakes which sacred jugglers. . .
>
> Comme un bétail pensif sur le sable couché. . .
> Like a pensive animal lying on the sand. . .

The imagination is no less effective by refusing to do violence to the reader's capacity for dream. Delacroix had noted, in a statement in his *Journal* in October 1853, the great value in art of this amplitude which prolongs the effect produced:

> The arts are not like algebra in which abbreviation of figures helps to successfully solve the problem: success in the arts is not achieved by abridging, but by amplifying, if it is possible, by prolonging the sensation by all possible means.

Recollections of the decorative and artificial similes of the eighteenth century, found in the works of Milton's imitators, descriptive poets, and even Chateaubriand, make us smile at the artificial and old-fashioned similes in the very early poems of Hugo or those of Vigny. But neither of them stopped there. Now and again at least, Vigny managed to blend the metaphor and the simile, the idea, which normally precedes the symbol in his work, and the musicality of expression, in lines full of a beautiful, suggestive resonance:

> Pleurant comme Diane au bord de ses fontaines
> Un amor taciturne et toujours menacé.
>
> Weeping over Diana at the edge of her fountains
> Over a silent love that is always threatened.

SEARCH FOR CORRESPONDENCES, INTUITION OF THE
ROLE OF THE SYMBOL

The preeminent quality of the image, according to certain theoreticians of poetry in the last century, was expressing with immediacy rather than communicating, drawing on the sources of life which lie hidden within our unconscious and scaling at the same time the heights where the invisible is found. Once again, it was Baudelaire who formulated that concept with penetrating force. Partially for this reason and because of the sonnet *Correspondences* which is probably unduly famous, he has been considered as the first of the symbolists. A great deal could be said about such a view which detached Baudelaire from those to whom he was, and felt, most akin: Vigny, Nerval, Gautier, Sainte-Beuve, and even Banville and Pétrus Borel. He has been credited with the quasi-paternity of a group of poets, those of 1888–1895, who were not very familiar with his work and had not really understood him. This search for mysterious correspondences between the carnal and spiritual, the Earth and Heaven, was certainly not something radically new in 1800, or among the illuminists and Swedenborgians of the end of the eighteenth century. In a scholarly work entitled *La Mystique de Baudelaire* (Belles Lettres, 1932), Jean Pommier has shown how many antecedents this aesthetic mysticism—if it deserves such a name—had: St. Paul, various Church Fathers, undoubtedly theologians of the Middle Ages, and unorthodox thinkers of the Age of Enlightenment. Just as for the term "imagination," the precise history of the word "symbole" ("symbol") in France between 1800 and 1890, and the briefer but just as curious history of the word "hiéroglyphe" ("hieroglyph") remain to be written. It is certainly risky to read too much into the use of vague words, sometimes thrown out at random, the full significance of which is not recognized by the person using it. But, here again, French romanticism does not have to envy German romanticism. Court de Gébelin, Fabre d' Olivet, and Saint-Martin had had the idea of a universal symbolism without having read Swedenborg and long before Creuzer's *La Symbolique* was contemplated. Ballanche, about whom the important work that he deserves has not yet been written, had initiated formulae which have remained graven on the memory of many: "Everything is a symbol" or "the material order is a hieroglyph of the spiritual world." Pierre Moreau has pointed out[6] that, in *La Muse Française* of 1824, it was said: "Everything is symbolical in the eyes of the poet." A remarkable man, Jouffroy, in his *Cours d'esthtique* of 1822, published in 1843, recognizing the full value of his statement, had declared: "Poetry is only a series of symbols present in the mind to make it conceive the invisible." *Les Pensées de Joseph Delorme* include a few observations on the essence of poetry, which reveal in Sainte-Beuve the theoretician a much greater comprehension of what symbolic poetry might be than his poetic creations seemed to promise. "The artist has received at birth the key to symbols and the understanding of forms," he wrote. In a poem found in *Consolations* (1830), dedicated to a confused but prophetic mind, of which there were many at that time, Pierre Leroux, the future critic, praised poets in terms that Baudelaire and perhaps Nerval were able to retain in their minds:

> They understand the waves, hear the stars,
> Know the names of flowers and for them the universe
> Is only a single idea expressed in different symbols.

The following year, from August to September 1831, *La Revue encyclopédique* published a series by Pierre Leroux, "De la poésie de notre époque." In them, he solemnly called upon the poets of the then-triumphant romanticism not to persist in turning to a past that was over and to the extremely negative and pessimistic philosophy of the eighteenth century. Distracted by their complacency in only considering themselves and their "egotistical sublime," according to the felicitous expression used by Keats to characterize Wordsworth, they did not want to serve posterity. In spite of their occasional professions of faith in Catholicism (or at least those of Lamartine until then), they believed in nothing; they described, narrated, but they did not know that art is symbol and that, by these symbols, poetry must express the sensibility, anxiety, and hope of their epoch. The task of the poet should be to draw his creative inspiration from the sight of forests and mountains, establish new harmony between the world of nature and man, and suggest a spiritual sense beyond his paintings of reality; such was Leroux' thesis, and he concluded in striking terms:

> Thus the entire world, including Art which is part of it, like the natural monuments to which it is added, becomes *symbolic.*

> The symbol. Here we touch on the very principle of art ... The principle of art is the symbol.

Much later, Leroux, the companion in exile of Victor Hugo at Samarez, near Saint-Hélier, on the island of Jersey, expressed many opinions to the author on what his poetic mission should be and, among other things, he tried to make him admire Shelley, the "Polyeucte of atheism," a true Greek and creator of myths. Hugo himself, in the strange poem with the provocative (and debatable) title: "Que la musique date du XVIe siècle," published in *Les Rayons et les ombres* (1840), which Baudelaire had probably read, said: "Under the universal being, see the eternal symbol."

We cannot ask to whom Baudelaire owed the use of this word or the fascination that the concept of the symbol seems to have had for him, for he only owed that to himself. Delacroix's conversation was able to help him to read into certain statements made by the painter more than Delacroix himself had indicated in them. Of course, he had forgotten the bond shared by two friends, one of whom has received the hospitality of the other, which henceforth ensures mutual recognition. Not very keen on Greek, he did not speculate any further on the sense of the verb which could mean "to throw together," to blend into one unity the sign and the thing signified, appearance and reality, the superficial meaning and the hidden meaning reserved only for the initiates. Generously, he attributed to Victor Hugo, whom he admired only at times, the talent of a visionary decoder of symbols. What is more surprising is that he admired in Gautier, his elder and his friend, "a tremendous innate understanding of universal *correspondence* and symbolism, this repertory of any metaphor" (article of 1859). At other times, however, Baudelaire seemed to use the words "symbol" and "allegory" without any discrimination. He extolled "the understanding of the allegory" due to artificial paradises, when "anything becomes a speaking symbol."

To the extent that one can generalize, it is undoubtedly right to say that only Nerval, Hugo, and Baudelaire, of the poets before 1870, were aware of the multiplicity of suggestions that the use of symbols could bring into their art. They alone wanted to combine, as Baudelaire again has said, the exterior world with the artist and his interior world in which imagination and reverie reign. In the symbols employed by Vigny (bottle in the sea, flute, house of the shepherd) and in the less imposing and more scholarly poems of Hugo, like "La Vache," the moral lesson is drawn extremely clumsily from the symbol. One has the impression that the symbol was added on as an afterthought, to embody a preexisting idea, instead of having appeared in the subconscious of the artist. But that does not mean that only the symbolists after 1870 or 1885 knew the secret of the use of the symbol. "La Maison du berger," in spite of its awkwardness and, here and there, its rhetoric, is just as good, when all is said and done, as the sonorous and eloquent "Bateau ivre." Certain poems of Henri de Régnier, Francis Jammes, Mallarmé himself, and Valéry, who dearly loved the symbolist period which had revealed poetry to him—or beyond the frontiers of France the poems of George, Rilke, Yeats— are nothing but expert intellectual riddles, in which the poet's ingeniousness in combining his enigmas is altogether too obvious. In our opinion, the difference between symbolism and romanticism, set up in total opposition, has been much too emphasized, and what these two movements in France had in common has been neglected. We believe that an essay which could and should be written on "Le romantisme vu par le symbolisme français" would show this. The main element which makes these two movements similar, in spite of the differences of historical and philosophical context and particularly of manipulation of the syntax and of the line of poetry, is that both were, in the last resort, an invasion of all literature by poetry or, one should say, by the poetic.

9 The Survival and Vitality of Romanticism

Ernest Seillière, one of the most "romantic" prophets of the past in our century, and one of the most stubborn adversaries of European romanticism, had given the name "imperialism" to what he considered most to be dreaded in romantic sensibility. We would not like to be guilty of another sort of imperialism by trying to connect with romanticism all that followed this tremendous agitation of the nineteenth century. There were many Frenchmen who repudiated romanticism's aesthetics, its search for very obvious effects, its cultivation of excess and horror, its immodesty at times, and its tolerance of a plebeian sentimentalism. Furthermore, no literary or artistic period ever consents to being only the imitation or banal continuation of one which has preceded it, the grandeur of which overwhelms it; and no writer, however little ability he may have, willingly resigns himself to being a mere follower. The very exacerbation of individualism, which was one of the romantic traits, drove the successors of Byron, Schiller, Hugo, and Delacroix to become themselves as much as possible.

THE END OF ROMANTICISM

We are concerned here with another aspect of romanticism. We maintain that romanticism can no more be limited by very clearly defined dates than it can be restricted to any definition. One cannot, without artifice, hold up the date of 1843, or consider Victor Hugo's failure in the theater or Ponsard's short-lived success as a reason for entitling a chapter of our textbooks "the end or the death of romanticism." Sainte-Beuve, in one of his moments of anti-romantic bitterness which clouded his clearsightedness, made a mistake about this. Other critics, misled by their conservative and moralistic prejudices, have also rung the knell of a movement which had always seemed dangerous to them. But neither Balzac, nor Vigny, nor Delacroix, nor above all Hugo had ceased to be of consequence in the period 1843–1850. Gautier, Nerval, Pétrus Borel had continued to write. And it was these masters, born around 1800 or 1810, that the young generation, which was preparing a new literary period, ecstatically admired. They did not care about *La Préface de Cromwell* or the old quarrel about unities and noble or proletarian words. But René, Obermann, Raphaël of *La Peau de chagrin,* Lucien of *Illusions perdues,* and Musset's Octave were their elder brothers and their heroes.

REACTION AGAINST THE DOCTRINES OF
THE ROMANTIC AESTHETICS

It is almost inevitable that a rising literary generation should try at first to assert itself by opposing those who immediately precede it and by indicating forcefully its differences in point of view, ideals, and method. For sons to act differently towards their fathers, for gifted disciples to act otherwise towards their masters, would be to confess that their presence in the world was quasi-useless and that everything had been said and accomplished before them and for them. So they join forces to emphasize the deficiencies of their elders and repudiate the doctrines (romantic, impressionist, symbolist, cubist, existentialist, structuralist) that their predecessors have professed and sometimes used. That is all the more natural as any generation which is thus going to assert itself sees immediately before it not the giants who had triumphed in their time and imposed their successful innovations, but their followers, daunted by the greatness of their elders: those who had exploited already conquered territory, applied the new tricks of the trade, and often exaggerated the mannerisms or peculiarities of those who had been the true literary conquerors.

In France in particular, where journalists, critics, and professors find it convenient to group writers by "schools," a second generation of romantics, born around 1810, who have been mentioned above, had, about 1835–1840, caused some stir by its peculiar behavior and by some of its literary lucubrations. They have been called by different names: "groupe de la rue du Doyenné," "Jeunes-France" (after an amusing book of Théophile Gautier), "the generation of art for art's sake" (to the extent that the aggressive preface of *Mademoiselle de Maupin* was their manifesto). They have not been studied very much in painting or literature, and that is a pity: for they were often more unhappy than true rebels and they suffered from their bohemianism, their relative lack of success (nobody had any idea then about the apotheosis which would one day transfigure Nerval into a sacred monster!), the isolation to which the literary and almost official success of Hugo, Balzac, Vigny, and Delacroix was going to relegate them. It was against these minor romantics, considered as humbugs or incurable failures, that a part of literature between 1850 and 1870 reacted—the part which was taking shape mainly in Paris and preferred to look beyond these "minor romantics," as they are called today, to the great men who had preceded them and were more powerful and prolific. Chateaubriand, Hugo, Balzac, Delacroix continued to inspire respect in the men of letters of the Second Empire, and even in their envious contemporary, Sainte-Beuve.

PROVINCIAL WRITERS AND ROMANTIC SENSIBILITY

But it was provincials, both important and insignificant, who had moved to Paris, who left their mark on French literature, particularly in the nineteenth century, young men who were champing at the bit in the Grenoble of Stendhal and Berlioz, the Touraine of Balzac, the Normandy of Flaubert, the South of Daudet and Zola. Fromentin experienced in his Charente a youthful and melancholy love and dreamed of painting in a Parisian studio; Leconte de Lisle, in his distant island and later at Rennes, balked even more at the dull middle-class; Renan and then Taine remained, even in Paris, the hardworking natives of their province and gathered knowledge and reflections to later force their way into the academies and change the insipid philosophy of their predecessors. All of them, intoxicated by what they read, even more Byronian at the start of their career than the men of 1820 or 1830 had ever been, borrowing from Byron a few themes and a type of conventional hero, experienced romanticism through their sensibility and the dreams of their senses or their mind.

In spite of all that unites a generation[1] at its beginnings—shared disdain, hatreds, and admiration—each of those who are a part of it remains an individual. As soon as he feels he has found himself in his first books or pictures, he accentuates the features which distinguish him from his contemporaries, whose passions and ambitions he had shared when they were together at school, at cafés, or in the same studio. Each of the writers who asserted their authority in France during the Second Empire, and each of the painters of the Salon des Refusés (exhibition of rejected works), almost all of whom drew inspiration from Delacroix without imitating him, deserve a study of their connections with romanticism and the romantics, and of what was romantic in them: this last point of course presupposes an agreement on the main elements of a definition.

SENTIMENTALISM AND DISPLAY OF PERSONAL EMOTION

There was one failing of the romanticists that almost all their successors noticed and vowed they would avoid: a cheap display of emotion. It is very difficult to decide at what moment the expression of personal sensibility becomes a slightly puerile sentimentality, and finally a display of one's sufferings, of one's intimate life, of the pity inspired in us by others, and of the self-pity that the term "maudlin sentimentalism" evokes. Even the greatest writers have not been able to avoid it; these include the first great English romantics, for example, Wordsworth in "The Idiot Boy" or "The Afflictions of Margaret," or the moving story in verse of his encounters with Simon Lee, an old hunter, or with an old beggar of Cumberland. Shelley, in some of his slightly over-facile songs, also lays himself open to the reproaches of those who criticize a certain mawkishness in art. The aesthetes that professors of literature quickly become, lovers of refined art and of a certain irony which cures the self-pity of every lyricist or elegist, severely criticize this "keepsake" literature appealing to young British girls. This is perhaps a necessary stage in the formation of taste and one which it would be foolish to be ashamed about later. From Tennyson's *Enoch Arden,* Poe's "Ulalume," or Verlaine's musical expression of tears shed over a town and his own heart, the lover of poetry then comes to more restrained works. He guesses fairly rapidly that, as Verlaine himself remarked maliciously about E. A. Poe, the immodest poet or the devout painter who manages to move him is the one who is smart and wily. Traditionally, in the last hundred years or more, we have rejected, as the most discomfiting and outdated aspect of romanticism, the excessively languid poems, embarrassing to our sense of modesty, of Longfellow, Heine, Lamartine, and Musset, the emotion of Hugo about his children and, of course, patriotic poems. We reserve our tears for the sentimental songs sung at cafés or played on the barrel-organ. This involves curious problems of the psychology of taste, or perhaps of psychoanalysis, which literary critics have preferred not to tackle so far. They prefer to make fun of the poor taste displayed by Goethe in admiring Béranger or even by Taine writing with deference to that old song-writer in June 1853; or they treat as the tall stories of a dandy or the mistaken ideas of a young man the very embarrassing praise that Baudelaire bestowed on that detestable woman poet Marceline Desbordes-Valmore, on Hégésippe Moreau, and on Pierre Dupont in 1861. And yet at that time he was forty years old.

The same Baudelaire attacked elsewhere the display of personal emotion by Musset. It may even be, as he insinuated in a letter to his mother in which he boasted about being extremely good at lying, that he had been repulsed by the sentimentality and social pity of *Les Misérables* even as he was praising the work in public and in writing. Leconte de Lisle and Rimbaud likewise rejected Musset as just good enough for high school adolescents, and were barely lukewarm in their attitude towards Lamartine's elegies. Furthermore, they thus distorted the image of Musset, a poet even more damned than those whom Verlaine called "les poètes maudits" (more than Mallarmé certainly, and Corbière), and a virtuoso artist who, in his better moments, demanded much from himself. There continued in fact to be a great deal of sentimentality in the works of the Parnassians and Verlaine, Samain, and Laforgue, as well as in Gide, who was always ready to weep over what he read, and Proust, who was moved by *François le Champi* and by *Mill on the Floss*. But this sentimentality is expressed slightly differently. The immodest naivety of the romantics lost popularity. In about the middle of the twentieth century, immodesty is transferred from the heart to the body and endeavors to be more brutal, or more wholesome.

IMAGINATION AND REVOLT OF THE WRITERS OF THE SECOND EMPIRE

It was not only against the tendency towards sentimentality, but also against what was at times slipshod, vague, and limp in construction and expression (among poets and novelists) in romantic literature, that the following generation protested—the generation that is sometimes called Parnassian, giving too much honor to a poetic collection that was on the whole very modest. A great deal, if not all, has been said about the cult of impassivity on the part of some of these poets, about their substitution of history, archaeology, and a review of defunct religions and past centuries for the expression of the wretched and egotistic self of the romantics. The determination of Flaubert, who had been extremely sentimental and hyperbolic at the start of his career, to compose an objective, well-ordered novel, almost the antithesis of the novel of Balzac, is well known. There is no doubt that there was unfairness in some of his peremptory judgments, in his *Correspondance,* or in Leconte de Lisle's prefaces. In actual fact, in the best works of Balzac, Hugo, and Vigny, there had been organization, structure, and deliberate adaptation of means to the goal aimed for. It was against the failings and excesses of its elders that the new generation, very naturally, stormed, as it was anxious to mark the difference between them and to take their place. Nothing would have been worse for the Parnassians than to have been contented with imitating Hugo; for Flaubert, Fromentin, the Goncourts, and Zola than to have done over again works like Balzac's or George Sand's. It was not by their aesthetics, but by their sensibility, that the writers of 1845–1875 were still romantics, and by the dreams of their imagination dissatisfied with the present and their country. They too were rebels. The development of society, between 1830 and 1860, having brought about a reinforcement of the state and the growth of technology, made their revolt only more hopeless. They did not fall into line later, as Hugo, Mérimée, and Sainte-Beuve had done when they had become peers of France or senators of the Empire, or like Lamartine, when he was minister for a while. None of the novelists of the period 1850–1880 were even admitted to the Académie. The Parnassian poets were only admitted into it later, and the painters were poorly treated in the official art exhibitions for an even longer period.

THE ROMANTICISM OF BAUDELAIRE

It would take an entire book to appreciate as one should the romanticism in Baudelaire's sensibility, aesthetics, and poetry. He borrowed shamelessly from Stendhal. He was impressed by the personality of Balzac, and probably he envied in him (as well as in Delacroix and Hugo) the creative force, inventiveness, and broad inspiration which he felt were lacking in himself. He loved Gautier for having been the friend and survivor of the romanticists of 1830 as well as for other traits. To be sure, he was not equally fascinated by everything about his predecessors, and his few observations on Hugo were clearly ambivalent. But at least he had read him closely and involuntarily recalled some of his expressions; he was one of the first who, with rare lucidity, extolled in Hugo the visionary, the decoder of correspondences, the author of the "Pente de la rêverie," the daring painter of "the extravagant, the immense . . . , all the monstrosity which surrounds man." (These words are found in his article of 1861.) From the immense heritage of the romantic generation, which was going to fall to the lot of Baudelaire, Banville, Ménard, Flaubert, and Bouilhet, when they reached manhood in about 1840, the poet of *Les Fleurs du mal* was going to retain, exploit, and transfigure the strange and the morbid, sensuality combined with spirituality. He was going to preserve the determination to be modern and to extract beauty from what was common and even ugly, as Hugo and Sainte-Beuve had done. In a famous essay, Valéry, starting from a statement outlined in a draft of the preface to *Les Fleurs du mal* (and which was probably based on a suggestion by Sainte-Beuve), supposed that, since "famous writers had divided the poetic domain among themselves," Baudelaire was forced to turn to a distant, unrecognized writer, the American Poe. But actually Poe was not at all opposed to the French romantics (whom he barely knew, apart from Eugène Sue). Poe and, after him, Baudelaire, declared that there is no true beauty without a taste of misfortune, that poetry is a yearning to reach an impossible sphere, and that inevitably love is intimately related with death and the women loved with ephemeral creatures and dream-like apparitions. But that had been said before by Coleridge, Shelley, and Lamartine. However, in Poe, who was unknown in France and not appreciated in his native country, Baudelaire found a mysterious older brother whom he made it his duty to rehabilitate. There was nothing left to discover in the French romantic poets.

From the start of his career as critic and poet, Baudelaire examined his position and that of his generation with respect to romanticism. His sonnet "Le Coucher du soleil romantique" was written belatedly (in 1862); it was a work written for a special occasion, to please his friend Asselineau and Banville: the latter was to evoke "the rising of the romantic sun" in a sonnet with which Asselineau's book would open, while Baudelaire wrote an epilogue in verse for the same work. But his respect for the romanticists who were his seniors had not diminished, even after he had fully asserted his originality as a poet. At the time when he was still far from being famous, in the second chapter of his *Salon de 1846,* the young critic had thought that, as a prelude to his task as commentator on works of art, he should seriously ask himself "what is romanticism?" and offer a few well-thought-out and forceful formulas in response to this preliminary question.

Right away, he decided that its essence was "neither in the choice of subjects, nor in the exact truth, but in the manner of feeling." Therefore, the only valid definition of romanticism had to be an internal one. And Baudelaire had by no means dissociated himself from that group of romantics which a passing fancy, in 1843, had tried to relegate to a bygone past. Taking up again a sally by Stendhal, but expressing it with intense conviction, the poet added: "In my opinion, romanticism is the most recent, the most current expression of beauty." In painting, it was Delacroix, particularly as a colorist, who incarnated this romanticism.

What were its salient features? First of all, naivety. Several times Baudelaire had recourse to this term, and undoubtedly he did not borrow it from the aesthetics of German romanticism or from an essay by Schiller, which was then not widely known in France. In many respects, the praise of naivety is the very last thing one would expect from a dandy. This naivety seems to have been a form of spontaneity, a "childhood rediscovered at will," which was opposed to what was later stilted and coldly calculated in the doctrine of art for art's sake. Gautier's poem-manifesto, "L'Art," and the preface to *Poèmes antiques* had not yet been published when Baudelaire, who was still unknown, wrote this *Salon*. But elsewhere, in 1851, particularly in his first article on Pierre Dupont, he still remained the champion of romanticism and expressed regret that it had been followed so soon by "the puerile school of art for art's sake," which excluded passion and was doomed to sterility. In Chapter XVII of the same *Salon de 1846,* the critic attacked again the lack of naivety, which was the crime of his century "and naivety, which is the domination of temperament, in manner, is a divine privilege."

A form of this remarkable privilege consisted of not fearing intensity, "the passionate violence" which Baudelaire admired in 1861 in Wagner's works, full of extravagance and even the monstrous. "In art, I admit that I do not dislike excess. . . . I like the excesses of well-being, the outbursts of will which flow into works as burning lava pours out of a volcano." This very beautiful sentence was inspired by *Tannhauser,* which he championed against the timid and obtuse Parisian public. The same year (1861), in another essay, he extolled a similar grandeur in Hugo's work: "The extravagant, the immense . . . , the description of all the monstrosity which surrounds man." It was this kind of amazing and also overwhelming beauty that he tried to attain in his most confusing *Petits poèmes en prose* and in the most grandiose poems of *Les Fleurs du mal:* "Danse macabre," "Rêve parisien," "Femmes damnées." Without realizing it clearly and, perhaps through Poe, having got wind of certain theories of Coleridge, Baudelaire followed in this case the example of the English romanticists. He quoted in English the sentence "It is a happiness to wonder," which he translated "C'est un bonheur d'être étonné." It is more the sense of wonder such as children possess that the English term implies. After Baudelaire, a British writer, Watts-Dunton, who was a friend of Swinburne, did in fact propose, as a definition of the word "romanticism," the "rebirth of the sense of wonder."

Everything could be found in romanticism, and among other nostalgias there was a nostalgia for the past, either primitive and paradisiac, or ancient and pagan. Baudelaire protested against the second, attacking, with the great knack that he had of making enemies or criticizing his friends, the "pagan school" which, in the eyes of his readers, was bound to include Gautier and Banville and former fellow-student of the Louis-le-Grand School, Louis Ménard. But it was in his immediate contemporaries that he perceived and criticized this love of losing oneself in the Greek or Roman past. In romanticism, Baudelaire preferred to look for an aesthetics of modernism and, in opposition to the bygone classicism or, in painting, to the disciples of Ingres, a new interest taken in the present. "When you are speaking of romanticism, you are talking about modern art," he declared as early as 1846. He was undoubtedly thinking about Balzac in particular, and the poems of Victor Hugo and Sainte-Beuve, who wanted to capture local color and poeticize the prosaic. It was to Hugo that Baudelaire later dedicated his "Petites Vieilles." The first impetus given to this magnificent aesthetics of the modern, which Baudelaire set forth in his long essay on *Constantin Guys,* undoubtedly came from what he thought he had found and what he loved in romanticism—the opening of the way to the modern and the future. "To call oneself romantic and to dwell systematically on the past is to contradict oneself." The aphorism was debatable, but it revealed what the poet thought as long ago as when he wrote his *Salon de 1846.*[2]

Finally, and in spite of Baudelaire's insistence on describing pessimistically one of the two simultaneous positions of man, the one which attracts us to evil and sin, he dreamed constantly of "the centralization of the ego," the concentration that Emerson had declared was the true sign of the hero, and even more of the development and advancement of this ego. The romanticists had spoken with some complacency of their yearnings for the infinite. Their dream had been to develop their being, to sell it to the devil, if necessary, to acquire superhuman powers, to become "at the same time cause and effect, subject and object," in a word, to be in contact with the infinite. In *Du Vin et du Haschisch* and *Paradis artificiels,* Baudelaire described this Faustian state with a mixture of envy and terror. Already in his translation of Poe's "Mesmeric Revelation," the first short story of the American story teller that he published, he had come upon this extraordinary state in which the mesmerized person believes and feels that he has become God. "All contradiction has become oneness. Man has 'become God,' " he wrote (after De Quincey) in Chapter IV of *Du Vin et du Haschisch* in 1851. And in the volume of 1860 he returned to the subject of this love of the infinite or perhaps this "deprivation of the sense of the infinite" which stimulates our perception of symbols and our understanding of the allegory. The drug addict joins the two worlds, natural and spiritual. He finally utters the supreme cry: "I have become God." It is undoubtedly a costly price to pay. More moralistic than some of his contemporaries (opium was not forbidden in France in the nineteenth century and laudanum was often given to children to alleviate their afflictions), Baudelaire condemned this manipulation of the personality. He dreaded the evaporation of the will, as Balzac and Hugo had feared insanity. But he was grateful to romanticism for not having been contented with the prosaic banality of the self-satisfied middle-class man. He accepted the heritage of romanticism to enrich him, as a semidivine grace. In his *Salon de 1859,* he stated about the romantic artist Célestin Nanteuil: "Romanticism is a grace, from heaven or hell, to which we owe eternal stigmas."

LECONTE DE LISLE: CRITIC OF THE ROMANTICS
AND PERSONAL POETRY

The peremptory statements with which Leconte de Lisle, as early as 1852, in his Preface-Manifesto, attacked personal poetry, which the romanticists had used and abused, have remained famous. It took only a few years for this haughty poet to be considered the leader of a literary school. When, fourteen years later, he brought together disciples and young poets who were still trying to find themselves (among whom were Verlaine and Mallarmé) in the first series of *Le Parnasse contemporain,* one was led to believe that there was a general reaction against the aesthetics and works of the romantic poets. Nevertheless, a closer look made one quickly realize that "Madrigal triste," "Hymne," "Le Jet d'eau," and "Recueillement" by Baudelaire, published in this first *Parnasse,* were not the work of an impassive author who drew his inspiration from archaeology and the science of religions. The poetry of Léon Dierx, or Verlaine's "Mon rêve familier," the first poems of Mallarmé and those of fifteen other young writers represented in this volume of 1866, did not conform any better to the declarations categorically formulated by the master of the future school in 1852: "In the public confession of the anguish of the heart and its no less bitter delights, there is a gratuitous conceit and desecration." In the same text, he railed against the poets, "inconsistent and bragging race, enamored of yourselves, whose ever acute sensitiveness only becomes irritated about a narrow personality and never on behalf of eternal principles." He demanded from his colleagues an ascesis of meditation and purification which would be brought about by the renunciation of personal themes and a return to the Greeks before Socrates and Euripides. Poetic form should become more rigorous and turn its back on the "paroxysm of raving" which had been indulged in by a literary generation acting "a brilliant comedy for the benefit of an assumed self-idolatry." Leconte de Lisle's second preface of 1855 to his *Poèmes et poésies* no longer condemned the egocentrism of the romantic elegists so much as realism and modernism, the poetry of industry and of the vile present (recently advocated with some pomposity by Maxime du Camp). Influenced by Louis Ménard, the severe poet deplored in this preface the abandonment by humanity of polytheism, the only fruitful source of art and beauty. He condemned Byron especially and repeatedly, the same Byron from whom he had drawn inspiration on occasion in his poetry, particularly in his *Qaïn.* Finally, in 1864, in a series of articles which were just as peremptory and trenchant as his manifestos, Leconte de Lisle heaped contempt on Béranger and added harsh criticisms to a few praises of Lamartine: lack of vigor displayed by his excessive wailing, limpness of verse, slipshod language, above all, "the lack of religious respect for art" and, later on, the sponsorship of very bad descendants. On the other hand, Leconte de Lisle made no reservations about Victor Hugo, who was, however, in *Les Contemplations,* a personal poet and, in other works, a sonorous echo of a modern century. Much later, in 1887, when he succeeded him in the "Académie," he recalled how, when he was still very young, he had been ecstatically impressed by the beauty and splendor of form of *Les Orientales.* He extolled the tremendous imagination manifested in his novels and, with more lucidity than many professional critics of the time, he considered that the true greatness of Hugo lay in his work "as an evocator of the supernatural dream and apocalyptic visions. He is exalted by the eternal mystery."

To be sure, the chief of the Parnassian school condemned the vulgarity to which the sentimental and too complacently personal poetry of the romanticists had often descended and the lack of finish and clearcut style in the very facile form with which this poetry had often been satisfied. In some of his poems, particularly in the scornful sonnet of "Les Montreurs" *(Poèmes barbares),* he humiliated the men of letters who consented to perform for the crowd "with its play-actors and its prostitutes," and he did this in a very personal manner, opposing his "I" to the carnivorous common people. But, as in his articles on the poets Byron and Lamartine, who had sought and too quickly won popularity, he attacked the crowd. It was his age, which was decadent and incapable of discerning or being aware of beauty, that he criticized. Condemned to remain unappreciated, the true artist could only smile bitterly at the "illusory whirl of appearances." By seeking his aspiration in the past and by peppering his poems with difficult terms, he tried to get rid of profane vulgarity. Théophile Gautier had declared more playfully: "A page should contain about ten words that the bourgeois does not understand."

But there was still a great deal of romanticism in the sensibility and work of this poet who is still considered impassive by casual readers who refer only to "Midi" or "Les Eléphants." He never got over the setback of his youthful republican dreams by the events of June 1848 and then by the election of Louis-Napoléon. The word "Liberty" returned to favor in his poems, but he associated this "virgin liberty" with a dazzling Greece and the dawn of civilization. His Fourierist dreams of culture, liberation of desire, and universal harmony established when tyrannical governments and religions have finally been overthrown always continued to haunt him. Annoyed at the destruction of his dreams, forced by life and poverty to repress the impulses of his heart, he then railed against this desire that the wise man should know how to reduce to nothing in Nirvana. But he knew that man and himself were incurable. His fate was always to long for and reach out to some impossible infinite, as Goethe and other Faustians had said:

It is the bitter cup of desire that we need!
It is the fatal bugle which sounds in our passions:
Up! Walk, run, fly, further, higher!

He cried out thus with mockery and yet with nostalgia, evoking the immense, unsatisfied aspirations of the child he had been and had remained, in one of the most romantic of French poems, "Ultra Coelos" *(Poèmes Barbares)*. He never wanted, like others, to resign himself to success, or to the acceptance of the modern world, much less find something beautiful in the modern which he spurned as vulgar. The adjective "pure" was often repeated in his poems. He steadfastly dreamed of a luxuriant nature, of beings living in harmony with it, of a return to purer sources and to something grandiose and excessive which would overwhelm puny mortals eager for useless activity and profit. He loved, just as much as Hugo had done, the great, the monstrous, wild creatures, massacres, the vastness of ancient India, sacrificing the puny insignificance of beings. This "librarian and pastor of elephants" has been jeered at. But this poet, reduced to working in a library, carried with him to Paris, just like Baudelaire, his dream of animal and human savagery, his visions of blood ("Le Soir d'une bataille," "Le Coeur d'Hialmar," "Le Massacre de Mona"), terror, and hatred. He used these terms to hold this world up to public obloquy in the imprecations of "Solvet seclum." His heroes were rebels (Qaïn, Niobé, Adam in "La Fin de l'homme," at war with their God whom they denied, even more romantic than Vigny's Moses or Christ.

Those who had known Leconte de Lisle most intimately had not been mistaken regarding his galled sensibility and this undercurrent of romanticism: revolt against the world and human destiny, nostalgia for the great and gigantic, anguish that his work and the impulses of his passionate heart were misunderstood. Louis Ménard, the friend of his youth as well as of his entire life, wrote in 1897, when the poet had just died, in *La Critique philosophique,* that passion had been the constant source of his inspiration. He continued:

But passion is not limited to the narrow bounds of real life. It is in vain that one takes refuge in the exalted spheres of the intelligence; there, too, are found again insatiable desire and futile regrets and anguish about the irretrievable. Is it an impassive poet who has written this poignant self-examination of history which he has called "Dies irae"?

When he evokes the radiant recollections of the youth of the world, it seems as if the heart of humanity is beating in his breast; and when he turns back from the joyous cradle of the pure races to the desperate melancholy of the present, his regrets resemble remorse.

The woman writer who signed herself Jean Dornis, in the book that she wrote about the poet who had been very close to her, reported the confession that this supposedly impassive man had made to her, in his old age, on November 3, 1893:

The solitude of a youth deprived of intellectual sympathy, the vastness and unceasing complaint of the sea, the splendid calmness of our nights, the dreams of a heart filled with tenderness that was inevitably unexpressed have, for a long time, led people to believe that I was indifferent and even a stranger to emotions which have more or less been felt by all, when, on the contrary, I was choking with the need to shed passionate tears. I did shed a few later on, knowing that women pity us willingly for the sorrows which other women make us endure and enjoy those that they themselves inflict on us.

His work itself amply bore witness to the sensibility of this man who was hurt by the lack of understanding of his contemporaries, of his friends, and at times of women, and who was too proud or too timid to beg for understanding. Sometimes, it was in the indirect lyricism of Heracles climbing on to the funeral-pyre, a centaur condemned to solitude, an Indian ascetic listening to the doleful complaint of suffering humanity that he incarnated himself. At other times, and in his most moving poems, which have an assured place in any anthology of the melancholic poetry of the romantics, Leconte de Lisle gave direct vent to his complaints, by generalizing his personal sorrow. These poems were "Dies Irae," "La Fontaine aux lianes," "Le Manchy," "Ultra Coelos," "L'Illusion suprême," "Le Vent froid de la nuit." He was, as much as Leopardi and Novalis or Keats, a melancholic lover of death, and he made numerous references to nothingness. "The secret of life is in the closed tombs,/What no longer exists is so only because it has been," he repeated, as he ordered his heart to be silent, just as Baudelaire used to do. But even more than Baudelaire, he yearned too much for eternity ever to be consoled by the present. Proust, who liked him very much when he was writing *Jean Santeuil,* rightly saw an elder brother in this serious and melancholic poet who was inconsolable because love and friendship, the beauty of beings and things did not last and were therefore only deception. "What is the value of things that are not eternal?" was the undoubtedly puerile but pathetic question asked at the end of "L'Illusion suprême" and actually throughout the work of this unrepentant romantic.

FLAUBERT'S ROMANTICISM

Of all the writers who were ten years old when *Hernani* was presented, and thirty in 1850 when Balzac died, none has revealed his romantic frenzy more in his letters, none has loved his malady more dearly than Flaubert. He was himself in his thirties and forties when he repeated to Sainte-Beuve: "I was born lyrical" or "I am an old dyed-in-the-wool romantic," and to Turgenev "I am an old fossil of romanticism." The ennui of life, contempt for the present and for humanity, a nostalgia for the past which his imagination could wantonly idealize were more painfully and proudly felt by him than by Baudelaire or Leconte de Lisle. Like other romantics before him, he felt he had appeared too late in this aged world. He was convinced that he would have fitted in better in the century of Rabelais and Ronsard, or in the age when Roman generals returned as conquerors dragging their captives behind their triumphal chariot.

> Had I but lived in Nero's time! . . . If only I had lived in the age of Pericles and dined with Aspasia who was crowned with violets and sang poetry within walls of white marble! . . . I was certainly there in some earlier existence!

Thus did he write to Louise Colet in a long letter of September 4, 1852. His letters to the woman whom he called, half-jokingly, "the Muse," constantly expressed this nostalgia for a period in which she would really not have fitted. The woman, who was too demanding and inclined to complain and burst into tears, would have been in those ancient days a refined and obedient courtesan. She would not have rebelled against every repeated declaration by Flaubert that nothing is worth any trouble and that we, modern men, are only of consequence by "the feeling of human inadequacy and of the nothingness of life" (same letter to Louise Colet). In *Les Romanciers naturalistes* (1881), Zola rightly said that Flaubert was "the most sweeping denier we have had in our literature. He has not written a page in which he has not examined our nothingness." Many paragraphs of his letters consist of nothing but curses against life.

Like a true romantic, he had expected too much from this life. *Novembre,* which he wrote impetuously at the age of twenty-one, was full of the desire to love. As a young man, he had been steeped in poetry. Maxime du Camp related in his *Souvenirs littéraires* how fast the heart of his friend beat when he noticed on the yellow cover of a book the letter "g" of the name "Hugo." Flaubert himself wrote to the exiled poet on July 15, 1853: "Your poetry helped build up my constitution, just as my wet-nurse's milk did." He had been equally fascinated in the beginning by Musset, whom he later reviled, by Lamartine, whom he soon found too spineless and vague, and by Quinet (particularly by his prose epic, *Ahasvérus*). As much as his heroine of whom he said that she was he, he took part in the exaggerated and corrupt life of fiction. The hero of *Novembre* confessed in his delirium that he had read too much the poets who spoke of love. Timidly, he avoided women because he desired them, and he had a feeling that they were less maternal and tender than he would have liked them to be. "With the help of the imagination, I covered myself with their hair and I placed myself between their breasts and suffocated divinely there." He imagined himself as a conqueror, as Tamerlanc or Gengis Khan, "crossing rivers full of corpses, galloping over groveling nations." Such impossible dreams soon gave way, as in the case of other romanticists, to the love of death. The future could hold nothing in store for those who had cultivated such romantic visions. "So death seemed beautiful to me. I have always loved it" *(Novembre)*.

Flaubert never got over these crazy desires and this craving for the monstrous and excessive, any more than did the friends of his youth, Le Poittevin who died at thirty-one and over whose dead body Flaubert kept vigil with a morbid obsession while reading Creuzer's *Symbolics of Religions*, or Louis Bouilhet. "In spite of his strong classical education, Bouilhet accepted only romanticism," du Camp wrote about him. This provincial teacher had produced in Paris in 1856 a Romantic drama which would not have been out of place in 1830. The more education in the high schools in the reign of Louis-Philippe claimed to exclude the new writers, the more pleasure the younger generation took in reading them.[3] But he managed to rid his work of what was juvenile in this complacency in dreaming about exoticism and about a past that was happier than the present, and this insuperable attraction to misfortune. To be sure, *Salammbô* incarnated his dreams of the outrageous, of massacres and slaughters, and there was still much of Flaubert himself in St. Antony, tempted by lust, and in Julien indulging in his slaughter of animals. But his letters and his conversation provided an ideal outlet for these declamations on the futility of everything and for his pessimism. His correspondents, his mother, and his mistress offered him their sympathy, but with some exasperation. It was Flaubert himself who quoted in 1855 to Louis Bouilhet the following statement made by his mother: "The passion for language has desiccated your heart." Much earlier, in 1846, Louise Colet had irritated him by reproaching him "for making a display of his sorrows like a swashbuckler of his scars."

But neither the author of *René* nor any of the romanticists of 1820 or 1830 had taken so much pleasure in his dreams, his excesses of sentiments, and such impossible reveries. The earliest romantics had also been men of action. Even Vigny, the romantic who loved solitude most, had realized right away that there was a danger of every effort being paralysed by the conviction that one was alone against all others and trampled underfoot by civilization. The Quaker warned Chatterton that "if solitude is sacred, it is also embittered." Flaubert could not help approving of this idea, but his heart, or perhaps the obsession of his malady, would not allow him to follow the advice that he gave, as early as April 1846, to Maxime du Camp: "Only beware of reverie . . . It is the siren of souls: it sings, it calls, you fall a prey to it and you never get over it."[4] Flaubert realized, with some effort and grudgingly, that he had to curb these impulses, which were profoundly sincere but the expression of which could only be declamatory. The religion of art cured him of his nihilism. He became impersonal, cold, even sarcastic. He became resigned to not having been Greek or Oriental. He needed more courage than he had to become a true pagan. He attacked what he believed to be the basic principle of romantic aesthetics, that one has to be moved in order to move others. (This false advice really came from Horace, Boileau, and possibly Goethe's *Faust,* rather than from Musset.) He understood that one creates more durable works by going against one's bent than by allowing oneself to follow one's inclination. He remained a romantic even in his old age, but he repudiated the aesthetics of facility and egocentrism, which he attributed to his predecessors.

THE "MAL DU SIECLE" OF MAXIME DU CAMP AND FROMENTIN

Biographers and critics have laboriously exploited this inner contradiction in Flaubert and have analyzed the conflict of these two tendencies in him. They have been grateful to him for never having drawn to one side, even if writers today, basically as bourgeois as he was, have jeered at him for his middle-class inclinations. He did not cure himself of his romanticism as completely as others of his generation, and it is this intensity that we still find attractive in him. Other romanticists who, like him, were twenty-five years old shortly before the 1848 Revolution, learned more quickly that living means accepting a compromise with the conditions of life and that writing involves making the required concessions to the public and to one's colleagues. It is paradoxical that the critical biography that Maxime du Camp deserves has not yet been written. He later became a polygraph, brought upon himself the wrath, at times unwarranted, of the man he had formerly travelled with in Brittany and in the Orient, and only partially understood his greatness. But the autobiographical novels of his youth, *Mémoires d'un suicidé* (written in 1852, published in 1855) and *Les forces perdues* (1867) do have some value. They are a valuable document on the romantic "mal du siècle" experienced by a man born in 1822.

However, the best example of a romantic who tried to cure himself of his romanticism is that of Eugène Fromentin, who was two years older than du Camp. As a high-school student, he too had dreamed about Adolphe, Obermann, and René, and had enjoyed the picture of love presented by Ovid and Virgil. His father was a specialist in mental disorders, and he was as unfeeling about the artistic inclinations of his son, who wanted to be a painter, as about his adoration of women. His best school friend, Gustave Drouineau, became insane. Fromentin himself fell madly in love with a young Creole woman, who was nineteen when he was fifteen, and who married a sensible provincial servant, had two children, but undoubtedly encouraged Fromentin's compliments and responded to his passion. In 1844, at the age of twenty-eight, she died. Fromentin wept at her tomb and was so overcome by memories and grief that his parents feared for his health. He thought of entering a monastery. Finally, in spite of his parents' opposition, he proceeded with his training as a painter, always analyzing himself, having more of an intellectual than a visual perception, and adoring his sorrow. He was convinced that this complacency towards his romantic malady was the best part of himself and yet he had to rid himself of it for fear of being a perpetual failure. Already at the age of twenty-two, he had portrayed himself to a friend as one of those morbid people "always fascinated by the dazzling mirage of memories and hopes, and creating in this way an impossible world beyond the bounds of reality . . . , not living, as Pascal said, but preparing to live."

Fromentin lacked audacity as a man (and, like Dominique, as a lover) and also as an artist and writer. He has not been forgiven for this by posterity. If Gide, whose work *La Porte étroite* resembles in places *Dominique,* has praised the novel very highly, if Fromentin has been considered by some as an anticipator of Proust living by affective memory, others have been either ironical about his over-chaste novel, or severe about a man who, in Péguy's words, was "not good enough to be a sinner."[5] He knew he was too serious, too cautious, too distrustful of his very acute sensibility, too modest to allow himself to be carried away by his sensations or his passions. He had been able to note around him the damage that romanticism could cause if it was too complacently prolonged beyond youth. With some clumsiness, he presented an example of this in his Olivier, who ended by committing suicide. He had been a precocious Werther, but had understood the lesson of acceptance of reality, of resignation and of consolation derived from nature and from an active life, a lesson that the author of

Werther had himself applied and taught. His Augustin was a stubborn and headstrong man who had overcome his romantic impulses and spent his time achieving success. He also found some poetry in his well-ordered life of a bourgeois whose ambition had been rewarded. Already at the age of twenty-four, he had written to his friend du Mesnil: "The secret of life consists of knowing one's abilities. The goal is to find them. The means involves choosing a suitable sphere of action." He conquered his romanticism, as his hero had done when he became a country landlord, but he did not renounce it completely. He refused any posture, every technical dodge which could have heightened the curiosity of his readers, every finishing touch which might have communicated to his pages or his canvases an intensity which would have made them dramatic. Almost without his knowledge, he became, during the Second Empire, one of the masters (and the most sincere and discerning) of the anti-romantic novel and one of the creators of the anti-hero.

THE REVOLUTION OF 1848, A ROMANTIC REVOLUTION

No revolution in France, with perhaps the exception of the abortive student revolution of 1968, has been as chimerically romantic as that of 1848; and none has burst forth with as little apparent justification, other than the ennui in which the younger generation felt they were plunged. It was not a revolt provoked by extreme poverty, or hunger, or the exasperation of the poor against the propertied classes, or the irritation of citizens against a tyranny which they considered intolerable, but an exaltation sustained by literature and history. During the years which immediately preceded the downfall of Louis-Philippe, Lamartine's *Histoire des Girondins,* Louis Blanc's *Histoire,* and especially Michelet's stirring *Révolution française* had evoked various aspects of the great events of 1789 and had restored a nostalgia for them. The utopian romanticism of the socialists, in spite of all the raillery directed against it by persons of sane judgment, had convinced many citizens that a change was desirable and that a better order could be established. Tocqueville, who, thanks to this revolution, controlled the external affairs of France for a while and who left recollections on what he had observed around him, rightly noted that it was not poverty or wants which had caused the upheaval of February 1848, but ideas. The younger generation which had been experiencing this romanticism in its emotions and its dreams felt roused for a moment.

This moment did not last long for Baudelaire. It left an eternal mark on the young Leconte de Lisle who, as early as July 15, 1848, disappointed and bitter, described this Republic, which was already threatened by this time, as "the sacred dream of our life." It appealed to Louis Ménard, whose participation in the struggle had been more daring and who transferred to ancient Greece, "democratic" and free, the ideal which he no longer expected to be realized by his age. Even Renan, prudently and without jeopardizing his study of oriental languages, sided with the people in revolt. He had read some Michelet, but more Lamartine; and the reflections of the seminarist Jocelyn, pursued by the French Revolution, on the beauty of revolutions, a beauty mixed with horror and perhaps divine in its source, impressed him greatly. More adaptable and critical than the poets who were his contemporaries, he did not give way entirely to disgust with the present and to pessimism following the events of June 1848 and even the election of the Prince-President. He fought against the revival of clericalism in the review *La Liberté de penser,* and opposed the emperor with firm dignity when the latter dismissed him from office in 1862. But he soon realized that romantic and revolutionary enthusiasm could not by itself alone overthrow or reform the established authority. It was necessary to add to it the spirit of criticism and irony, and begin by reforming the very foundations of the structure which was to collapse finally in 1870; it was necessary to reorganize education and thus promote public feeling. From the frustrated romanticism of his youth, he retained a deep-rooted pessimism, which only diminished gradually by assuming the outward appearance of an amused smile. He noted in his *Essais de morale et de critique* how much he valued this pessimism, which he did not wish to feel lessening in his heart. In the same work as well as in his letters to Berthelot, he concluded that the role of the one who reflects upon the inevitable and sad setbacks of life is to save at least some of his youthful dreams by trying hard to fulfill them.

It would be a long and tedious task to review a great number of writers of the period 1850–1870, and show all the romantic elements which tormented their sensibility, kept alive their dislike for the present and for life, and plunged their vast dreams into such bitter disillusion that they became lovers of death and nothingness. Flaubert evoked this affliction of an entire generation in his preface to *Dernières chansons* by his friend Bouilhet. Those writers who had great talent or who found in the cult of art a faith that could substitute for their lack of religion or devotion to some political or social chimera, were consoled in spite of everything. This was so in the case of Renan, Flaubert, Baudelaire himself, and his senior by thirteen years, Barbey d'Aurevilly, who he called "an old Romantic like me" in a letter to Jacques Crépet, dated March 9, 1865. This was also true in the case of one of the most passionate of these pessimists, Taine. But Le Poittevin (the uncle of another sick soul who suffered from a disgust of life, Maupassant), for example, or Jean Lahor, who was to be the confidant of another pessimist, Mallarmé, were acutely conscious of the abyss which separated their poetic creations from their dreams. *La Gloire du néant* was the title of Lahor's best collection, which was at least second-rate; "Nada," "Suicide," "Maladie régnante" (the subject of which was ennui) were the titles of some of his sad poems. He cursed life and modern man who was out of tune with an indifferent society and an absurd universe, with as much conviction as Leconte de Lisle but with less success in expression.

TAINE, A PASSIONATE BEING

If our only acquaintance with Taine were based on the conventional portrait of him found in textbooks or on the distorted presentation of his image and his thinking by Barrès, Bourget (in *Le Disciple*), or Brunetière towards the end of the nineteenth century, we would be led to believe that this man, enamored of positive science and the rigorous explanation of works of art, had experienced none of the so-called romantic anguish and aspirations. However, this was not at all the case. He was a complex figure. He did not reveal his personality in his works and avoided the intimate confessions and the exaggeration in form which had spoiled many of the works of his predecessors. He liked accurate investigations and striking formulas by which an artist or a nation could be characterized. He anticipated some of the assertions of the structuralists by introducing coherency into the many-sidedness of a character and by singling out one facet, with some artifice of course, and making it the dominant faculty which would account for everything. It is at least to his credit that, in front of a work of art, he did not slip away with a pirouette or swoon at the sight of the sublime. With a Faustian ambition, he was bent on taking it to pieces in order to appropriate its secrets. His entire critical work aimed at combining the best of the analytical and associationist psychology of eighteenth century (Hume, Condillac, and behind them and before their time, Spinoza) with the contribution of German romanticism: that of Hegel and Goethe, with its bent for synthesis and its intuition of the organic. He was the first of the literary critics of his time to give Stendhal, Balzac, and Michelet their rightful place, the highest place of honor. In this respect, he proved to be superior to Sainte-Beuve, as he appeared morally more generous, less scheming and calculating than the critic of *Lundis* in his *Correspondance,* which was one of the richest of the century.

The romantic element that was most apparent in him was an intense, passionate, and pantheistic love of nature, and he was more open in his attitudes and his statements than Chateaubriand or Hugo. No one perhaps has spoken better than he about trees and forests, both as a naturalist who observed and as a poet who identified with these forces which grow and rise. Deeply Byronian, he could have said with Childe Harold that he loved man (with a certain pity for his pettiness), but that he loved nature and solitude even more.

This great sensitive man had been tormented at a very early age by a craving for love. "I love, I would like to love," he confided in one of his letters, written on March 2, 1849, when he was twenty years old. He had read and enjoyed Lamartine and only became alienated from him (and his very limp form) over a long period of time. He was impressed by Musset, about whom he wrote a touching eulogy, when he was well past the age of thirty, in his chapter on Tennyson in his *Littérature anglaise*. In exile at Nevers in 1852 after he had been rejected at the competitive examination of the "agrégation" due to the reaction of the conservatives and Catholics who were frightened by his thinking, he studied Hegel every morning and found in him, to his delight, "Spinoza, multiplied by Aristotle." Above all, he consoled himself by rereading Musset and Marcus Aurelius. "In the work of the former I find all my anxieties and the latter speaks to me of the universal remedy," he indicated to Prévost-Paradol, on February 22, 1852. Later, in 1854, dismissed from office for having refused to take the oath of allegiance to the government, poor and sick, he went back to his Musset, whom he "knew by heart." Every word of this poet as well as of Goethe, Byron, Beyle, and Balzac "is like a wound to the heart," he wrote on May 12, 1854. His nephew André Chevrillon reported that for years he liked to repeat to himself the despondent statement found in *Fantasio* (Scene 2):

> Eternity is a great eyrie from which all centuries, like young eagles, have flown away in turn to traverse the sky and disappear. Our century, in its turn, has stood at the edge of the nest; but its wings have been cut, and it awaits death looking out at the infinity into which it cannot fly away.

The "mal du siècle" affected few victims more deeply than it did Taine. He described and analyzed it in a beautiful page of the fourth volume of his *Littérature anglaise,* a book of confessions beneath its appearance of cold dissection:

> Dissatisfaction with the present, a vague desire for a superior beauty and an ideal happiness, heartrending yearning for the infinite. Man suffers from doubting, and yet he doubts. . . . It is "the beyond" that he desires. Sceptics, resigned souls or mystics, have all caught a glimpse of it or imagined it [ideal happiness], from Goethe to Beethoven, from

Schiller to Heine. They ascended to it to fully agitate their swarm of
great dreams; they could not be consoled for falling down from it.
                                        (*Les idées et les oeuvres,* IV, 243)

In his great chapter on Byron, in a very fine development, Taine
returned to the subject of the same malady which undermined him
and other descendants of romanticism. Its origins lay in "a horrible
disproportion between the elements of our structure," a lack of harmony which spoils the entire human destiny. But he was not complacent about this malady. Should we revolt by exacerbating the vehemence of our sensations to the point of morbidity? Should one forget
by cultivating one's garden, prosaically, like a beast of burden? Ought
we to genuflect and believe? Ought we to fall into line and run after
power and wealth? He repudiated each of these solutions and chose
Goethe's: "Try to understand yourself and comprehend things." He
cried out then: "Let knowledge attack the soul itself! Let us get to
know more truth about beings, things, and ourselves!"

At the age of twenty, on March 6, 1848, he was already writing an
outline of a treatise entitled *De la destinée humaine.* He craved for
certitude, since he needed to replace the Catholic faith which he had
lost at an early age. With the beautiful confidence of youth, he wrote
on March 30, 1849, from the "Ecole Normale," to Prévost-Paradol:

> I am making headway every day in the knowledge of truth. I see, I
> believe, I know. I believe with all the strength of my being. I cannot fail
> to believe, since all the logical, psychological and metaphysical cer-
> titudes join together to strengthen me in the certainty in which I have
> found perfect peace of mind.

By his own confession, thinking, linking up thoughts, writing them
down were for him "a delightful thing: the tête-à-tête of love." If
everything leads to a dead end, if society rejects the thinker who
refuses to compromise his values, if man, as soon as he is free of the
constraint of manners, reveals that he is fundamentally "a ferocious
and lustful gorilla," Taine saw but one remedy for the terrible pessimism which was his basic element, when he had extended his romantic malady to the dimensions of humanity: always to think more
courageously, more lucidly, and undoubtedly against the tide of opinion. Even at the end of his life, not at all spoilt by the honor and respect
shown him by Nietzsche, Brandes, the English thinkers, and many
French admirers, he added proudly: "I am the opposite of a sceptic. I
am a dogmatic man. I believe that everything is possible to human
intelligence." He had transposed to the interior, to the brain, the
devouring passion which had consumed the heart of other romantics.

"Nobody is more capable of passion than men who live within themselves," he had noted one day. He was one of those men.

THE ROMANTICISM OF THE FOLLOWING GENERATION: ZOLA, MALLARMÉ, REDON, VAN GOGH

There had undoubtedly been adolescents tormented by dire anxiety, eager to experience life but refusing the conditions that their social sphere imposed on them, inclined to ruthless self-analysis, long before those whom we call the preromantics. But if Virgil, Botticelli, El Greco, Shakespeare, Racine, or Montesquieu had suffered from being in conflict with the world, they had not revealed it. Rousseau and his contemporaries greatly enlarged the domain of psychology and analytical literature by authorizing what one of the enemies of romanticism, Ernest Seillière, called *Le Mal romantique (The Romantic Malady)* in the title of one of his works. There have been very few men who have not been affected by it, among those whose correspondence and intimate works have given us information about their youthful crisis. One could mention in this context the Goncourt brothers, Huysmans, Mallarmé, Claudel, Gide, Suarès, Alain Fournier, Mauriac, Lyautey (who, according to the letters he wrote as a young officer, was bored to death in his garrison), and many more contemporary men.

Of course, this youthful period of revolt and despair can only be a passing crisis. Those who have gone through it later become angry with themselves for having uttered adolescent complaints and having felt a disgust for life before having lived or acted. Sometimes, they turn in shame and anger against those romantic poets in whom they had felt they could see themselves. They punish themselves for having been taken in by them. This was what happened with Zola and to some extent with Valéry after his "Nuit de Gênes," when he resolved not to feel any more pity for women and himself. At the same time, they repudiate in romantic aesthetics what seemed to encourage facility, doleful complaints, flabbiness of style, and a lack of rigor in thinking. They hold up to ridicule love elegies, idealizations of the angelic woman, and protestations of sincerity. Mallarmé and Valéry made fun of that poetry based on the theme of love, written by men (Lamartine, Musset, or Hugo) who were fully aware of carnal realities. And Mauriac himself, in spite of the fact that he was inspired by Maurice de Guérin, Baudelaire, and Barrès, sometimes spoke harshly about the romanticism which he had fostered in himself.[6]

But what writers might have said for a century for or against their romantic predecessors counts for less in our opinion than the traits of

their sensibility and their temperament by which romanticism is recognized: literary, moral, and metaphysical revolt; solitude and despair; lack of moderation, a passion for the great and tremendous; a
need to embrace nature and the world in their fierce "imperialism";
finally, an implicit or instinctive patheism. In the generation which
was born around 1840 and grew up during the Second Empire,
Cézanne (born in 1839), Monet or Redon (born in 1840), Rodin
(1840), and in literature, Villiers de L'Isle-Adam (born in 1838),
Mallarmé and Charles Cros (1842), Verlaine (1844), Corbière (1845),
Lautréamont (1846) could be chosen as examples. Daudet (in books
like *Le Petit Chose* or *Sappho*) and Zola, both born in 1840, were the
most typical of them all. A few lines on Zola will have to suffice here.
The letters he wrote, when he was young, to his three friends from
Aix—Valabrègue, Cézanne, and especially Baille—give us a clear
picture of him.

Brunetière, who bluntly opposed him but who was basically fascinated by him, said very rightly somewhere: "Flaubert, whom I would
call the last of the romantics if Zola had not existed." Seillière, who
was a supporter too of tradition and morals, entitled the first chapter
of his book on Zola (Grasset, 1933): "The stigmata of the romantic
temperament." By that he meant faith in the natural goodness of man,
the will for power, and even nervous instability, which in Zola's case
was undoubtedly real. Zola had confided his constant anguish about
his work to Dr. Toulouse, who had observed and studied him as a
nevropath: "Oh! what a poor hurt soul I am!" The first of Zola's novels
which are of consequence, *La Confession de Claude* (1866), is indeed
the still maladroit work of a hyper-romantic, eager, notwithstanding,
to react against the romantic clichés. *La Faute de l'abbé Mouret* (1875),
the work of his maturity, was undoubtedly the most luxuriant and
exuberant of the romantic novels of the entire century. Nature was
even more ardently alive in it than in *Les Misérables* or *Les Travailleurs
de la mer.* Meadows, flowers, birds—everything was stamped with a
diffuse sensuality and sang a hymn celebrating the love of the priest
and the wild and tender young girl, a new Daphnis and Chloe as they
have been called, but much less soft-spoken than the characters of
Longus' pastoral novel.

> The vine plants trailed like great insects; the thin corn-stalks, the
> wilted plants were like batallions armed with long spears; the trees were
> dishevelled by running, they stretched out their limbs, like wrestlers
> preparing for a fight; the fallen leaves and the dust of the roads were
> marching forward.

And in another part of this work, he described the pagan ecstasy
which took possession of the sense of sight, the sense of smell, of all

the senses of the young priest captivated by this sweet-smelling Garden of Eden in which the sense of sin disappeared:

> A warm joy of light filtered into a floating gold dust, a certainty of perpetual greenery, an attraction of continuous perfume.

Like so many others at that time, the adolescent Zola had begun by being intoxicated by Hugo and Musset. He knew entire poems of Hugo by heart and, he reported in those curious articles written for a Russian newspaper and later published in France under the title *Documents littéraires* (1881), his friends and himself, returning home in the evenings, recited Hugo and synchronized their steps "to the rhythm of his verses which were as sonorous as trumpet blasts." In the same work (p. 89), he evoked his escapades with his two friends in the countryside of Aix. One wet morning, one of them had brought along a volume of Musset, a poet about whom one took good care not to breathe a word in high school. The rain was falling in torrents. The wind was making the branches creak. But "in the ditch . . . , in the little room of the village inn, Musset was with us and was enough to make us happy." They thus reread "Rolla" and "Les Nuits" more than twenty times, in the midst of nature. Michelet, at the end of his career, when he wrote *La Femme, L'Amour, L'Oiseau,* impressed him just as much, as he also impressed Van Gogh and many others at that time, by sentimental and sensual exaltation and the confused yet deferential cult of woman, which had been diffused in these works by the historian who became a naturalist and was more than ever a romantic. From his first works which were filled with declamatory sincerity, Zola showed himself to be what he always remained: a romantic, dissatisfied with the present, worshipping the purity which he attributed to woman, strangely chaste and puritanical, drunk with that despair which, from the time of *René* onwards, he declared in his essay on Chateaubriand, "has blown for a while over all the summits of the mind."

Perspicacious as he was (he proved to be one of the best critics of his century on Stendhal, Balzac, Hugo, and Manet), he soon realized that he had too much creative energy, too great a passion for certain aspects of the truth which had not struck his predecessors, to remain a mere follower of romanticism. *La Débâcle, Nana* particularly, and even *La Terre* with its poetry of ugliness were great romantic novels. Sandoz, in *L'Oeuvre,* uttered wild pantheistic cries to the world. But Zola understood that one had to destroy in order to replace and that the most fruitful message of romanticism urged him to imitate, not the aesthetics or the work of the romantics, but the daring they had shown in renovating everything. So he included romanticism in his "hatreds." Naturalism, of which he was the theoretician, was a product of romanticism, and he recognized this. Its role was then to move away from romanticism and fight against it, if it was to take its place. A fig for the mess of the poorer romanticism! An end to the total condemnation of their age begun by the romantics! They had been too enamored of the past and the idealization of reality. In a strange statement (in an article on Gautier, reprinted in *Documents littéraires*), he even accused romanticism of having been "a leprosy which has corrupted our national genius. . . . A school of rhetors, battling for form, without trying to base its conquest on the scientific evolution of the century" (pp. 139, 153). He was surprisingly hard on Baudelaire himself. In his *Roman expérimental* (1880), he proposed as a goal: "Reality being accepted and then dealt with in poetry." Again elsewhere, without suspecting how romantic he was in the statements that he made as leader of his literary school (*Le Naturalisme au théâtre*, 1881), he exclaimed:

> Poetry is everywhere, in everything, even more in the present and reality than in the past and abstraction. Every act, at every hour, has its poetic and splendid aspect.

And in his correspondence, he found a more poetic and striking formula to specify his aim as a novelist:

> A leap to the stars from the springboard of precise observation. Truth rises to the level of symbolism in one rapid leap.[7]

It would be almost too easy to indicate the points of similarity between the "damned poets" such as Verlaine, Corbière, or Rimbaud, and the romantics who had been the first to express their revolt against the world, their yearning for a more or less reinvented love, and their frantic attempt to broaden man's horizons and change life. The "damned poets" too could have cried: "I revolt against death," and cursed western civilization for what was bourgeois and pettily commercial in it. On the other hand, from the point of view of aesthetics, they were not satisfied with the techniques or efforts of the romantics. The romantics had opened the way for them. It was now up to them to be more daring than their predecessors, to make poetic language more familiar and popular, and to dislocate the verse by adding meters which were opposed to the alexandrine or the octosyllable. Verlaine, an artist who was very conscious of his means and a virtuoso metrist, succeeded marvellously in doing this. Rimbaud had been impressed by the poems of Hugo the visionary, and even more by *L'Homme qui rit* from which he borrowed his allusion to "comprachicos," and certainly by *Les Travailleurs de la mer*. But it was in the youthful poems of Mallarmé that all the feelings of tenderness, ideal purity, and melancholy of the romantic poets and their heir Baudelaire were expressed with the greatest emotion and charm. The earlier volumes of his *Correspondance* show him to be one of the most moving and subtly ironical letter-writers of his century. Like Zola, it was in his youthful letters that this man revealed himself most. Alas! after he was forty, too often he only wrote letters to editors, notes to colleagues, and advice to disciples. Once past that age, few men can still lay bare their hearts.

It is well known that Mallarmé, with his exquisite politeness but also undoubtedly in all sincerity, had a very high opinion of Zola and exchanged several letters with him. "As for me, admiring as I do a designed and colored poster . . . , as much as a ceiling or an apotheosis, I do not know one point of view in art which is inferior to another," he wrote to Zola on November 6, 1874, after having attended one of his plays which the public had not liked. He felt that Zola was a poet in his own way and sought the ideal. However, at the same time, Zola, who was less observant or less lucid, only considered Mallarmé as a Parnassian who was so enamored of pure art that he became a bit cracked because of it. Mallarmé's letters about the young German girl with whom he fell in love and whom he finally married after many tears shed on both sides were full of sentimental effusions (very natural at the age of twenty), of tenderness nicely tinged with irony and moral idealism. She gave herself to him and this only made her seem purer in his eyes. Would she understand his poetic dreams? His friend and confidant Cazalis (Jean Lahor) asked him this question. Like all lovers who have a bent for teaching, he replied that he would bring her up to his level:

> She is as intelligent as a woman can be without being a monster. It is I who will make her an artist. Moreover, to whom does the pleasant task of teaching fall? To the husband. . . . After two years spent with me, Marie will be my reflection.
>
> (Letter of September or October 1862.)

Both of them were very poor when he was in a position, as he expressed it very nicely, to "legalize the throbbings of their two hearts." But at least, said Mallarmé, who was as scornful of the bourgeois as his romantic predecessors or Flaubert, his children "would not have the blood of merchants in their veins." For he could not bear to "feel running through his hair a hand which had served customers and had rattled coins on a counter." How could he "drink infinity" in the eyes of a tradesman's daughter? For shame! He already had a love of unhappiness and knew that he was predestined for it, just like the hero of Byron. But the sentimental tone of his letters brings to mind Lamartine. To the young conscience-stricken governess, fright-

ened by the future and already by the "what will people say" around
her, the only consolation he offered was Victor Hugo's advice: "you
who suffer because you are in love, love even more."

He declared to his friends, who were, like him, just beginning their
poetic careers and were just as obscure and poor at that time: "Happiness in this world is ignoble" (June 3, 1863). One of his first poems,
"Les Fenêtres," published in the *Parnasse contemporain* of 1866, expressed a great dislike, similar to that professed by Leconte de Lisle,
for "the hard-hearted man/Wallowing in happiness" and avid for
wealth. And that was not a literary complaint made during one particular moment of spleen, for there were many such moments in the days
of the young devotee of "the bitter ideal." Villiers had declared, in the
same year, 1866, that Mallarmé and himself were both equally indifferent to happiness and would remain so. Such was the destiny of
these heroes of a rejuvenated romanticism. Their dream was too
idealistic and had to devote itself to preserving its purity. Twenty
years later, in 1886, in a magnificent and revealing "divagation" on
Hamlet, a character who, he confessed, exercised over him "a fascination akin to anguish," Mallarmé stated solemnly: "For, rest assured,
that is the question: the conflict between man's dream and man's fate
as decreed by a higher Fate." Delacroix, Musset, Baudelaire had
already suspected this in their insistent meditation upon the Shake-
spearean character.

There is obviously no question of reducing Mallarmé completely to
the young melancholic man revealed in his confidential letters to his
friends, and to this elegiac romanticism. At the same time, in his
letters of July 1866 to Théodore Aubanel, this anguished man in exile
at Tournon released the most glorious bulletins of victory that any
poet has ever written:

> I have laid the foundations of a magnificent work . . . I have died and
> come to life again with the key to the precious stones of my last spiritual
> casket . . . I have found the key to myself . . . a center where I remain like
> a sacred spider on the main threads which have already emerged from
> my mind . . .

The expressions he used (cult of beauty, for example) still recalled
the Parnassians. Moreover, Mallarmé was sincere in his long-lasting
admiration for Banville and even more for Gautier. Claudel reported
how, at one of Mallarmé's Tuesday receptions, the poet had cast a
withering glance at him and rebuked him when the young man had
dared to make a blunt statement against Victor Hugo. Later, he broke
away from a certain Parnassian aesthetics which had become static and
had been spoilt by clumsy followers, whose virtuosity was only formal.
We know that he criticized them in his famous reply to Jules Huret's

inquiry in 1891; and in those few lines, and in another even more striking declaration to Léo d'Orfer, he assigned to poetry the goal of expressing "the mysterious meaning of existence." But if he reproached the descendants of the Parnassian school for lacking tremendously in mystery, he proposed a definition of symbolic art very similar to those which various romantics, including Vigny, had presented in a more clumsy fashion. The mood that the object evokes or that poetry "draws from the subject by a long deciphering process" counts for much more than the skill in making a few gems sparkle.

THE PAINTERS' CULT OF THE ROMANTIC DELACROIX

Similarly, the painters contemporaneous with Mallarmé and Verlaine did not turn very much for inspiration to their immediate predecessors, Courbet (who was, however, most romantic in temperament) and the Impressionists, but to the romantics and especially to Delacroix. The history of the fortunes of Delacroix and of his influence on painting, from Cézanne to the Fauvists, remains to be written. The young Cézanne was intoxicated by the audacity and violence which he found in the work of Delacroix, whose last words noted in his *Journal* and reported orally while he was still alive by those who had heard them, inspired the young artists, in revolt against the disciples of Ingres: that a picture should be above all a feast for the eyes. Cézanne, Monet, Gauguin, more particularly Van Gogh, and after them, Rouault and Matisse, held up to ridicule the claims of art to imitate nature. On January 6, 1875, a survivor, Corot, who was then sick but kind to the younger artists, encouraged Gauguin in his rebellion and in the complete expression of his ego. "Courage . . . I interpret as much with my heart as with my eye." Gauguin made numerous telling statements to assert that he was fond of evasion, of the primitive, of "barbarianism which is . . . a rejuvenation," (to Strindberg, who was a painter of talent as well as an intensely romantic dramatist, on February 5, 1895), of nature whose image the poet should distort without scruples in order to express his ego. Writing on May 24, 1855, to Schuffenecker, a friend whom he asked for a photographed copy of Delacroix's "La Barque de Don Juan," he added this revealing comment:

> Have you noticed how much the temperament of this man was like that of wild animals? That is why he has painted them so well. Delacroix's drawing always reminds me of a tiger with its supple and strong movements. His "Barque de Don Juan" has the force of a powerful monster and I would like to feed on this spectacle.

On the other hand, Gauguin, Odilon Redon (the second more prone to languid reverie and a victim of the romantic sentiment of the ennui of life), and many others repudiated, in the interest of a return to the best aspects of romanticism, the impressionism which, about 1880, had finally just been accepted by the French. In their opinion, such an art was too devoid of the tragic sense of life. It did not emphasize mystery, "the unfathomable mystery which remains unfathomable," wrote Gauguin. The very romantic term "mood" persistently reappeared in their writings. "Why should we not come to the point of creating different harmonies corresponding to our moods?" asked Gauguin. Redon, who discovered his individuality as a painter through the dramatic element of a particular oilpainting by Delacroix ("Desdémone maudite par son père"), wrote to Sérusier: "I refused to embark on the impressionist adventure, because I found it led nowhere." He preferred to examine his subconscious and, even more, to yield to it, and expand the object, "elevate the spirit . . . in mystery, in the confusion of the unsolved and its delightful anxiety." The only critic of the time who understood these painters and unfortunately died at the age of twenty-seven, too soon to convert the public, Albert Aurier, declared in remarkable hyper-romantic articles that "the only way to understand is through love."[8]

The most remarkable case of literary romantic exaltation among these grandchildren of romanticism was indisputably that of Van Gogh. Of all these painters, he was the one who expressed himself with most effusion in his letters (to his brother) and whose correspondence has been preserved for us, by some lucky chance. He was enthusiastic about a few English novelists and especially about Michelet (his *Jeanne d'Arc,* his books on *La Femme* and *L'Amour* in particular), Zola, and Daudet. He did not rest till his brother shared his admiration for Michelet. Even though he was the son of a pastor, he considered Michelet superior to the Bible. "Michelet says openly what the Gospel, which only contains a few germs of these ideas, whispers softly in our ears" (letter to Théo, November 23, 1881). He became imbued with Hugo's poems and *Les Misérables.* The most terrible misery, moral solitude, and lack of understanding increased his anguish. He knew he would never attain harmony in this world. But he retained one belief: in love, the source and purpose of all things, the reason for all art. "Working, loving, living, that is all the same," he wrote to his brother, to his sister, and to another correspondent, Rappard. "I tried to express with the colors red and green the terrible human passions." Yearning for faith, intolerant of the clergymen who believed that they could strengthen faith by sermons, he rediscovered without suspecting it a famous piece of advice given by St. Augustine, and as a romantic devotee he explained to his brother that "the best way to know God is to love deeply."

Among the painters who had preceded him, while he had a high opinion of the artists of Barbizon and of Millet in particular, it was really Delacroix to whom he was attached and to whom he always went back for inspiration. He alone really influenced him, he assured us. He found in his paintings the crazy movement, the chaos of agitated nature, the whirlwinds and eddies which his nature needed. Like Delacroix, he needed to project his ego on nature in order to interpret it. "I paint the infinite," he declared one day in Provence. It seems that, without having read Baudelaire, he saw in this painter who had thought he did not like the romantics and who had kept aloof from their literary battles, someone whom he resembled.[9]

CELINE, CAMUS, ELIE FAURE,
APOLLINAIRE, AND THEIR
ROMANTICISM

Few critical doctrines are more casual, and more misleading, than those which attribute to a certain epoch a spirit or an essence of the epoch, a unique *Zeitgeist,* which makes it easy to label it forever. Everything must conform to this allegedly dominant current, which is also considered the tide of the future, and must move in the direction of history. Dissident doctrines or nonconformist talents that do not move in the direction which is proclaimed inevitable are, metamorphically at least, excluded or suppressed, as they could be in politics by a dictator or a single party. Zola had believed that his Naturalist novel alone followed thus the direction of history, between 1865 and 1880. He became rapidly undeceived, both by disciples who disowned him and by the continuing existence around *Les Rougon-Macquart* of other types of novels, of imaginative poetry and painting, and of an idealistic philosophy. What we consider here as romantic in the symbolists is of course only one of the many elements of their credo and their personality. Moreover, many other quests and creations coexisted at that time with symbolism.

But the romantic current continued to overflow into the last twenty years of the century. From time to time, it broke out with a temperament that was excessively fond of self-expression (Barrè professing his cult of the ego for a while, Loti with his monotonous laments, Mme de Noailles with a heart filled with wonder, who enchanted Proust) or of passionate vitality. Nietzscheism, which was then spreading in France, exacerbated even more this revival of egotism, and it was believed that German thinkers or Stirner, the prophet of the unique, provided a philosophical justification for this arrogant solipsism. In the case of Verhaeren, Loti, Mme de Noailles, or Barrès, it was not merely a question of a youthful outburst; they were just as romantic at the end of their lives as at the beginning. Barrès created a great stir with his conversion to nationalism and came to praise above all the French and Lorraine tradition. But, until the end of his life, he was obsessed by the romantics, in whom he recognized his elder brothers. He romanticized Pascal. His last project was to recount, with some addition of imaginative fantasy, the relations, which might have been amorous, and which he considered very romantic, of Descartes and Princess Elisabeth. In an article in *L'Echo de Paris* (September 28, 1912) on "Les Maitres romantiques," he confessed:

> I love and admire always the great romantic works. I consider them useful as a description of the suffering endured by elite beings, trying to reach the bank through storms and raging waves . . . I would like to write a history of the romantics.

To be sure, personalities whom we have been able to call "classiques" (in painting, Seurat or Signac) or who considered themselves as such after having sown their wild oats (Moréas) coexisted perfectly with the hyper-romantics (also called expressionists) between 1885 and 1910. Cubism, in which may be seen a return to the priority of form over color, to David and Ingres rather than Delacroix, and its quasi-scientific quests through still-life coincided very exactly with Fauvism about 1905–1910. Fauvism, however, was an outburst of exuberance, a return to the sentiments of tragedy and anguish, a will of aggressive coloring, of which Géricault and Delacroix were the most authentic distant ancestors. Vlaminck (whose little book, *Tournant dangereux,* published by Stock in 1929, is one of the most explosive and naive works ever written by a painter), and Delaunay, and more than anybody else the great tormented romantic Soutine, all of them in love with brute sensation and intensity, were the most genuine romantics in art in the first half of the twentieth century.[10]

In the literature of the twentieth century, there are so many authors with a romantic sensibility that one is forced to choose, almost arbitrarily, two or three of them as examples. Proust had been inspired by the poets of the first half of the century and by Baudelaire. On the other hand, he seemed to have taken little interest in the efforts of Mallarmé, the minor reviews of symbolism which Valéry loved, the first works of Apollinaire and Claudel. For his aesthetics of enchantment, dream, and assiduously cherished memory, for his love of long, involved sentences with their rich train of adjectives, for the Balzacian sense of mystery in his characters, he deserves to be styled "romantic." He was also romantic by his faith in art reinterpreting and immortalizing life, and his cult of the artist as the true hero. In a note (p. 267) in his *Pastiches et mélanges* ("Journées de lecture"), he even added that "the classicists have no better commentators than the romanticists. As a matter of fact, only the romanticists know how to read classical

works, for they read them as they were written, romantically." Gide
took some time to get rid of what he knew was disturbed and maudlin
in him; after having given free rein to this plaintive romanticism in
André Walter, and to a more exalted and pagan romanticism in *Les
Nourritures terrestres,* without ceasing to cultivate his ego and to pursue
his quest of sincerity, he had preferred to bring to light another facet
of himself, that of irony. Suarès, who was his friend for a while,
impetuous and proud, draped in his haughty solitude, fond of brilliant
prose, preferred all his life to cherish his loneliness as a social misfit
and a despiser of the modern world. He was one of the most nobly
Byronic Frenchmen. Bernanos, so different from him, but just as lost
in his century, against which he vituperated with verbosity and outbursts of anger, did not attain the so-called classical serenity either.
Malraux, from his earliest works which were very like those of
Chateaubriand and Barrès, then through his heroes who, too, were
proudly aloof and obsessed by their fight against fate, and by his often
sumptuous prose, is certainly the great romantic of the middle of the
twentieth century; he is also romantic by his meditations on art and the
artist who is the rival of reality and emulator of God. Perhaps, in the
opinion of posterity, the best aspects of Camus, once that part of his
work which has ideological pretensions has been excluded, will be
found in the bitterness of *La Chute* and in the romantic resonance of
his first essays and travel accounts in *Les Noces* and *L'Été.* Aragon's
novels, his poetry of war and love, the Moorish décor of the love
poems in *Le Fou d'Elsa* (1963), everything in him indicates an impeni-
tent romantic, who is by no means embarrassed to recall at times the
indiscreet opulence of Hugo, at other tims the tones and display of
sentiments of Alfred de Musset.

The excesses, aggressiveness, and transports of a certain romanticism, proliferated further by the audacity of the Naturalists, were
found again in the most obdurate of the romantics of this period,
Céline. More than any of his predecessors, Céline proclaimed his
need to revolt coupled with a feeling that the only outlet for modern
man is to fume and curse. The restraints of society and administration
blocked all the openings around him. As early as October 4, 1933, in
an article "Hommage à Zola" in *Marianne,* Céline saw on all sides
around modern man a quasi-mystical passion for death.

> The current unanimous sadism arises above all from a desire for
> nothingness which is deeply embedded in man and especially in the mass
> of men, a sort of amorous, almost irresistible and unanimous impatience
> for death. With coyness, of course, and a thousand denials, but the
> tropism is there, and it is all the more powerful as it is perfectly hidden
> and silent.

The omnipresence of death (in the work of Céline as well as in that of Julien Green, Malraux, Camus, and Bonnefoy) is indeed one of the obsessions which, after the great slaughter of 1914–1918, recalls the obsession of death which afflicted the romantics after the Napoleonic wars. But the rebound to hope in the future had been more rapid one hundred and fifty years ago. Finally, Élie Faure, one of the first men in France to have understood and helped Céline (who was not at all grateful to him for this), one of the most perspicacious art critics of his time and, in his best moments, a profound and passionate essayist, was not afraid to reveal his personal sentiments in his work and to express himself with vehemence and often with turgidity. In the fourth volume of his *Histoire de l'art* (p. 298), he made the affirmation which pervaded his entire thinking: "France would not be France without French romanticism." In France, even rationalism, while trying to impose the reign of reason, becomes romantic.

> From David up to and including cubism, all of French painting, or almost all of it, has been romantic, even in those of its internal movements which were born with the avowed purpose of opposing romanticism . . . Zola is the most romantic, not only of the disparagers, but also of the champions of romanticism.

Whatever might have been said about it, it is very seldom by its classical qualities of lucidity, order, moderation, and respect for venerable traditions that French art and literature have exercised such a powerful influence over Germany, England, and America. Dreiser who admired Balzac and Zola, Faulkner who rewrote a *Comédie humaine* in the South of the United States, Henry Miller who was intoxicated by Rimbaud, Giono, and Céline, twenty disciples or translators of Apollinaire, so many admirers of surrealism who reinterpreted this movement, the first enthusiasts of Claudel, all these men have sought in the France of today the country par excellence of a romanticism which has never been stamped out and is always renascent.[11]

It is in poetry just as much as in painting, however, that a romantic sensibility is manifested most fully, and for the observer that the critic becomes in these matters, the advantage lies in the fact that he has at his disposal many more confidences and written testimonies than in the case of painters, who are less inclined to explain themselves clearly, or in the case of sculptors or musicians. Here again, a few references relating to poets as diverse as Apollinaire, Breton, and Claudel will have to suffice for illustration.

Few poems are as personal as those of Apollinaire. He himself remarked that each of his poems commemorated an event in his life. His personality, which was moreover engaging and which had won

him so many warm friendships among artists and poets, was exposed
in his poems, at times smiling in its melancholy and weeping over a
dead love ("Love died in your arms") with accents which brought back
to mind Musset or Heine, at other times tragically anguished, as in his
long autobiographical poem *Zone,* written after the break with Marie
Laurencin:

> The anguish of love chokes you
> As if you were never to be loved any more . . .
> I have lived like a mad man and I have wasted my time . . .

Also, like so many romantics, he combined his intimate memories
and his impulses of evasion with fragments of popular songs
("Rosemonde," "Marie") and visions of chimerical palaces. Nobody
since Baudelaire had expressed sadness in more poignant verse. But
he was peculiarly hard on Baudelaire in the few notes which he wrote
about him, and he was even more distant from the symbolists. He had
more affinity with Verlaine and Musset than any other Frenchman.
He was romantic in his exalted conception of the poet as the supreme
creator, the one who creates or recreates for us a world which, without
him, would remain uninteresting or incomprehensible to us. "To
contrive a new universe" was one of his definitions of the function of
the poet as seer and architect of a more harmonious world than the
one in which we struggle. To one of the women whom he courted and
loved, Madeleine Pagès, when she showed herself incapable of understanding a poet as a lover, he wrote the following very solemn lines:
"Poets are creators. So nothing is born on earth, nothing is presented
to the eyes of women, if it has not first been imagined by a poet."

He was well aware of the fact that every true romantic, once
adopted by posterity if not by his contemporaries, became a classic.
And he never spoke ill of the so-called classical values, and certainly
not of the poets of the seventeenth century called "baroque"
(Théophile or Maynard), whom the romantics had rediscovered. In
his aesthetics, he always fought for "the most energetic art" of a
period, the one which has the best chances of survival.

SURREALISM
REINCARNATION OF THE ROMANTIC REVOLT

If, from Rousseau to Rimbaud, the great romantic outburst had
been a revolt against the world and a tremendous impetus to transform it by transforming man, none of the revolts since that time equals
in verbal violence and in bitterness that of the surrealists. They
dreamed of nothing less than a total remodeling of man. Their revolt
was social, like that of the romanticists who had come into contact with

Saint-Simonism and Fourierism, had been eager to change religion with Lamennais, and had understood that one had to "cure the universal human malady" not only by theories but by political action. It was moral to an even greater degree, in its effort to transform the relations between the sexes, as George Sand and Michelet had no doubt dreamed of doing, and this on the strength of passion loudly asserting its rights. In the text entitled "La Confession dédaigneuse" (*Les Pas Perdus,* 1924), Breton had asserted this, when he was still very young, invoking his favorite moralists, Vauvenargues and Sade:

> The moral question preoccupies me. . . . Morals are the great conciliator. To attack them is to still pay homage to them. It is in them that I have found my main subjects of exaltation.

He had proclaimed very emphatically the unique influence of Rimbaud, more profound in the moral sphere than in the poetic domain, in his *Position politique du surréalisme.* Even before he became an acknowledged admirer of Fourier, he had wished to establish morals on desire, distinguished from animal lust. The sexual revolution which the young people of several countries prided themselves on in 1970 could justly have claimed him as their most direct precursor.

Like the romantic revolt, which had constantly come up against the limits assigned to the human condition and had been fond of the image of man as a bat, colliding incessantly with the walls and roof of his prison, the revolt of Breton and his friends was metaphysical. Against the "ridiculous conditions of all existence," according to another sentence of *Les Pas perdus,* Breton wanted to retrieve all the psychic forces which lie, untapped, in us. He had recourse to the coincidences of objective chance, to automatism (much less, in fact, to automatic writing than he had seemed to announce in a few statements which had aroused a great deal of interest), and particularly to the unconscious and dreams. Here again, Breton turned, not to the symbolists (about whom he spoke unkindly, preferring the naturalist novelists to the "symbolists who, during the same period, endeavoured to stun the public with their more or less rhythmical lucubrations (*Les Vases communicants,* p. 107), but to Nerval, Hugo, and a few German romanticists for a few features which he tackled with a more fierce persistency. With the impeccable virtuosity in reasoning which characterizes French revolutionaries in all spheres, he proposed to exalt the method of analogical thought at the expense of the use of logic. He cast out the word *"car"* as the most baneful of the language. Elsewhere, *"Signe ascendant"* (1947), he expressed the desire to destroy forever the little word *"donc"* "with all the vanity and morose enjoyment that it involves." He went as far as to suppose, and soon to affirm, the existence of a connection between real automatism and forms of poetry, between personal automatism and universal automatism, borrowing from Friedrich Engels his enigmatic expression "objective chance" to describe it.

The task that he proposed for his combative energy was a Herculean one. Fighting against and going beyond reason, man, transformed and craving for liberty (as the German and French romantics had already described him), could only avoid sinking into despair by struggling against the skeptics and rational logicians, against corrupt society and against God. He had to have recourse to powers which were perhaps magical and at least mythical, and to believe (as Balzac had done) that miracles themselves are within our reach. Man, carrying out the vertiginous descent into himself that Novalis and Nerval had asked, had to draw from there the force required to rise much higher. "Every artist must resume on his own the pursuit of the golden fleece," this new argonaut declared in his *Prolégomènes*. . . . Here again, the symbolic names of Prometheus and Icarus, heroes of the romantics, were those which were recalled by the exhortations of Breton, who wished to attain, and help others attain, a state of grace. He said himself in a very important article, "Le Merveilleux contre le mystère" (1936), included in *La Clé des champs* (Sagittaire, 1953), what a high regard he had for romanticism, from which dates—and not from Baudelaire or from symbolism—"the will for the total emancipation of man." A glimmer of this had shone in "the gigantic façades of Hugo," in "Musset's admirable song of February 3, 1834" (undoubtedly "A saint Blaise, à la Zudecca . . ."), in Nerval, and lastly in Lautréamont. Again, elsewhere, he expressed his admiration for *Bug-Jargal, Han d'Islande,* and for the poems of Hugo's twilight years. How romantic still was the famous precept that concluded *Nadja,* which, along with *Arcane 17,* was the most romantic work of the twentieth century: "Beauty will be convulsive or it will not be."

The most constant preoccupation of Breton and of those who, for a while at least, were his disciples—Eluard, Desnos, Péret, and Char— was even more romantic, and without any fear of ridicule: the preoccupation of restoring total, deified love to its true place, by far the foremost position, both in literature and in life. As early as 1924, in *Poisson soluble,* Breton exclaimed: "We will reduce art to its simplest expression, which is love." In 1929, repeated: "There is no solution outside of love," and he would agree to receive into the surrealist clique only those who could answer to his own satisfaction the question: "What sort of hope do you place in love?" Much later still, at the age of fifty-six, in his *Entretiens* (Point du jour, 1952), Breton showed that he had not wavered on this central point of his credo: "All subjects of exaltation peculiar to surrealism converge . . . toward love.

The highest human ambition lies in elective love" (pp. 139–140). It was not a question principally of eroticism and, in spite of the admiration proclaimed for the divine Marquis, there was even less a question of anything sadistic, but entirely of sentiment and deferential declarations to woman, which were generally chaste, even in the quasi-Petrarchan enumeration of the charms of the partner (Union libre). Sentences like the following from Arcane 17 could have been written by Chateaubriand pursuing the sylph of his dreams, by Lamartine to Elvire, by Hugo to Juliette:

> Before knowing you, I had encountered unhappiness and despair. Before knowing you? Nonsense! These words have no sense. You know very well that when I saw you for the first time, I recognized you without the slightest hesitation.

The love that the poet celebrates in prose and verse, that "crazy love," idealizes woman as a fairy Mélusine, a woman-child or even a woman-serpent, an intermediary between man and nature. She unites existence and essence in herself, declared Breton. She brings him faith. She alone can inspire and guide him in his struggle against the menacing war and the governments which threaten to reduce half of humanity to slavery.

She is always the same, even though those to whom the adoration of the male is directed are continually changing. This is not quite the same as Musset's not very gallant cry, "What does the flask matter provided one gets intoxicated!" or Goethe's epigram comparing women to plates of crockery or silver on which men place their golden apples. Rather, it is faith in the future, in the infinite possibilities that this future offers us, faith that love creates and renews. Old age and death are conquered:

> Men despair stupidly of love. They live a slave to the idea that love is always behind them, never before them. . . . And yet, for each one, the promise of this hour to come contains the whole secret of life, capable of revealing itself one day, accidentally, in another being.
>
> (L'Amour fou, p. 64)[12]

CLAUDEL, A ROMANTIC AGAINST HIS WILL

At the time when he was writing Partage de midi, Claudel had spoken of love with as much passion as, and with more dramatic force than, any of the surrealists. The surrealists had no great fondness for Claudel, who had given the impression that he considered himself Rimbaud's heir. Claudel himself, however, had been partial to that great sentimentalist and that marvel of marital fidelity in literature, Aragon. After the magnificent love duets of Partage de midi, he soon became very afraid of the despotic power that passion can gain over us, and of the ease with which it can suddenly open all the floodgates for the most perilous of romantic outbursts. Claudel had been very fond of Wagner in his period of maturity; as he declared in his usual familiar language, he had "wanted to take in the whole tetralogy. . . . The tetralogy swallowed without taking a breath is terrible," he confided to Henri Guillemin. He laughed several times at the performances of Wagner, so easy indeed to hold up to ridicule, but as a man who could not manage to completely suppress in himself his exacerbated romanticism, and who was punishing himself for his childish enthusiasm. He repudiated "Tristan's wrigglings" and moralized late in life that "it is not fitting to die for love of a woman. It is more than ridiculous. It is really indecent" (*Oeuvres complètes, XVI,* p. 307). But on this theme as on so many others, Claudel did not fail to pile up contradictions, according to his moods, or simply out of a love for whims and the roguish pleasure of startling the bourgeois who had feared him for such a long time as the wolf who was invading the sheep-pen. An ambassador, a pillar of the Church, a supporter of the Pope, and in the autumn of his life, a member of the "Académie française" and the lord of a manor, he nonetheless crushed the bourgeois with his antipathy, just like the writers of the romantic century. In 1922, he confided in the notes of his *Journal:*

> I am struck by the bourgeois character of French literature, by its callousness, its insensibility, its hatred for the common people, its lack of sympathy, its affectation of hardness and detachment.

If there was one ever-prized quality which he had, in the aesthetic domain, it was the quality of vehemence in inspiration and of creative intoxication. He noted in 1911 during a stay in Germany: "To be an artist, it is no use having God in one's heart if one is not possessed by the devil." Throughout his life, he praised disorder, the delights of the imagination, in contrast, according to the preface of *Le Soulier de satin,* to order and the delight of reason. Resorting to a questionable etymology, he assured us that "trouver" means the same as "turbare," to disturb everything, to upset order and create confusion, to agitate, first of all, the bottom of the basket or the vat. A confused disorder on the desk of a writer or a diplomat forces him to shake everything helter-skelter and thus to make some discovery, instead of leaving unresolved business lying in well-arranged, neatly piled up files (*Journal,* 1924). Much earlier, in accents resembling those of a pythoness in a state of trance, or in the tone of a person inspired by the Muses, he had extolled this bounding liberty which resists being curbed in any way.

Oh, my soul, you must not arrange any plans!
Oh, my wild soul, we must keep ourselves free and ready,
Like the immense frail flocks of swallows when, without
a sound, autumn's call resounds!
      ("Les Muses," *Cinq grandes Odes*)

and, in the same volume ("La Muse qui est la grâce"):

Ah! I am intoxicated! Ah! I have surrendered to God!
I hear a voice within me, and the rhythm which becomes
faster, the movement of joy!

By temperament, Claudel, was in fact a passionate man, a Nietz-schean who longed for power (without having read Nietzsche), and the first of his heroes, Tête d'or, embodied this aspect of combative nature which he knew was his own. Several times, he alluded to the verse in Chapter II of St. Matthew's Gospel, in which "it is written that the meek will inherit the earth, but the passionate will conquer heaven" (*Journal,* 1936). The drama of the possession of the earth, as he called *Tête d'or,* was also his own. He hated the weak and submissive, perhaps even the humble. "We are not created to be understood; we are in this universe to conquer it." It was literally "a surprise attack on God" that he had wanted to carry out, and which he transposed to the one character whom he created most like himself, Mésa. He had feared the discovery, which was delayed for a long time, of woman and of his own passionate nature. He had wished to find peace and protection against himself, in 1901, by entering a Benedictine monastery. He reported that God responded to him with a very firm "No." Certainly his confessors were not mistaken about his true nature: he loved force and fighting. With some audacity and at the risk of shocking his most timid readers, he made Acer, one of the interlocutors of his strange and often forceful *Conversations dans le Loir-et-Cher,* present a passionate eulogy of war "which has taught us to love what is not ours and to count as nothing what we possess. It is war which establishes between men relationships other than those based on money."

Since Claudel's death, it is no longer indiscreet to mention the great influence which had been exercised over him by his sister Camille, who was born four years before him and died in 1943. More than half of the life of this woman, a sculptress of exceptional talent, an impetuous and passionate woman, an unbeliever from an early age, had been spent in a mental hospital. Claudel spoke with terror, as if he himself felt threatened by it, of this "insanity brought on more rapidly by a dreadful violence of character and a terrible talent for mockery." He himself always admired the daring of great creators, and of great sinners, the only men fit for salvation. In art as well as in life, he took up again Danton's cry, always demanding more audacity: *Quantum potes, tantum aude* was also his formula in art. He did not quote very much from the Gospels, and even less from St. Francis, just like another man who praises fighting and war, Teilhard de Chardin. Buddhism, with its lesson of resignation and its total condemnation of matter and created things, was almost as repulsive to him as Jansenism, which he so often attacked. In his opinion, the "Messieurs de Port-Royal" whom he called "those bad men," and Pascal most of all, who were incapable of hearing the music of the heavens and who declared them eternally silent, only represented "a stunting of Christian thought instead of the great inspiration of the Church Fathers and St. Thomas" (statement cited by Henri Guillemin in *Pas à pas,* 1969). He considered the Protestants even worse; they wish to stifle this "romanticism" which is man's most precious element.

Like those men of 1820–1850 who had been inspired by Rousseau, like more than one modern pagan (D. H. Lawrence or Giono) whom Claudel would not have liked (however, it is true that he enjoyed Ramuz, who was more biblical), this great Catholic felt a nostalgia for a primitive innocence and for a world that was still pure. In spite of some internal hesitation, he had to believe in original sin, without which there would be no need for a Redeemer. But, contrary to Mauriac and other Catholics, he did not consider that nature itself was full of traps into which aegipans, satyrs and nymphs try to make us fall. He always repeated that creation was beautiful and undefiled. "Open your eyes," he exclaimed in his *Art poétique,* "the world is still untouched, it is as pure as on the first day of creation, as fresh as milk! Man gets to know the world, not by what he steals from it, but by what he adds to it of himself." There is no need to call "pantheistic" this faith of a man for whom everything was imbued with the divine. But, according to him, one of the tasks of the poet was to give meaning to things by giving them a name. "Through him, all things become explicable"), he said of the poet in *La Ville.* Mallarmé's statement had impressed him: "Poetry is a hymn that everything creates with everything." He was not very fond of Lamartine or Shelley, whom he did not consider courageous or masterful enough. Goethe, with his wisdom which was too prosaic for his liking, his Faust who became an engineer and a swamp clearer, or the characters of *Affinités électives* and their petty worries as provincial landlords, was, for many reasons, his pet aversion. But he felt and expressed the poetry of the sea as Byron, Lautréamont, and Michelet had been able to do. "And, the whole day, I study the sea as one reads the eyes of a woman who understands" (*Connaissance de l'est*). He did not really like Mozart, but he adored Beethoven's last quartets and, above all, Berlioz. He did not use the words "gouffre" ("abyss") and "vertige" ("dizziness") as dramatically as Hugo or Rimbaud had done. But he made room for the invisible without rejecting anything visible. "The object of poetry is the universe of visible things to which Faith adds the universe of invisible things" *(Positions et propositions).* He liked storms as much as René, and, like Hugo, he treated haughtily those who only used words of so-called classical moderation, simplicity, and order. Gide, he stated on one of his less charitable days (there were quite a few of them), "imagines that he is simple because he is dull and that he is classical because he is colorless."

Finally and especially, in spite of his immense pride and his conviction that God had chosen him on the famous night of conversion and had assigned to him the mission of a converting apostle, Claudel was always troubled by the feeling that nothing in him, or by him, was finished, complete. He reworked, or would gladly have reworked, some of his dramas, two, three, or even four times. Behind the grumpy dogmatism which he readily displayed, he hid great doubts about himself. He spoke ill of romantic love because he had been its hero and victim and had estimated its full force. The work of this apparent despiser of woman was, as early as *Tête d'or* and *La Ville,* obsessed by the need and temptation of woman who was absent at that time:

> There is in us something unused, something which has not emerged, and perhaps, just what is best and most profound in us.

It is precisely the woman's role to draw that out of us. He declared to woman: "You are the promise which cannot be kept and therein lies your charm." In *Le Soulier de satin,* Rodrigue, who also was a conqueror of the soul, as well as an adventurer and knight of the impossible, confided to his Chinese servant that he loved and desired *everything* in Prouhèze, her body as well as her immortal soul. Claudel returned to the subject of this immoderate demand, impossible to satisfy in this world: "What she demands is everything in him who demands everything in another; a man should give himself completely to her.")

When Mésa, who bore the name of a king of *La Légende des siècles,* discovered himself, he greedily demanded everything from Ysé with no less romanticism and materiality than the Wagnerian Tristan. He knew the power of a woman's hair, just as well as Baudelaire and Mallarmé, and the Baroque poets before them. "Keep that horrible hay well tied," he exclaimed at the end of the great lyrical drama. Finally, when he was close to finding God, he cried out in a supreme swoon:

Ah! This is the same hair, ah! I recognize its
odour.
When my face and nose were buried in you as in a deep hole,
The same hair!

Thanks to this crazy need for woman, man has understood how
divided and alone he is, and has constantly yearned for a whole, an
infinite which he could only find in God. "The unextinguishable idol,"
as Claudel called woman, spreads darkness in the conscience of man.
But she is also "one who revives paradise."

Claudel, whose critical faculty could be most keen, at certain times
one of the most lucid and even wisest of his century, did not conceal
his romanticism in his literary judgments either. Sometimes he
showed himself to be terribly unjust to the French classicists of the
seventeenth century and particularly to Corneille. He preferred *La
Tour de Nesles* to *Le Cid. Polyeucte,* which Péguy had extolled as the
great Christian drama, seemed even worse to him; of course, Claudel
considered Péguy insufferable. Claudel thought that the author of
Polyeucte was "false, affected, declamatory, dramatic, and artificial."
He was just as hard on the Racine of *Bérénice:* ("This sentimental
affectation of style . . . is what I detest most in French literature. . . . It
is refined and boring.") It is true that, at another time, he wrote a
booklet to extol Racine: *Conversation sur Jean Racine* (1954). He
doomed the souls of Renan, Michelet, Hugo, and other infamous men
to hell and decay, along with dead dogs. But elsewhere, he hailed
Michelet as a sublime visionary, the greatest of French prose-writers,
"our great Michelet" (*Oeuvres complètes,* Vol. XVIII, pp. 85–90), and
that was in the course of an extravagant eulogy of romanticism: "The
period 1830–1870 witnessed the most powerful imaginative movement which had appeared in the world since the 'chansons de geste'."
He detested Stendhal, who was undoubtedly not romantic enough for
his liking, but he praised to the skies Balzac, George Sand, Alexandre
Dumas, and . . . Paul Féval and Eugène Sue. His attitude towards
Victor Hugo was curious. In 1908, in his *Journal* he declared that he
was "a great poet, if it is possible to be one without intelligence, or
taste, or sensibility, or order." But when he was at the Copenhagen
Museum, meditating in front of the bust of Victor carved by Rodin, he
wrote *(Positions et propositions)* admirable lines of this "great suffering
soul" and on Hugo's most customary sentiment, which was fright. He
concluded: "He has not seen God, but no one has drawn so many
things out of the darkness brought about by the absence of God."
Elsewhere, Claudel mentioned what a lasting impression *Hernani* had
made on him, especially the final scene of the horn. It was to this

drama that he owed his revelation of the theater. Again, in another work, he ranked very high *Les Travailleurs de la mer* and *L'Homme qui rit.*

> The Romantic muse teaches us that indignation too is a necessary and noble sentiment, that dissatisfaction with egoism and injustice is something wholesome and beautiful, and which deserved to rouse in a strong soul all the powers of expression.
>
>   (Vol. XVIII, cinq morceaux sur Hugo.)

Claudel's judgments were so spontaneous, so violent, like the contradictions of an irritable man, that one must undoubtedly treat them lightly, as they were formulated. Henri Guillemin has certainly not attributed a lie to him when he quoted him as saying: "It is so much better not to know what is in the books one is speaking about. That allows us to be more peremptory." But the publication of Claudel's letters, in particular to an American friend, Agnes Meyer, in whom he confided more than in anybody else, reveal him to be more passionate—tenderly passionate at times—than one had suspected. The ambassador to Washington, worried and often feeling that he was misunderstood, declared to her on May 15, 1929: "Dear Agnes, the important word is not *action,* nor *enjoyment,* nor even *creation,* but *love." (Cahier canadien Claudel,* VI, Ottawa, 1969).

CONCLUSION

This outline of what we call the survival, and often the exacerbation, of romanticism since 1840 has been centered on the one modern literature we feel we know, the French. But it would not be difficult for scholars of other literatures of this century to show that the vitality of romanticism has been even more evident in Germany, where one has rightly been able to deplore in Hitlerism a destructive explosion of the irrational[13] and an outbreak of Faustian elements, enamored of the colossal and of nihilism, which Germany has often paradoxically associated with its genius for meticulous organization and obedience to the administrative hierarchies. The America of the mid-twentieth century, after having witnessed a few attempts, begun by sober-minded academics, to establish a neo-humanism favoring moderation, order, and moral and aesthetic restraints, proclaims itself incurably romantic through its Black, Jewish, Southern, and other kinds of writers, swearing only by the sexual, social, political, moral, or supramoral revolution. As one of its novelists and critics, Leslie Fiedler, has admitted, at the end of long discussions on the rules with which the novel should comply, the American writer, no matter how hard he tries to be "classical" with conviction, always ends up by becoming romantic.[14] Never before had the youth of the country, which was considered to be dedicated to the qualities of efficiency and hard work, fed so much on utopias (some of which had been revived from Fourier's and Cabet's times) as after 1965. England had witnessed, after the First World War, especially with the most uncompromising anti-romantic, T. S. Eliot, a systematic attempt to extol the cult of traditional and intellectual values. The attempt soon proved abortive. Twenty years after his death in 1930, D. H. Lawrence became the idol of readers, even of academics and—supreme ratification—of film directors. Stephen Spender did not manage to avoid in his poetry the romantic clichés of former times; he was a better essayist than poet, and he campaigned on behalf of a more accurate appreciation of romanticism in *The Destructive Element, a Study of Modern Writers and Beliefs* (London, Jonathon Cape, 1935) and especially in his sympathetic presentation of the English romantics in an article published in *The English Review* (XIV, March 1947, pp. 288–300). Francis Scarfe, a scholar of French literature, a poet and a discriminating commentator of poetry, was one of the first to protest, as early as 1942, against the excessive sophistication of English poetry of the period between the two World Wars, in his work *Auden and After: the liberation of Poetry, 1930–1941* (London, Rutledge, 1945). The experience of life after he had lost his father in the First World War, his brief encounters with surrealism and communism, the shock of the Civil War in Spain had opened his eyes. He wanted to testify for the younger generation which was attracted by the expression of ardent emotions in literature. Several of these young men of 1945–1960 had assembled in groups with the slogan of *La Nouvelle Apocalypse* (1939) or *Le Cavalier blanc* (1941). Their motto was total freedom in art and the individual pursuit by each artist of his creative originality:

> The Romantic artist is in the vanguard of human sensibility; he leaves the world richer than he had found it. . . . Romanticism is the spirit which springs into life; it is the spark of the Creator, which, one day, will flash like lightning from tired eyes and perceive the paradise that God has tried to create.
>
> (Introduction by the two authors, Stefan Schimanski and Henry Treece to *A New Romantic Anthology,* London, Grey Walls Press, 1949)

The most sonorous and the best virtuoso among the neo-romantic poets, who, on the other side of the English Channel, had undoubtedly rallied to surrealism, is the Welshman Dylan Thomas. His poetry—rich in sounds, in images, in leaps over the links of coherent language, and obsessed by death—and his intense life, which had been foolishly wasted (he died in 1953 at the age of thirty-nine), consist of the purest romanticism of Byron or Beddoes relived a century and a half later.

In all these countries, the romanticism of the twentieth century constitutes, like the romanticism of the previous hundred and fifty years, a claiming of spontaneity in art, of creative liberty against the forces which, more and more, want to reduce man to a mere cog in the machinery of compartmentalized civilization. The greatness of this romanticism lies in having taught us that harmony does not necessarily exist between the order of things (or perhaps their fundamental disorder) and the consciousness of man, eager for clarity and for well-ordered security in his thoughts. Camus saw in this irremediable discord the great source of the sentiment of the absurd which should drive modern man first to revolt, then to the creation of a different universe, that of art. There is sometimes a certain affectation in this revolt and some intoxication of words in this return to emotion, to the irrational, to the forces of instinct, which can only be savagely destructive. But in all this, there is also a legitimate protest against traditional humanism, which, until the irruption of these romantics, enjoyed its intellectual complaisance too indolently and imagined itself free from anguish in its firm belief that the reign of rational progress had begun. By repressing or avoiding this romanticism, too many artists risk growing poorer or condemning themselves to a dull barrenness. One of the most genuine poets of this century, Pierre Reverdy, whose style is severe, and who, more than anyone else, has avoided any declamation and flamboyant histrionism, has rightly stated in his *Gant de crin* (Plon, 1926):

> It is difficult for the artist to live without romanticism. If he does not introduce it in his works, he introduces it into his life; if he does not introduce it into his life, he preserves it in his dreams. . . . When one has got rid of romanticism, one has generally lapsed into a distressing dullness.

Notes

INTRODUCTION

1. Frederic Saint-Aubyn, "Entretien avec Michel Butor", *The French Review* (New York), XXXVI, No. 1, October 1962, pp. 1–12.

CHAPTER 1

1. The best work on the eighteenth century concept of poetry is that of Margaret Gilman, *The Idea of Poetry in France, from Houdar de la Motte to Baudelaire* (Harvard University Press, 1958). The author alters slightly the commonly held point of view by considering Baudelaire as the result, and also the model, by which everything that preceded him must be judged. It is only with him that she sees poetic theory in France focusing on the role of imagination as "queen of all faculties," and she looks upon Diderot as his most inspired precursor. Before Diderot, Abbé du Bos and Rémond de Saint-Mard had established themselves as apologists of enthusiasm, which is one form of imagination (and sensitivity). Another important work, which is also written in English, is that of Robert Finch, *The Sixth Sense. Individualism in French Poetry, 1686–1760*. He has borrowed his title from Abbé du Bos who meant by "sixth sense" an intuitive sense of taste that allows the appreciation of poetry. But the author does not really succeed in rehabilitating Gresset, Lefranc de Pompignan, and Louis Racine, or even their sometimes ingenious views of what poetry should be.

2. A work by Henri Potez, which was written a long time ago, *L'elégie en France avant le romantisme (1778–1820)* (Calmann-Levy, 1897) is still an excellent one. An American, Henry A. Grubbs, has written, with as much courage as good judgment, a fairly long and very sensible work about *Jean-Baptiste Rousseau* (Princeton University Press). Jean Roudaut has tried, most daringly, to rehabilitate the poetry of the eighteenth century in a perspicacious article in *Cahiers du Sud* (No. 350, April 1959). He opposes

this poetry of logical thought to that of analogical thought, and he insinuates that the poems of Valéry, Bonnefoy, and Breton's *Ode à Charles Fourier* are not so different as all that from this poetry that has been much too discredited. A less assertive article, but one that is equally discriminating, by Léon-Gabriel Gros, in the same issue of *Cahiers du Sud,* is entitled: "Poésie bien-disante, poètes maudits." M. Guitton is completing an important work on descriptive poetry of the same period, that of Delille.

3. We have tried to consider several aspects of this question of sincerity in literature (in the works of Diderot, Rousseau, the romantics, Gide, and modern writers, among others) in *Literature and Sincerity* (Yale University Press, 1963).

4. We are referring to the scholarly and also prudent work of the Englishman J. G. Robertson, *Studies in the Genesis of the Romantic Theory in the Eighteenth Century* (Cambridge University Press, 1923).

5. Diderot's frequent statements on passion, which anticipate Musset, are well-known: "A man without passion is like a musical instrument of which the strings have been cut or which never had any strings," and "Forceful ideas also have their sublimity . . . the bull is finer than the ox . . . , crime, perhaps, than virtue, cruel gods than good gods."

6. Three very detailed and interesting articles, among many others, have clearly brought out this anguish of the preromantics. Their authors are Armand Hoog for the first two, Mauzi for the third: "Un cas d'angoisse préromantique", *Revue des sciences humaines,* No. 67, July-September 1952; "L'âme préromantique et les instincts de mort", *Bulletin de la Faculté des Lettres de Strasbourg,* 1952; "Les Maladies de l'âme au XVIIIe siècle", *Revue des sciences humaines,* No. 100, October-December 1960.

7. Julien Green, "Au seuil des temps nouveaux," *Fontaine,* Nos. 27–28 (Algiers), August, 1943. *Ecrivains et poetes des Etats-Unis.*

8. It was not a Frenchman of 1968, but Goethe in 1812, who declared: "The incredible arrogance of the young will result in a very few years in the worst kind of follies."

CHAPTER 2

1. See Blanchot, *La Nouvelle Revue française,* January 1956.

CHAPTER 3

1. It is not easy to consult the seven quarto volumes and the two in-folio volumes of Le Globe; but Pierre Trahard, in *Le romantisme défini par le Globe,* Presses Françaises, 1925, has quoted the most significant definitions of romanticism contained in them. The most valuable work on the chronology of romanticism is René Bray's *Chronologie du romantisme* (Boivin, 1932). Pierre Martino and Edmond Eggli had begun a very useful series of volumes, only one of which has been published, along with an excellent preface: *Le débat romantique en France (1813–1830). Pamphlets, Manifestes, polémiques de presse,* Les Belles-Lettres, 1933.

2. Mrs. C. Roe, in a well-written article "Les véritables origines du roman-

tisme français," *Revue d'histoire littéraire de la France,* 36 (1929), pp. 202–220, had stressed this point.

CHAPTER 4

1. A very interesting study could be done on the German men and women who became French nationals at the end of the eighteenth century and throughout the nineteenth century; some of them changed nationality due to marriage with Frenchmen (Mme de Bernis, the person who became Flaubert's Mme Arnoux, the wives of Edgar Quinet and Mallarmé); others were scientists (including several Jews), bankers, and philosophers (from d'Holbach to H. Heine or Alexandre Weil). The few allusions or quotations that we have inserted here are partly taken from Jacques Droz' remarkable work, *L'Allemagne et la Révolution française* (Presses Universitaires de France, 1949). An excellent series of articles, by Henri Focillon and Adolphe Guéroult among others, on "La Révolution de 1798 et la pensée moderne" appeared in the *Revue philosophique,* 1939, Vol. CXXVIII, Nos. 9–12.

2. Henri Guillemin, a critic who, although Catholic, disapproves strongly of the established order and of reassuring views, has dwelt on eulogies of the Revolution by Lamartine (after 1830) and by many of his predecessors, in the second part of his long thesis *Le Jocelyn de Lamartine* (published by Boivin in 1936).

3. Virgil, or perhaps a pseudo-Virgil, angry at a Bathyllus who had appropriated his verses, had compared him to birds which take possession of the nest of other birds or to bees who distill their honey for others, in famous lines which begin with the words *Sic vos non vobis.*

4. There is a vast amount of literature on economic history in different languages. The most comprehensive recent work is *The Unbound Prometheus* by the American David S. Landes (Cambridge University Press, England, 1969). It traces technological changes and industrial development in Western Europe from 1750 onwards. The same author had edited a collection of essays by several authors in 1966, entitled *The Rise of Capitalism* (New York, Macmillan). Consult also W. O. Henderson, *The Industrial Revolution on the Continent* (London, Frank Cass and Co., 1914).

5. His study, "Early Use of the Term 'Industrial Revolution' ", appeared in the *Quarterly Journal of Economics* in 1922 (Vol. XXXV, 343 sq.) and was greatly praised by an eminent English historian, George Norman Clark, in his booklet *The Idea of Industrial Revolution* (Glasgow, Jackson and Son, 1952).

6. The English literary historian, Herbert J. Hunt, went as far as writing in the foreword of his book, *Le socialisme et le romantisme en France* (Oxford, 1935): "Extreme industrialism or, if you like, 'irrational imperialism,' which was a dominant trait of romanticism, led logically to socialism."

7. Here is an example: "Germany, with its marvellous treasures and its wise philosophy which are hidden from us by the mystery of its language, a modern orient, which like the phoenix, rises out of the dead ashes of the ancient orient . . . , Germany is beginning to partly open its doors and disclose to us the sanctuaries of its philosophy." It is commonly known that,

later on, both Victor Hugo and Michelet (as well as Ernest Hello) hailed Germany, with awe, as "the India of Europe."

8. *Procès du saint-simonisme,* Librairie Saint-Simonienne, 1832, p. 278.

9. Consult Herbert J. Hunt, *Le socialisme et le romantisme en France: étude de la presse socialiste de 1830 à 1848,* Oxford, Clarendon Press, 1935; David Owen Evans, *Social Romanticism in France,* 1830–1848, Oxford, Clarendon Press, 1951; Frank E. Manuel, *The Prophets of Paris,* Cambridge, U.S., Harvard University Press, 1962.

CHAPTER 5

1. George Sand, in her book *Histoire de ma vie,* which although it was unequal in quality and disorganized, revealed romantic sensibility very well, related how, drawn by water, when she felt a similar adolescent disgust for life before really having lived, she advanced on horseback to drown herself in a river and was saved only by her tutor who held her back.

2. An article by an Englishman has dwelt on this ambiguity of *René:* D. G. Charlton, "The Ambiguity of 'René' ", *French Studies* (Oxford), XXIII, 3 (July 1969), 229–243.

3. A maidservant had poisoned two of his brothers and sisters with arsenic and almost succeeded in poisoning both his parents. His father killed himself out of grief after the loss of his son, and another of his brothers. His few poems, like so many others at that time, were filled with his complaints: "I am young and yet I am robbed of gaiety."

4. Article reprinted in Francis Dumont, *Les petits romantiques français,* 1949.

5. He vehemently refused to allow himself to be called "the Victor Hugo of painting" and declared "I am a pure classicist," from the beginning of his *Journal;* at the same time, he added: "If one understands by romanticism the free manifestation of one's personal impressions, not only am I a romantic now, but I was one at the age of fifteen"; on May 8, 1824 he remarked about himself: "If I am not agitated like a serpent in the hands of a pythoness, I am cold."

6. In his *Ahasvérus* (1833), Quinet, who was also very romantic and has been unfairly neglected by literary history, wrote: "The world is bored; it no longer knows what to do. . . . A strange malady plagues us without respite today." Joseph de Maistre, a philosopher who endeavored to be a prophet of the past but who admired more than he realized the Revolution in France, from his native Savoy, had noted in his *Soirées de Saint-Pétersbourg:* "Man today no longer seems to be able to live within the former limits ascribed to human abilities. He wants to go beyond them; he gets agitated like an indignant eagle in his cage."

CHAPTER 6

1. On the attitude of French writers and scholars of the seventeenth century toward the Middle Ages, there is an elaborate work written in English by Nathan Edelman, *Attitudes of Seventeenth Century France toward the Middle Ages* (New York, King's Crown Press, 1946), which was to be fol-

lowed by a second volume on the attitude toward Medieval art. René Lanson has written a short illustrated work on *Le goût du Moyen Age en France au XVIIIe siècle* (Paris and Brussels, Architecture et Arts décoratifs, 1926). A cautious article on Alexandre Lenoir has weighed his merits and faults: Yvan Christ, in *Jardin des Arts,* No. 172, March 1969, 2–13.

2. Georges Poulet has written a charming and suggestive meditation on "Nerval, Gautier et la blonde aux yeux noirs" in his *Trois essais de mythologie romantique, Corti,* 1966. It would take more than one volume to deal with the concept that the romantics had of the sixteenth and the beginning of the seventeenth centuries and the sense of affinity which they felt with the Renaissance. It is a well-known fact that Balzac has been credited with using the word "renaissance" (and no longer "renaissance des lettres") for the first time in *Le Bal de Sceaux* (1829).

3. Hugo has used the term "surnaturalisme" ("supernaturalism") twice in the little known but revealing notes published after his death with the title *Post-scriptum de ma vie* or *Promontorium Somnii:* "The poet par excellence has three visions: humanity, nature, supernaturalism." Of course, Baudelaire, who has also spoken of "surnaturalisme", was not familiar with these notes.

4. The literature dealing with the interpretation of mythology and the romantic visions of antiquity is vast. Only a few titles can be mentioned here: Pierre Albouy, *Mythes et mythologies dans la littérature française* (A. Colin, 1969); Paul Böckmann, *Hoelderlin und seine Götter* (Munich, Beck, 1935); Douglas Bush, *Mythology and the Romantic Tradition in English Poetry* (Harvard University Press, 1937); E. M. Butler, *The Tyranny of Greece over Germany* (Cambridge University Press, 1935); Henry Hatfield, *Aesthetic Paganism in German Literature* (Harvard University Press, 1964); Henri Peyre, *Louis Ménard* (Yale University Press, 1932) and *Bibliographie critique de l'hellénisme en France* (1843–1870) (Ibid.); Albert Py, *Les mythes grecs dans la poésie de Victor Hugo* (Droz, 1963); J. G. Robertson, *The Gods of Greece in German Poetry* (Oxford Press, 1924); Fritz Strich, *Die Mythologie in der deutschen Literatur von Klopstock bis Wagner* (Halle, 1910).

CHAPTER 7

1. Note to a scholarly and precise article, "L'évolution de la pensée religieuse en France," *Revue de littérature comparée,* XXIX, No. 1, January-March 1965, 135–144. On Christ's role in the poetry of the four most representative poets of romanticism, there is an American thesis by Mother Maria Consolata, Bryn Mawr, Pennsylvania, 1947.

2. On the subject of romanticism and religion, besides Auguste Viatte's book, various articles or works are mentioned in the bibliography at the end of this volume, under the names of Victor Giraud, Joussain, etc.

3. Paul de Musset related that his brother had planned to analyze himself, perhaps in order to cure himself, in a work the title of which was first to be *Le rocher de Sisyphe* and later *Le poète déchu.* As a matter of fact, Alfred de Musset had declared to him, in one of those unfulfilled promises of which there are so many also in Baudelaire's correspondence: "Today, I placed my early youth, my laziness, and my vanity in their coffin and nailed it shut with my

own hands. I seem about to speak and it is as if there is something in my soul that demands to be let out."

4. Found in an appendix to Volume II of Marius Guyard's edition of *Les Misérables,* Garnier, 1957.

5. Albert Béguin, who has written sympathetically and objectively about him, rightly says: "Spiritually as well as with regard to temporal problems, Lamennais is a romantic: an emotional, intuitive and warm-hearted person—not a rigorous man at all"), *Esprit,* April 1954, p. 580.

6. It was often foreigners rather than their own compatriots who were drawn by their lucubrations and their profoundness: David Owen Evans, *Le socialisme romantique, Pierre Leroux* (Marcel Rivière, 1948); David Albert Griffiths, *Jean Reynaud, encyclopédiste de l' époque romantique* (Marcel Rivière, 1965); R. J. North, "Alexandre Weill," in *Currents of Thought in French Literature, Essays in memory of G. T. Clapton* (Oxford, Blackwell, 1965); Frank Bowman, *Eliphas Lévi, visionnaire romantique* (Presses Universitaires de France, 1969).

7. Albert Béguin, with the greatest insight, has drawn the attention of the Frenchmen of this century to the role of the dream in the works of the German romanticists, and has given importance to the lines, quoted above, by Novalis. Maeterlinck, during the symbolist period, and later excellent German scholars (Spenlé, Lichtenberger) had already understood and loved Novalis.

8. Consult "Le panthéisme dans les lettres françaises au XVIIIe siècle," by Hassan El Nouty, *Revue des sciences humaines,* No. 100, October-December 1960, 435–457.

9. Teilhard de Chardin has often cited, as the sentence on which was based his vision of a future which would substitute christogenesis for biogenesis, the verse from the First Epistle to the Corinthians (XV, 28) which ends with the words: "that God may be everything to everyone."

10. Henri Focillon, *La peinture au XIXe siècle* (Henri Laurens, 1927, Vol. I, Preface).—The works to which our text implicitly refers are: Michel Carrouges, *La mystique du surhomme* (Gallimard, 1948); Léon Cellier, *L'epopée romantique* (Presses Universitaires, 1954); Herbert J. Hunt, *The Epic in Nineteenth Century France* (Oxford, Blackwell, 1941); Maurice J. Schroder, *Icarus, The Image of the Artist in French Romanticism* (Harvard University Press, 1961).

CHAPTER 8

1. The reputation that regions of the South have of being inclined to verbal inflation and great oratorical flow is, all the same, not really justified by their poetry. Neither Dante, nor Leopardi, nor Montale, nor the Spanish mystics nor the poets of the productive generation of 1898 have misused words. On the contrary, they are masters of suggestive condensation and almost of a deliberate baldness of style that one usually terms "classical." Reverdy, born like Valéry in the department of Hérault, has been more on his guard against amplification than Claudel, Breton, or Eluard, who are from the Northern half of France, and Char is very fond of aphorisms.

2. These are the magnificent and stirring alexandrines which begin with "Amour, être de l'être, amour, âme de l'âme . . ." ("Love, being of the being, love, soul of the soul . . .")

3. The author of this work, without being a scholar of English literature, feels he could be classed among them. In a book entitled *Shelley et la France: lyrisme anglais et lyrisme français au XIXe siècle* (Le Caire, 1935), he has declared that English romantic poetry was superior, in many respects, to the French. We are thinking here particularly of Emile Legouis, *Défense de la poésie française à l'usage des lecteurs anglais* (London, Constable, 1912) and of Louis Cazamian, "Retour d'un infidèle à la poésie française," *Essais en deux langues* (Didier, 1938).

4 A long work by François Germain, in 1961, has dealt with *L'imagination d'Alfred de Vigny.* On the other hand, one of the best Hugo scholars, J. B. Barrère, has written with great finesse, in three volumes, *La fantaisie de Victor Hugo.*

5. We have dealt briefly with this point in an article on "Le peu d'influence de Baudelaire," *Revue d'histoire littéraire de la France,* Vol. 67, No. 2 (June 1967), pp. 424–436. The references to the frequent eulogies of the imagination by Vigny are in *Journal d'un poète* and *Stello:* "Imagination, with its elect, is as superior to judgment, alone with its orators, as the gods of Olympus are to the demigods", said Dr. Noir (1832).

6. In the article "Le symbolisme de Baudelaire", which appeared first in the American review, *Symposium,* in 1951, and was republished in *Ames et visages romantiques* (Corti, 1965), pp. 231–245. Consult another article by the same author, "De la symbolique religieuse à la poésie symboliste," in *Comparative Literature Studies* (University of Maryland), Vol. IX, Nos. 1–2, 1967, pp. 5–16. Let us cite here a few curious texts of the many that one could collect on premature symbolism portended by various minds of the Romantic era: "The true, the good, and the beautiful are only forms of the infinite. What do we love by loving truth, beauty, and virtue? We love the infinite itself. Love of the infinite substance is hidden beneath love of its forms. . . . Art is a reproduction of the infinite by the finite." Victor Cousin, *Du Vrai, du Beau et du Bien,* Lesson 8 (published by Adolphe Garnier in 1836). "Our poetry . . . is a symbol, and this is what all true poetry must be" *(Orphée)* and "All senses are mutually aroused. There would be as it were, onomatopoeia of colors, as everything is so harmonious in man and the universe" *(La Ville des expiations,* Ballanche). "Poetry is only a sequence of symbols present in the mind to make it conceive the invisible . . . Every object, every idea is, to a certain degree, a symbol. Every idea that we understand effectively arouses in us the concept of what it is, and the idea of something else besides which it is not . . . The romantic prefers vague symbols to precise ones. . . . The romantic tends to spiritualize material nature, and the classicist to materialize spiritual nature. . . . All visible things are symbols." (Jouffroy, *Cours d'esthétique de 1822,* published by Damiron in 1843, Lesson XVIII, pp. 133, 137–138.) "The aim of art is not the exact reproduction of nature, but the creation, by means of the forms and colors that it gives us, of a microcosm in which dreams, sensations, and ideas, inspired in us by the aspect of the world, can live and be produced." (Théophile Gautier, *Le Moniteur,* November 18,

1864). There is scarcely any difference between such declarations and, during the period that is called symbolist, those of Rodin (repeating that everything is symbol, in his book on art, Chapter VIII), of Huysmans, *La Cathédrale* (assigning a divine source to the symbol, after Hugues de Saint-Victor), and of Paul Adams, who repeats in his *Vues d'Amérique* (Ollendorf, 1906, pp. 468, 470) "art is the work of expressing a thought by means of a symbol . . . , art is the work of inscribing a dogma in a symbol." But the language of the symbolists was often more veiled and filled with strange neologisms.

CHAPTER 9

1. On this subject of generations and the way in which they seem to be divided or grouped in different literatures, we have written a work, *"Les générations littéraires"* (Boivin, 1958). Richard Chadbourne has written a suggestive essay on "The Generation of 1848," in *Essays in French Literature* (University of Western Australia Press, No. 5, November, 1968).

2. In this modernness of romanticism, Baudelaire also perceived undoubtedly the interest taken in the representation of the ineradicable evil in man, the diabolical elements in him. In his article of 1852 on "L'essence du rire", he praised the romantic school "or one of its subdivisions, the satanic school, for having understood the primary law of laughter" (that laughter arises from the arrogant conviction that the one who laughs has of his own superiority).

3. Maxime du Camp, a member of the *Académie française* and a methodical man, was dismissed from two Parisian high-schools and placed "under arrest" for four days in one of these schools, for having dared to praise *Les Feuilles d'automne,* and this was in 1838! "Abominable book," he was told. He had to copy both Horace's and Boileau's *Poetic Art,* "to develop his taste," declared the headmaster. He recalled what a great impression the play *Chatterton* made on Flaubert and himself. Du Camp has written in his very romantic personal novel, *Les Forces perdues:* "We develop from our early reveries such an exalted idea of existence that we demand from it more than it has the capacity for and we do not forgive it for only offering to us what it comprises."

4. Jacques Monge has emphasized the "Proustian" aspect (before its time) of *Dominique* in "Un précurseur de Proust: Fromentin et la mémoire affective, *Revue d'histoire littéraire de la France,* Vol. 61, No. 4, October-December 1861, pp. 564–588. The rather severe reservations that *Dominique* can give rise to in a modern reader have been expressed with the greatest insight by Philippe Garcin, "Le souvenir dans Dominque," *Nouvelle Revue française,* January 1957, pp. 111–121.

5. We do not claim to analyze here all the writers affected by the romantic malady among those who, born between 1820 and 1829, were steeped, during their youth, in romantic literature and dreams. But let us recall, however, Taine's friend, Prévost-Paradol, who entered the *École Normale* a year after him, a talented thinker, who, while ambassador to Washington, committed suicide in 1870. Émile Montégut, born in 1826, was one of the most remarkable essayists of the last century and has written a short master-

piece, "Les confidences d'un hypocondriaque", in his *Types littéraires et fantaisies esthétiques* (Hachette, 1882). He has also written with feeling about Musset and Gautier, and, with a rare finesse blended with irony, on *Hamlet* and *Werther*. The *Journal* of Amiel (born in 1821) has revealed on numerous occasions the Faustian impulses of the Genevan. On July 14, 1859, for example, having reread Faust, he confessed: "I too am reduced to nothingness and I shudder on the brink of the great empty abysses in my interior being, in the grip of nostalgia of the unknown, craving for the infinite, dejected by the ineffable. I too experience at times those secret passions of life, those desperate transports of happiness, but much more often I suffer from complete depression and silent despair. And from what does that result? . . . from an uneasy and gnawing doubt which makes life impossible and laughs derisively at every hope." The history of this "mal du siècle" long after 1840 or 1850 would make a fine and sad book.

6. In his *Mémoires intérieurs* (Flammarion, 1960), the elderly novelist who had begun by writing the ultra-romantic poems of *Mains jointes* (1909) and passionate stories like *La chair et le sang* (1920), wrote sternly: "The history of French romanticism is that of an unsuccessful attempt to escape beyond the limits of reality. In its worst aspect, its theater, it escapes from the observable only to fall into the trap of showiness and shallowness; and in its best aspect, its lyric poetry, it continues to be the effusion of the most ordinary and completely superficial sentiments. The sadness of Olympio is the most banal and widely shared thing in the world." (p. 242). Mauriac's contemporary Jacques Rivière, who was, however, an agitated soul himself as well, was even more severe in 1913 in his great article on "Le roman d'aventure," reprinted in the posthumous collection of *Nouvelles études*.

7. See Carl Frake, *Zola als romantischer Dichter* (Marburg, 1914) and John C. Lapp, *Zola before the Rougon-Macquart* (University of Toronto Press, 1965).

8. A volume of posthumous works of Aurier (who died in 1892), presented by Rémy de Gourmont, appeared in 1893 *(Mercure de France)*. In it, the critic seemed to be hard on the impressionists; he had become the spokesman for a symbolism enamored of romantic passion and also ideas. He praised especially Redon and "his terrible, bewildering, and alarming work," Van Gogh, and Gauguin. He said of Gauguin: "One would say Plato interpreted by a savage of genius." Aurier's credo was formulated on page 201: "The only way to fathom a thing is through love. . . . Understanding is proportionate to love. . . . So, the only way to understand a work of art is to become its lover."

9. Delacroix had confided in his *Journal,* on May 8, 1824: "I do not like sensible painting. I see that my unmethodical mind has to be agitated, to disassemble, and to try in a thousand ways, before reaching the goal, the craving for which torments me in everything. . . . If I am not agitated like a serpent in the hands of a pythoness, I am cold. One must recognize this and submit to it, and that is a great happiness. All the best work I have done has been done in this way."—Baudelaire, in his essay on *L'oeuvre et la vie d'Eugène Delacroix* (1863), had remarked: "There is nothing in his work but affliction, massacres, fires; everything bears witness against the eternal and incorrigible

cruelty of man. . . . This entire work . . . resembles a terrible hymn composed in honor of fatality and irremediable grief."—But Van Gogh, to whom Emile Bernard cited in 1888 the quatrain on Rembrandt in *Les Phares,* did not forgive the poet such a characterization of his compatriot: "These are sonorous but very hollow words," he exclaimed.

10. Verhaeren was himself a talented art critic. His criticism, which was very personal, defended the romantic values which suited his own temperament. Furthermore, he defined the romantic movement and what followed it (realism and impressionism) as "a continuous manifestation of liberty and spontaneity against official servitude and crystallization" (article of August 1900 in *Mercure de France,* included in *Sensations,* Crès, 1927). Maupassant, born in 1850, five years younger than Verhaeren, should be studied as a victim of the romantic malady which was manifested in him by a morbid pessimism, distress, and a disgust for life, an inclination towards nothingness and death. In an article in *Le Gaulois,* written to promote *Les Soirées de Médan,* this gloomy pessimist declared: "For the great masters of the romantic school, I have a tremendous admiration, to which is often added a revolt of my reason" (1880).

11. One modern critic, René-Marill Albérès, who has done extensive research and who is bent on not separating literature from life, that is, from the philosophical and moral preoccupations of the writers, has studied in the work *La Révolte des écrivains d'aujourd'hui* (Corréa, 1949) about ten authors: Bernanos, Malraux, Camus, Aragon, Anouilh, Sartre, *et al.* In all of them he has emphasized their soterio-logical inclinations and their Promethean ambitions. They revolt like the Titan who rebelled against God, the hero par excellence of the romantics. In their anguish in the face of the present, they desire nothing less than to save this world or to allow it to be born again better.

12. Before the outburst of surrealism, as soon as the war of 1914–1918 was over, the young people of the period 1920–1925 felt at a loss, gripped by an anxiety which delighted in analyzing itself, by vague passions, and by their maladjustment to the world as it was after the great massacre. Drieu La Rochelle was one of these young men, and he never got over this. Men (who were later to become members of the *Académie)* felt that they were afflicted by a new "mal du siècle," as Marcel Arland called it, and they prided themselves (Daniel-Rops) on *Notre Inquiétude.* The surrealists suffered from this malady of the new century with a more bitter impatience. Jacques Rigaut, who later committed suicide, like René Crevel, wrote: "I am not free from ennui. Ennui is truth, the pure state." He made this despondent confession to his surrealist friends: "You are all poets, and I am on the side of death" (*Papiers posthumes,* Au Sans-pareil, 1934). We are reminded of the sad statements of another man who committed suicide, Jacques Vaché, about the disheartening uselessness of everything, and particularly of writing. Eluard knew better how to smile a little at his sadness and sing of his malady to enchant it. But he did not hide the fact that: "They are dismal truths that appear in the work of true poets: but they are truths, and almost everything else is a lie."

13. A long book of George Lukacs, which is not one of his best, is entitled

Die Zerstörung der Vernunft. It had appeared in German in 1953 in Berlin and a French translation was published in 1958 by the Editions de l'Arche.

14. Randall Jarrell, a poet and a discerning critic, who was by no means influenced by literary fashions, in a very impressive article on the so-called modernist poetry of his country (the poetry of Pound, Crane, Cummings, Stevens, and others), considered it "a continuation of romanticism, a culmination of the majority of romantic tendencies carried to their limits." The more critics have tried to fight against this romanticism, he added, the more poets have emphasized it ("The End of the Line", *The Nation,* February 21, 1942, pp. 222–228). Henry Miller, in *The Books in my Life* (New Directions, 1952), proclaimed: "My antecedents are types of romantic, demoniac and subjective writers," and he summarized his message in the formula: "Be what you are! But be so to extremes."

Bibliographical Notes

There are of course numerous works and articles dealing with some aspect or other of romanticism. We can only mention here a few works, which we consider particularly useful, grouping them according to the themes treated in the preceding chapters.

On *preromanticism* and the first romantic waves of the eighteenth century: Baldensperger (Fernand), *Le mouvement des idées dans l'émigration française (1789–1815),* Plon, 1925; Cellier (Léon), *Fabre d'Olivet,* Nizet, 1953; Estève (Edmond), *Etudes de littérature préromantique,* Champion, 1923; Fabre (Jean), *Lumières et romantisme. Energie et nostalgie,* Klincksieck, 1963; Fairchild (Hoxie Neale), *The Noble Savage. A Study in Romantic Naturalism,* New York, Columbia University Press, 1928; Folkierski (Wladyslaw), *Entre classicisme et romantisme,* Champion; 1925; Hoog (Armand), "L'âme préromantique et les instincts de mort", *Bulletin de la Faculté des Lettres de Stransbourg,* 1952, 22 p. and "Un cas d'angoisse préromantique", *Revue des Sciences humaines,* No. 67, July-September 1952, 181–198; Jacoubet (Henri), *Le genre troubadour et les origines françaises du romantisme,* Les Belles-Lettres, 1929; Manuel (Frank E.), *The Eighteenth Century Confronts the Gods,* Cambridge, Mass., Harvard University Press, 1959; Mauzi (Robert), *L'idée du bonheur au XVIIIe siècle,* A. Colin, 1960; Monglond (André), *Le préromantisme français,* Grenoble, Arthaud, 1930, 2 vol.: Mornet (Daniel), *Le romantisme en France au XVIIIe siècle,* Hachette, 1912; Pizzorusso (Arnaldo), *Studi sulla letteratura dell'età preromantica in Francia,* Pisa, Libreria Goliardica, 1956; Robertson (J.G.), *Studies in the Genesis of Romantic Theory in the Eighteenth Century,* Cambridge University Press, 1923; Trahard (Pierre), *Les maîtres de la sensibilité française au XVIIIe siècle (1815–1889),* Boivin, 1931–1933, 4 vol.; Van Tieghem (Paul), *Le préromantisme. Etudes d'histoire littéraire européenne,* Rieder, 1924–1930, 3 vol. and *La poésie de la nuit et des tombeaux en Europe au XVIIIe siècle,* Rieder, 1921; Viatte (Auguste), *Les sources occultes du romantisme (1770–1820)*, Champion, 1928; Wais (Kurt), *Das antiphilosophische Weltbild des französischen Sturm und Drang, 1760–1789*, Berlin, Junker und Dünnhaupt, 1934.

On the terms "romantique" and "romantisme": Baldensperger (Fernand), *"Romantique", ses analgoues et ses equivalents. Tableau synoptique de 1650 à 1810*, Cambridge, Harvard Studies in Philology, 1927, XIX, 13–106; Brown (Calvin S.), "Toward a definition of Romanticism", in Burnshaw (Stanley), *Varieties of Literary Experience*, New York University Press, 1962, 115–135; Egglie (Edmond) and Martino (Pierre), *Le débat romantique en France (1813–1816); Pamphlets, manifestes, polémiques de presse*, Les Belles-Lettres, 1933; François (Alexis), "De romantique à romantisme", *Bibliothéque universelle et Revue suisse*, Vol. 91, Nos. 272 and 273, August and September 1918, 225–233 and 365–376, and "Où en est romantique?", *Mélanges Baldensperger*, Champion, 1929, I, 372–381; Jost (François), "Romantique: la leçon d'un mot", in *Essais de littérature comparée. Europeana*, 1st series, Fribourg, Editions Universitaires, 1968 (pp. 181–258); Lovejoy (Arthur O.). "On the discrimination of romanticisms", article of 1924, and "The meaning of romanticism for the historian of ideas", *Journal of the History of Ideas*, article of 1941, reprinted in *Essays in the History of Ideas*, Baltimore, The Johns Hopkins Press, 1948; Smith (Logan Pearsall), "Romantic", in *Four Words*, Oxford, Clarendon Press, 1924; Trahard (Pierre), *Le romantisme défini par Le Globe*, Presses Françaises, 1925.

On the *romantic movement* considered in a *historical perspective* and from the point of view of its *nature:* Abercrombie (Lascelles), *Romanticism*, London, Martin Secker, 1926; Abrams (M. H.), *The Mirror and the Lamb, Romantic Theory and the Critical Tradition*, New York, Oxford University Press, 1953; Aynard (Joseph), "Comment définir le romantisme", *Revue de littérature comparée*, October-December 1925, V, 641–658; Babbitt (Irving), *Rousseau and Romanticism*, Boston, Houghton Mifflin, 1919; Béguin (Albert), *L'âme romantique et le rêve*, Corti, 1963 (first published in *Cahiers du Sud* in 1937); Benz (Richard), *Die deutsche Romantik, Geschichte einer geistigen Bewegung*, Leipzig, Philip Reclam, 1937; Boas (George), *French Philosophies of the Romantic Period*, Baltimore, The Johns Hopkins Press, 1925; Bray (René), *Chronologie du romantisme (1804–1830)*, Boivin, 1932; Emery (Léon). *L'âge romantique*, Lyon, Les Cahiers libres, 1960, 2 vol.; Evans (David Owen), *Le socialisme romantique, Pierre Leroux et ses contemporains*, Marcel Rivière, 1948, and *Social Romanticism in France, 1830–1848*, Oxford, The Clarendon Press, 1951; Farinelli (Arturo), *Il Romanticismo nel mondo latino*, Turin, 1927, 3 vol.; Frye (Northrop), *A study of English Romanticism*, New York, Random House, 1968; Frye (Prosser Hall), *Romance and Tragedy*, Boston, Marshall Jones, 1922; Grierson (H. J.), *The Reconciliation of Classic and Romantic*, Cambridge, Bowes and Bowes, 1925; Hugh (Ricarda), *Die Romantik, Blütezeit, Ausbreitung, Verfall*, Tübingen, 1899–1902; Hunt (Herbert J.), *Le socialisme et le romantisme en France*, Oxford, The Clarendon Press, 1935, and *The Epic in Nineteenth Century France*, Oxford, Blackwell, 1941; Landry (Lionel), "Classicisme et romantisme, essai de définition", *Mercure de France*, vol. 197, July 15, 1927, 257–276; Lucas (F. L.), *The Decline and Fall of the Romantic Ideal*, Cambridge University Press, 1936; Marsan (Jules), *La bataille romantique,* Hachette, 2 vol., 1912 and 1925; Moreau (Pierre), *Le classicisme des romantiques,* Plon, 1932, and *Le romantisme,* Editions Mondiales, 1957; Parodi (Dominique), "L'essence du romantisme", *Revue de Métaphysique et de Morale,* Vol. 38, No. 4, Oct.-Dec. 1931, 511–526; Pater (Walter), "A Postscript: classical and romantic", in *Appreciations,* London, Macmillan, 1889; Petersen (Julius), *Die Wesenbestimmung der deutschen Romantik, eine Einführung in die moderne Literaturwissenschaft,* Leipzig, Quelle und Meyer, 1926; Peyre (Henri), "Romantic poetry and rhetoric" and "Romanticism and French literature to-day: le mort vivant", in *Historical and Critical Essays,* Lincoln, University of Nebraska Press, 1968; Pouillard (Raymond), *Le romantisme (1869–1896),* Arthaud, 1968; Rodway (Allan), *The Romantic Conflict,* London, Chatto and Windus, 1963; *Romantisme et politique (1815–1851),* Colloque de l'Ecole Normale de Saint-Cloud, A. Colin, 1969; Schroder (Maurice), *Icarus, the Image of the Artist in French Romanticism,* Cambridge, Mass., Harvard University Press, 1961; Souriau (Maurice), *Histoire du romantisme,* 3 vol., Spès, 1927; Strich (Fritz), "Die Romantik als europäische Bewegung," in *Festchrift Heinrich Wölfflin,* Munich, Hugo Schmidt, 1924, 47–62, and *Deutsche Klassik und romantik, oder Vollendung und Unendlichkeit,* Munich, Beck, 1922; *Symposium, Syracuse University Press,* special issue on "Le romantisme français", XXIII, 3–4, Autumn and Winter 1969; Talmon (J. L.), *Romanticism and Revolt: Europe 1815–1848,* London, Thames and Hudson, 1967; Wellek (René), "The concept of romanticism in literary history," in *Concepts of Criticism,* Yale University Press, 1963, 128–198 (published in *Comparative Literature,* I, 1949).

On the *romantic "mal du siècle", religiosity, mysticism:* Antoine-Orliac, "Essai sur le tournant romantique", *Mercure de France,* Vol. 199, No. 704, October 15, 1927, 257–292; Bousquet (Jacques), *Les thèmes du rêve dans la littérature romantique,* Didier, 1964; Cazamian (Louis), "L'intuition panthéiste chez les romantiques anglais", *Revue germanique,* IV (1908), 414–455; Cellier (Léon), *L'epopée romantique,* Presses Universitaires de France, 1954; Fairchild (Hoxie Neale), *Religious Trends in English Poetry,* Vol. III: 1780–1830, *Romantic Faith,* Columbia University Press, 1949; Farinelli (Arturo), "La religion romantique et la pensée de l'infini et de l'éternel," *Revue de littérature comparée,* VII, 1927, 5–46; Giraud (Victor), "Catholicisme et romantisme", in *De Chateaubriand à Brunetière. Essais sur le mouvement catholique en France au XIX siècle,* Spès, 1939; Grillet (Claudius), *La Bible dans Victor Hugo,* Hachette, 1910, and *La Bible dans Lamartine,* Lyon, Vitte, 1938; Joussain (André), *Romantisme et religion,* Alcan, 1910; Mauzi (Robert), "Les maladies de l'âme au XVIIIe siècle", *Revue des sciences humaines,* No. 100, Oct.-Dec. 1960, 459–493; Milner (Max), *Le diable dans la littérature française de Cazotte à Baudelaire (1772–1861),* J. Corti, 1960, 2 vol.; Moreau (Pierre), "Romantisme français et syncrétisme religieux", *Symposium,* VIII, No. I, Summer 1954, 1–17; Nouty (El Hassan), "Le panthéisme dans les lettres françaises au XVIIIe siècle", *Revue des sciences humaines,* No. 100, Oct.-Dec. 1960, 435–457; Piper (W. H.), *The Active Universe. Pantheism and the Concept of Imagination in the English Romantic Poets,* London, The Athlone Press, 1962; Sagnes (G.), *L'ennui dans la littérature française de Flaubert à Laforgue (1848–1884),*

A. Colin, 1969; Viatte (Auguste), *Le catholicisme chez les romantiques,* De Boccard, 1922.

On the *romantic imagination, symbol, eloquence, image:* Barat (Emmanuel), *Le style poétique et la révolution romantique,* Hachette, 1904; Bonnet (Henri), *De Malherbe à Sartre, essai sur le progrès de la conscience esthétique,* Nizet, 1964; Borgese (Giuseppe), *Storia della critica romantica in Italia,* Milan 1920; Clayborough (Arthur), *The Grotesque in English Literature,* Oxford University Press, 1965; Gerard (Albert S.), *English Romantic Poetry; Ethos, Structure and Symbolism in Coleridge, Wordsworth, Shelley, and Keats,* Berkeley, University of California Press, 1968, and *L'idée romantique de la poésie en Angleterre,* Les Belles-Lettres, 1956; Gilman (Margaret), *The Idea of Poetry in France, from Houdar de la Motte to Baudelaire,* Cambridge, Mass., Harvard University Press, 1958; Houston (John Porter), *The Demonic Imagination, Style and Theme in French Romantic Poetry,* Baton Rouge, University of Louisiana Press, 1969; Kayser (Wolfgang), *Das Grotesque: seine Gestaltung in Malerei und Dichtung,* Hamburg, Stalling, 1957; Riffaterre (Michel), "Poétiques et poésie de Diderot à Baudelaire", *The Romanic Review,* LI, No. 2, April 1960, 115–122; Watts-Dunton (Theodore), *Poetry and the Renascence of Wonder,* London, Herbert Jenkins, 1916; Wilkie (Brian), *Romantic Poets and Epic Tradition,* Madison, University of Wisconsin Press, 1965.

On *romanticism and the arts:* Baldensperger (Fernand), *Sensibilité musicale et romantisme,* Presses Françaises, 1925; Barzun (Jacques), *Berlioz and the Romantic Century,* Boston, Little Brown, 1950, Brion (Marcel), *Schumann et l'âme romantique,* Albin Michel, 1954; Einstein (Alfred), *Music in the Romantic Era,* New York, Norton, 1947; Evans (Raymond L.), *Les romantiques français et la musique,* Champion, 1934; Focillon (Henri), *La peinture au XIXe siècle,* H. Laurens, 1927; Guichard (Léon), *La musique et les lettres au temps du romantisme,* Presses Universitaires de France, 1955; Locke (Arthur Ware), *Music in the Romantic Movement in France,* London, Kegan Paul, Trent, 1920; Marix-Spire (Thérèse), *Les romantiques et la musique: le cas George Sand (1804–1838),* Nouvelles Editions Latines, 1955; *Le romantisme et l'art,* J. Laurens, 1928 (series of essays); Rosenthal (Léon), *La peinture romantique,* Fontemoing, 1903; Rudrauf (Lucien), *Delacroix et le problème du romantisme artistique,* H. Laurens, 1942; Schneider (René), *L'art français au XIXe siècle. Du classicisme davidien au romantisme,* H. Laurens, 1929; Simches (Seymour), *Le romantisme et le goût esthétique du XVIIIe siècle,* Presses Universitaires de France, 1964.

On the *survival* of romanticism and some attacks against it: Adams (Robert Martin), *Nil. Episodes in the Literary Conquest of Void during the Nineteenth Century,* New York, Oxford University Press, 1966; Albérès (René-Marill), *La révolte des écrivains d'aujourd'hui,* Corrêa, 1949; Carrouges (Michel), *La mystique du surhomme,* Gallimard, 1948; Daniel-Rops, *Notre inquiétude,* Perrin, 1927; Eliot (Thomas S.), *After Strange Gods,* London, Faber and Faber, 1934; Fernandez (Ramòn), *Messages,* Gallimard, 1926; Friedrich (Hugo) *Das antiromantische Denken in Frankreich,* Munich, Max Hueber, 1935; Hoog (Armand), "Le romantisme et l'existence contemporaine," *Mercure de France,* No. 1011, November 1952, 436–448; Hulme (T. E.), *Speculations,* London,

Kegan Paul, Trench and Teubner, 1924; Lasserre (Pierre), *Le romantisme français,* Mercure de France, 1907; Maigron (Louis), *Le romantisme et les moeurs,* and *Le romantisme et la mode,* Champion, 1910 and 1911; Reynaud (Louis), *Le romantisme, ses origines anglo-germaniques,* A. Colin, 1926; Rivière (Jacques), "Le roman d'aventures" (1913), included in *Nouvelles Etudes,* Gallimard, 1947, 235–283; Scarfe (Francis), *Auden and After, The Liberation of Poetry, 1930–1941,* London, Routledge, 1942; Seillière (Ernest), *Le mal romantique, essai sur l'impérialisme irrationnel,* Plon, 1908; Thomas (Jean), *Quelques aspects du romantisme contemporain,* Les Belles-Lettres, 1927.

INDEX